Gothic Realities

Gothic Realities

The Impact of Horror Fiction on Modern Culture

L. ANDREW COOPER

McFarland & Company, Inc., Publishers
Jefferson, North Carolina, and London

LIBRARY OF CONGRESS CATALOGUING-IN-PUBLICATION DATA

Cooper, L. Andrew, 1977–
 Gothic realities : the impact of horror fiction on modern culture / L. Andrew Cooper.
   p.   cm.
 Includes bibliographical references and index.

 ISBN 978-0-7864-4835-7
 softcover : 50# alkaline paper ∞

 1. Horror tales, English — History and criticism. 2. Gothic fiction (Literary genre), English — History and criticism. 3. Horror tales, American — History and criticism. 4. Gothic fiction (Literary genre), American — History and criticism. 5. Horror in literature. 6. Popular culture and literature — History — 20th century. I. Title.
 PR830.T3C66   2010
 823'.0872909 — dc22   2010020163

British Library cataloguing data are available

©2010 L. Andrew Cooper. All rights reserved

No part of this book may be reproduced or transmitted in any form or by any means, electronic or mechanical, including photocopying or recording, or by any information storage and retrieval system, without permission in writing from the publisher.

Cover image ©2010 Arie van der Wolde

Manufactured in the United States of America

McFarland & Company, Inc., Publishers
 Box 611, Jefferson, North Carolina 28640
  www.mcfarlandpub.com

For James, who saw me through the horrors

Table of Contents

Acknowledgments ... ix

Introduction
Bad Influences and Gothic Realities ... 1

Part One: Gothic Threats ... 23

1. The Threat in the Gothic's Foundation: From John Locke to Horace Walpole ... 25

2. Gothic Threats and Cultural Hierarchy: The Critical Evaluation of *The Monk* and *The Mysteries of Udolpho* ... 39

Part Two: Gothic Sexualities ... 57

3. Pathological Reproduction: The Emergence of Homosexuality through Nineteenth Century Gothic Fiction ... 59

4. Romps in the Closet: The Persistence of Nineteenth Century Notions in Contemporary Pop Culture ... 81

Part Three: Gothic Ghosts ... 115

5. Ghost Stories and Ghostly Belief: Conventional Horrors That Make Good Truths ... 117

6. Ghost Epistemology: Five or Six Ways to Haunt the Senses ... 144

Part Four: Gothic Violence — 159

7. Fictions That Kill: Columbine, Virginia Tech, and Stephen King's Only Out-of-Print Novel — 161

8. Violent Self-Reflection: *Natural Born Killers*, Wes Craven's Nightmares, and Torture Porn — 184

Chapter Notes — 209

Selected Bibliography — 223

Index — 233

Acknowledgments

This book grew out of the dissertation I completed at Princeton University in 2005. Claudia Johnson was its director; in addition to providing copious advice and considerable patience, she also gave me the opportunity to teach a course with her on Gothic fiction that provided a fertile testing ground for my ideas in their earliest forms. Jeff Nunokawa, Deborah Nord and Mark Hansen joined the dissertation committee, providing a breadth of understanding that enriched my own thinking. In addition to the official advisors, Diana Fuss helped me by asking many excellent questions, and Sue Ellen Case provided formative suggestions when I presented some of the material about Gothic sexuality at the Q-Grad conference sponsored by USC and UCLA. Many of my graduate colleagues at Princeton also lent inestimable feedback and consolation, especially Hannah Johnson and Lia Lynch.

The process from dissertation to book took some time, but during that time Georgia Tech gave me more valuable opportunities to shape my thinking with the help of hundreds of bright and inspiring students. The students in my composition courses that examined debates about media violence in fall 2005 and summer 2006 helped me to realize that my feeling that texts don't have agency like people do — which had been controversial in some company — made a great deal of common sense and was therefore worth pursuing. Similarly, students in a spring 2006 course that looked at the multimedia legacies of *Frankenstein*, *The Strange Case of Dr. Jekyll and Mr. Hyde*, and *Dracula* helped me see that despite the mountains of criticism already available on these foundational texts, scholars at all levels are still capable of new insight. Finally, students in a course on horror films that I taught in summer 2008, in which many people skeptical about the horror genre's value got stuck, proved that even viewers who aren't fans can see the cultural significance in films dismissed as trash by so many ill-informed critics. For me, students are the real reason for academic writing — without them, nothing.

During the years when the book was silently percolating in the back of my brain, the journal I consider to be the greatest outlet for my area of specialization, *Gothic Studies*, was kind enough to publish in issue 8.2 (November 2006) an early version of the material that appears, with their gracious permission, in the second chapter. William Hughes, the journal's editor, was particularly helpful with this material. I also need to thank Carol Senf, Georgia Tech's resident expert on things Gothic and vampiric, for the encouragement she gave me as I pursued this publication and tinkered with others.

This book draws on hundreds of sources, so without the helpful staffs at Princeton's Firestone Library, the Los Angeles Public Library, the Huntington Library, and Georgia Tech's Library and Information Center, it would be an insubstantial wisp of speculation. For the information that is good, they get the credit; if any information be bad, I get the blame.

The same division of credit for the good (theirs) and blame for the bad (mine) applies to my parents, who have encouraged my odd intellectual proclivities since the beginning, and to the three people who have been most helpful in seeing this book to completion. First, I'd like to thank Levi Kafka, whose brilliant ideas shared in the 2008 course on horror films made his agreement to work as my research assistant seem like a gift far greater than I deserved. Second, my mentor and closest friend at Georgia Tech, Rebecca Burnett, gave me new appreciation for the heights a dedicated teacher and scholar can accomplish. Finally, my partner James Chakan, to whom this book is dedicated, has been reader, critic, best friend, and constant support.

Introduction
Bad Influences and Gothic Realities

Putting psychoanalytic platitudes aside, I can't explain why I was always drawn to the macabre side of popular culture. Even though I couldn't handle scary things — I had terrible nightmares from which I would awake screaming and crying, afraid to go back to sleep — as a kid I watched horror movies every chance I got. In a way this book, which officially started when I was a graduate student, really began at age nine, when I stole an opportunity to watch one of the 1980s' most notorious horror films. I offer this brief account of a childhood encounter with Gothic horror as a case history, evidence that supports many of this book's claims.

The encounter was only possible because my friend Chris invited me to spend the night at his house; he had a basement where we could romp until the wee hours. The basement had a television, and the television had a cable box, so after Chris's parents went to bed, we of course searched the channels for anything that might be forbidden. The most exciting thing we found was a movie, irresistible because it was rated R, that we had heard of but knew little about: *A Nightmare on Elm Street* (1984).[1] During the waking hours, nine-year-old-me tended to ignore what I knew about the consequences of watching scary movies, so I agreed to become acquainted with Freddy Krueger, the supernatural madman who murders children in their sleep.

I recall that when the movie got too scary, we switched channels until we thought the worst would be over, and we switched back inevitably in time to see Freddy's razors ripping through someone's flesh. Chris and I were giddy, exhilarated. We refused to go to bed that night not because we were scared (of course not!) but because we were having too much fun.

The next day I went home, and that night I went to bed when my mom told me to. Like *A Nightmare on Elm Street*'s characters, I felt terrified of going to sleep because I knew Freddy would be waiting for me in my dreams. When I closed my eyes, I instantly imagined him on the stairs leading up to my bedroom, brown hat, dirty sweater, and razor blades extending from a horrible gloved hand. Then I remembered how the movie ends: the teenaged heroine, Nancy, confronts Freddy and tells him he's only a dream. *She* has the power; a kid could be stronger than a seemingly invincible psycho-killer. In the last chapter, this book discusses the ambiguity of the film's ending, but nine-year-old-me wasn't aware of any ambiguity. I remembered Nancy winning her battle against Freddy, and I thought that if she could, I could. I chanted to myself, "It's just a dream, it's just a dream," and eventually I fell asleep. I didn't have any nightmares that night. In fact, though I still have dreams both good and bad, since that night I have never been terrified of going to sleep.

Thus *A Nightmare on Elm Street* helped a child to overcome his greatest fears.

With this formative experience occupying a hallowed corner of my memory, I always scoffed at the notion that horror movies are bad influences on kids, and when in 1999 people everywhere seemed to be blaming Gothic culture for the deaths of 15 people at Columbine High School in Littleton, Colorado, I was incredulous. I paid attention, and when the time came, I decided that the problem was worth a dissertation. Can violent fiction really be responsible for real-life violence?

The concrete ideas for this book, then, began where the book ends, with thinking about the causal agency people attribute to violent fiction in the present day. Since horror was my favorite genre, I decided to turn back the clock, reversing through a lineage that connects Wes Craven's Freddy to Horace Walpole's Manfred. Had people *always* attributed real-life horrors to horror fiction?

"Always" is a tough bill to fit. I started to realize that the word "ambitious" on the lips of graduate advisors isn't necessarily a good thing. When tackling questions about the relationship between fiction and so-called reality, one could investigate millennia of art and literature. Such questions take center stage when Plato's *Republic* turns to relationships between poetry and the ideal community. Socrates warns that representational poetry "deforms its audience's minds" and "irrigates and tends" strong emotions "when they should be left to wither, and it makes them our rulers when they should be our subjects."[2] The foundation of Western philosophy thus makes a strong case for severely limiting the reach of fictional representations because they can make people lose control. Gothic horror isn't the only type of representational art that Plato's view would paint as bad, but the very affect named in the generic marker "horror" is something that Plato warns people to avoid.

The idea that fiction can have a (de)formative effect is roughly as old as Western civilization, and although specific questions about art's formative potential have changed from age to age, Platonic reservations about representational art have been remarkably persistent. Reflecting on literature's power, T.J. Mathias writes in his late-eighteenth-century treatise *The Pursuits of Literature*, "LITERATURE, *well or ill conducted,* IS THE GREAT ENGINE, *by which all* civilized *states must ultimately be supported or be overthrown.*"[3] Literature, like an engine, propels action. The survival of civilization could depend on the actions it propels: literature's illness and wellness are also society's. In other words, bad literature makes bad civilizations.

All fiction has the power to shape the real world; the artistic imagination often provides models that the real world later adopts. In *Desire and Domestic Fiction: A Political History of the Novel*, Nancy Armstrong demonstrates ways "the domestic novel antedated — was indeed necessarily antecedent to — the way of life it represented."[4] The eighteenth-century domestic novel contributed to the structure of domestic life that emerged during the eighteenth century and persists in altered form in the twenty-first century. As Armstrong's work indicates, even fictions considered genteel by contemporary standards have the power to support or overthrow the governing norms of civilization. Unlike domestic ways of life, murder — one of the most powerful and common of fictional horrors — demands culprits, and if fictions can create reality, Gothic fictions about murder might reasonably be prime suspects. All fiction might be blameworthy, but Gothic fiction seems particularly reprehensible.

As Martin Tropp claims in *Images of Fear: How Horror Stories Helped Shape Modern Culture*, "The parallel development of the modern tale of terror and the modern world show us how literature and life create each other." Identifying Gothic horror as an exemplar of literature and life's interdependence, Tropp "examines how images of fear... helped give form and meaning to the frightening events that have come to mark modern culture... how and why a few very special stories have helped determine the way we see the world around us."[5] Thanks to the works of Tropp and others, that the Gothic provides a way of seeing is well-established. The importance of Tropp's work for my own is hard to calculate; the similarity between my subtitle and his is meant to acknowledge his work's significance. However, people who blame the Gothic for real-life horrors do so because the Gothic does more than shape the perception of events: the finger-pointers claim that the Gothic causes events, making things be in ways they would not otherwise have been.

Ultimately the huge questions that I started asking in the wake of Columbine — whether violent fictions can really be responsible for violent realities and whether people have always blamed horror fictions for horrific realities — had to be whittled down. I chose to limit this book to the aforementioned lineage that connects the first novel called Gothic, Horace Walpole's *The Castle of Otranto*, to the contemporary horror film. This book is emphatically *not* a representative survey of Gothic fiction. If it were, its neglect of great works such as James Hogg's *Confessions of a Justified Sinner* and Bram Stoker's *Dracula* would be a criminal, fatal flaw. Instead, this book offers broad consideration of more chiseled forms of my initial questions:

1. When Gothic horror became a recognized literary genre in the eighteenth century, what ill effects did critics associate with it, and why did they do so?
2. In the 245 years since the Gothic's birth, has the genre proven those critics right, and if it has, how has it done so?

The first part of the book, "Gothic Threats," examines what ill effects the Gothic threatened and why critics perceived those threats. The remaining three parts, "Gothic Sexualities," "Gothic Ghosts," and "Gothic Violence," examine how selected works in the tradition of Gothic horror might seem to carry out those threats.

Before launching into these lines of inquiry about how the Gothic shapes reality, I have two important tasks. First, I need to define two key terms: "Gothic," which in the preceding pages has already appeared in ways that some readers will find problematic, and "reality," which is perhaps the most ontologically and epistemologically vexed word in the English language. Second, I need to defend the genre, which I credit for saving my young psyche from torturous dreams, from a conclusion that might erroneously seem to follow from some of my claims: though I do argue that the Gothic shapes reality, making things be in ways they would not otherwise have been, I do *not* argue that the Gothic is responsible for its influence. I therefore need to make some theoretical distinctions related to causation, culpability, and influence.

Gothic

Referring to the difficulty of separating the genres of horror, science fiction, and fantasy, Stephen King writes candidly, "It's a trap, this matter of definition, and I can't think of a more boring academic subject."[6] "Gothic" is indeed a trap: as with all definitions, the definition of "Gothic" changes with its contexts, and while it does have a set of historical meanings and associations worthy of study, no academic writer will ever legitimately declare a decisive victory in the battle over its precise meaning. While the Gothic has roots in medieval romances, Renaissance tragedies, and early experiments in the novel based on the romance tradition, most critics agree that the Gothic tradition began in the eighteenth century. The more contentious question is the question of when and whether the Gothic ended. Seeking to limit the Gothic by historical period, many critics confine the term "Gothic" to the heyday of the Enlightenment, the period stretching from the 1760s to the 1790s, roughly from Horace Walpole's *The Castle of Otranto* to Ann Radcliffe's *The Italian*. Others give it a slightly more distant endpoint, figuring the Gothic as the embarrassing underbelly of Romanticism and cutting it off around 1820, with Charles Maturin's *Melmoth the Wanderer*, or around 1824, with *Confessions of a Justified Sinner*.

Giving the Gothic such endpoints creates a need for a host of new categories for works that continue, sometimes self-consciously and sometimes not, to carry on the tradition of horror that began in the eighteenth century. For some, Gothic after 1824 becomes gothic, and little-g gothic names the uses of conventions derived from eighteenth-century Gothic in works such as Emily Brontë's *Wuthering Heights*. Little-g gothic appears in the works of Charles Dickens, George Eliot, and many other major nineteenth-century writers, and G/g-othic elements from Edgar Allan Poe and Mary Shelley often get credit for spinning off the detective and sci-fi genres. So many G/g-othic elements appear in the works of Wilkie Collins and his ilk that he sometimes appears as part of the Sensation novel tradition — which owes a great debt to the Gothic — or the beginning of neo-Gothic, a category that includes such fin-de-siècle works as Robert Louis Stevenson's *The Strange Case of Dr. Jekyll and Mr. Hyde* and Bram Stoker's

Dracula. In the century plus since *Dracula* combined eighteenth-century infested-castle terror with neo-Gothic urban horror, the revived Gothic tradition has continued. It has morphed into the horror novel and the horror film, and more recently it has produced Goth rockers such as Marilyn Manson and survival horror video games such as *Resident Evil*, which is set in an old mansion highly reminiscent of one of Ann Radcliffe's Gothic edifices.

This book does very little to acknowledge such fine demarcations: in *Gothic Realities*, "Gothic" refers to everything from Ann Radcliffe to *Resident Evil*, Horace Walpole to Marilyn Manson. In his seminal study *The Literature of Terror*, David Punter identifies fear as the "one element" that unites all Gothic fictions, a fear that "is not merely a theme or an attitude [but] also has consequences in terms of form, style and the social relations of the texts."[7] My own definition of Gothic derives from Punter's argument: a Gothic fiction is a fiction that primarily represents fear, the fearful, and the abject, even if the representation is comic; every work that this study labels with the big G makes fear and the fearful its main business. Works that use Gothic conventions (such as creepy old houses that hide dark family secrets) but do not focus primarily on the representation of fear and the fearful don't get the big G, and for that reason the only work mentioned in the previous paragraph that does not wear the Gothic label as used here is *Wuthering Heights*. Shelley, Poe, Collins, Stevenson, Stoker, and King all wear the G, perhaps with pride. The section of this book titled "Gothic Sexualities" gives Oscar Wilde's *The Picture of Dorian Gray* the Gothic label, which some critics would dispute; if they're right, my argument in that section is completely incoherent (naturally, I think they're wrong). The problem with defining the Gothic as a form focused primarily on representations of fear, the fearful, and the abject is that "fear," "the fearful," and "the abject" are unstable terms themselves, and therefore any claim of classification invites debate. "Gothic Sexualities" justifies Wilde's inclusion with different terms; Stephen King, sage bestseller, politely excuses himself from the table.

Realities

What is reality? Undergraduates might ask this question in smoky lava lamp-lit rooms; as moviegoers exit screenings of *The Matrix*, their brains pulse with the film's riff on Jean Baudrillard's ideas about simulacra, hyperreality, and "*the desert of the real itself.*"[8] "Reality" is far more slippery than "Gothic." The consequences of its meaning reach farther, and speculations about its meaning have incensed and inflamed both professional and amateur philosophers since its coinage. As a result of these controversies, defining "reality" requires engagement with some heavy theoretical thinking. The title of Ian Hacking's *The Social Construction of What?* frames the question of "reality" and its "social construction" as somewhat risible. Pointing out the wondrous vagueness of "reality" in such a context, Hacking states, "the social construction of reality... sounds like the social construction of everything." Hacking legitimizes only arguments about the social construction of specific things, arguments "that aim at displaying or analyzing actual, historically situated, social interactions or causal routes that led to, or were involved in, the coming into being or establishing of some present entity or fact."[9] *Gothic Realities* has such an aim: "Gothic Sexualities" and "Gothic Ghosts" analyze the Gothic's interactions with other social (or in a different idiom, discursive) factors involved in the coming into being of homosexuality and of the specific realities accorded to ghosts.

Like many others, I use "reality" as a label that signifies status. The label "reality," like the label "Gothic," announces the quality of a thing, its deservingness of a place within a category. Hacking refers to "reality" as an "elevator word," a word that conveys higher status or legitimacy, and argues, "Facts, truths, reality, and even knowledge are not objects in the world... [but] are used to say something about the world."[10] In "The Discourse on Language," Michel Foucault observes a "will to truth" in discourse that is a "system of exclusion," a way that discourse elevates the true and excludes the false according to its own "rules."[11] As elevator words, "reality" and "truth" have similar exclusionary functions within discourse. The label "real" grants the "real" thing—"the real thing!"—superior validity according to the rules of the discourse within which the label is applied. "Real" friends are more loyal than "false" friends and are supposed to be better company than "imaginary" friends. "Real" problems oppose inferior, "trivial" problems. "Real" in this study refers to things that discourses elevate with ontological or epistemological status, things said either to exist or to be perceived as existing. As a product of discourse, "reality" collapses the ontological into the epistemological because saying something is real results from a perception of existence governed by discourse's rules. In other words, when we say a thing is real, we are drawing a conclusion that results from our perception of the thing, a perception that is shaped by our cultural contexts. "Gothic Sexualities" examines the rules for the reality of homosexuality, a purely discursive entity, and "Gothic Ghosts" examines the rules for the reality of ghosts, entities with prediscursive existence according to a belief, itself a product of discourse, that dramatizes reality's collapse of the ontological into the epistemological. "Gothic Violence" examines more urgent claims about how the Gothic relates to a reality that consists not merely of discourse but of life and death.

Causality and Culpability

Attacks on Gothic fictions as bad influences, from the eighteenth century to the present, depict the Gothic as a culpable causal agent, framing it as a monster intent on destroying society in general and children in particular. This depiction informs the way David Grossman and Gloria DeGaetano's *Stop Teaching Our Kids to Kill* represents the media industry's "complete and total contempt for the people of the United States"; this representation simplistically imagines "the media" as a unified entity capable of a concentrated hatred for the people who both produce and consume its wares.[12] Madeline Levine's contribution to the student-friendly *Media Violence: Opposing Viewpoints* clarifies that blaming the media for its influence does not necessarily involve claiming a simple and direct causal link between fiction and crime: "The question is not whether the media are the cause of crimes like these (they aren't), but whether the media are an important ingredient in the multiple causation of crime (they are)."[13] The notion of multiple causation, explored more fully in "Gothic Violence," suggests that a contribution to a crime's many causes is blameworthy.

Most views that find violent fictions culpable for real-life violence are problematically deterministic: they strip agency away from the violence's human perpetrators and assign it to inanimate causal factors. This transference of agency from the animate to the inanimate is an unnecessary byproduct of constructivist thinking. If, as I argue, phenomena like homosexuality and ghosts, and even historical events like the tragedy at Columbine, have been shaped by the Gothic, then the Gothic made those phenomena and events be in the ways that they are. True — looking back, we can't see these phenomena and events fully without also seeing the Gothic, but at the same time, we wouldn't necessarily see the Gothic in these phenomena and events if we weren't looking back. The multiple causation associated with historical events and phenomena is retrospective. Retrospectively observed causal factors are not the same as causal *agents*. My arguments do not support the leap from retrospective causality to culpable agency, to the Gothic being guilty for the violence that people do.

The judicial concept of criminal guilt in the United States and elsewhere relies on the concept of free will; without a concept that grounds responsibility in the agency of human actors, criminal justice unravels. A dilemma appears: if art bears the ultimate responsibility for crime, then the criminal is little more than a conduit of influence, deserving pity rather than punishment. W. James Potter doesn't hesitate to blame media violence for undesirable social phenomena, but he nevertheless detects this dilemma and explains why it's false:

> [In] cases in which the defendant tried using the "media made me murder" defense, the jury convicted the defendant, reasoning that people have free will and should be held accountable when they decide to commit a serious crime. Do people have free will? Of course. Should people, even adolescents, be held accountable for their actions? Yes. But concluding that people should be held accountable for their actions is not the same thing as saying that the media exert no influence on people. Accountability and influence are two distinct issues.

After making this distinction between accountability and influence, Potter argues that "the media are in fact responsible for negative effects — that is, the media exert a negative influence."[14] Accountability here refers to whether something can be charged legally for a crime, and thus it differs from influence because an influence isn't necessarily chargeable. Potter links both accountability and influence to responsibility, but he distinguishes influence from the accountability of "free will" that can justly earn "people, even adolescents" imprisonment and possibly execution.

This link between influence and responsibility is problematic. Potter asserts that "of course" people have free will — the self-evidence of this notion supports the ethical "should" with which he bolsters the criminal justice system. Sensing the difficulty of positing the existence of free will within a deterministic model of causality, Potter distinguishes between "probabilistic causation" and "deterministic causation," associating the former and not the latter with media violence. "One of the implications of shifting thinking away from determinism," Potter explains, "is to recognize that there are no 'sufficient conditions' for an effect — that is, no single factor is sufficient to guarantee an effect."[15] In this view, the influence of media violence does not guarantee real-life violence, but it does, along with other influences, make real-life violence more probable. Herein lies one of the problems in Potter's attempt to link influence to responsibility: multiple causation makes absolute prediction of cause-effect relationships between fictional and real violence impossible, so the retrospective model of causality is the *only* model that indicates the responsibility that supposedly belongs to influence. This temporality frustrates Potter's assignment of responsibility to the media because it nullifies his distinction between probabilistic and deterministic causation. In retrospect, the probability of history having happened is by definition one hundred percent.

The distinction between accountability and responsible influence that Potter makes in order to demonstrate the legal relevance of free will relies on his false distinction between probabilistic and deterministic causation, and it therefore lacks validity. It is at best undemonstrable and at worst self-contradictory. Without addressing this problem, Potter goes to great lengths to show how violent art does have accountability before the law, employing a two-pronged attack. First, he cites the notion of clear and present danger that in U.S. law makes some speech acts criminal, and he argues that some violent fictions qualify as criminal speech. Second, he cites the notion of product liability that in U.S. law makes manufacturers of defective products or products that lack sufficient warning labels responsible for the harm they cause, and he argues that some violent fictions qualify as defective and/or insufficiently labeled causes of harm.[16] By claiming that the liability falls on artists (such as Wes Craven) rather than artifacts, Potter avoids hyperbolic personification of the media as a hate-filled entity bent on the destruction of society, but he nevertheless ties accountability to the influence provided by artists through the media of their art. The problem here is that the artists can't control or, according to Potter's own argument, entirely predict how people will respond to their art. In fact, the artists are usually nowhere near their artifacts when people experience their influence. By themselves, movies don't kill people. They don't do anything. My argument here may seem similar to the National Rifle Association's famous argument, "guns don't kill people, people do," but it's more than that. People can directly use guns to kill people. Unless they choose to batter their intended victims with a DVD or book, people can't use fictions to hurt anyone directly. Linking culpability, accountability, or responsibility directly to the influence of art gives it an agency that, while not necessarily human itself, impinges on human agency and creates a problem for a criminal justice system that seeks the prosecution of human perpetrators.

A different approach — blaming violent fictions because they contribute to the construction of social norms — is even more problematic than Potter's appeal for the media's culpable agency under U.S. law because it disperses the media's agency so broadly that it renders the law or any other institution that would enforce responsibility impotent. Michael Medved exemplifies this approach:

> I never stress the pernicious power of one movie, or one TV show, or one hit song; what concerns me is the accumulated impact of irresponsible messages that are repeated hour after hour, year after year. The most significant problems of the popular culture stem from the pervasive presence of antisocial material, not from a few isolated examples of offensiveness.[17]

If the pervasiveness of "antisocial" art causes the most significant problems, then art's culpable agency belongs not to specific artworks but to an aggregate. In effect, blame must spread throughout the entire field of culture. This general culpability not only removes individual human agency but all individual agency, leaving criminal justice with virtually no place to start. When influential ideas are criminals, criminals go free.

I don't claim that fictions lack roles in the multiple causation of events that we can observe retrospectively, and I don't claim that human agents possess a free will that is independent of cultural determination. Though it does for many thinkers, deterministic thinking for me does not preclude individual — and prosecutable — agency and responsibility. I readily grant that fictions teach people ways they might live; they can provide role models that shape how readers and viewers behave. Allowing that fictions can be role models posits a role for fiction in identification and consequent subject formation. In the remainder of this introduction, I'll examine theories of identification and subject formation that allow us to understand how fiction can participate in these processes while lacking the causal agency necessary for fixing blame. Because it deals with a number of difficult theoretical texts in a relatively short span, this examination involves some of the densest material in this book, a great deal of abstraction for which the concrete examples are deferred until later chapters. If you don't care for such stuff, please skip ahead. If you do, consider that identity and consciousness are, like causal influences, retrospective formations, but they are focused on the body: the body is the site that makes the effect of influence present. The embodied human agent alone has an agency sufficient for culpability. As bodily action influenced by Gothic fiction passes into history, the influence passes into reality.

Influence and Identification

Granting that fictions can provide role models means admitting that people can learn how to behave from fiction, and this learning becomes a facet of who they are. Building on the ideas of Kendall Walton, Thomas Pavel's study *Fictional Worlds* notes how "we participate in fictional happenings by projecting a fictional ego who attends the imaginary events as a kind of nonvoting member," and "after their return from travel in the realms of art, fictional egos... effectively melt back into the actual egos, sharing with them their fictional growth."[18] Readers enter fictional worlds with an ego whose relative passivity makes it highly impressionable. The intermediary "fictional ego" provides the conduit for influence to cross from the realm of fiction into reality, bringing with it fiction's formative potential. Reading Cervantes, Foucault discusses "madness by romantic identification" in *Madness and Civilization* as an exemplar of anxieties about "the relationships, in a work of art, between the real and the imaginary," relationships that allow "chimeras" to be "transmitted from author to reader."[19] The madness that readers contract from fiction reshapes their actual egos, creating new and dangerous forms of subjectivity.

Warning about fiction's corrosive role models, Medved states, "Children and adolescents regularly imitate heroes from television in shaping their styles of speech, dress, and grooming; it is only to be expected that they will similarly try to follow the lead of these role models when it comes to intimate relationships."[20] The phrase "follow the lead" suggests a unidirectional pathway of identification in fictional influences. For expectations based on this unidirectional model of identification to hold, fictions must present not only a leader who clearly invites identification but who also determines how readers will interpret and implement the model supplied. The unidirectional model of identification must remain remarkably simple, relying, perhaps, on pseudo–Freudian accounts of how individuals identify with and embrace the behaviors of models based on a perception of similarity between model and self. Carol Clover's *Men, Women, and Chain Saws* demonstrates that horror films confound such simplicity; Clover explains ways a single horror movie can invite spectators to identify both within and across gender boundaries, both with and against perpetrators and victims of violence.[21] Gerard Jones shows how "a girl can identify with both Indiana Jones and the female sidekick in love with him," and a boy can both want and want to be the adventuress Lara Croft, selecting models based on sexual and other kinds of difference as well as sameness.[22] No fiction, horror or otherwise, offers singular, unidirectional models for identification. Identification depends on the shifting and multiple relationships that a reader establishes with a text.

In some media, a fictional ego may be powerless to alter events in a fictional world, but the ego's passivity in that sense does not mean that it will grow in response to those events in a way determined by the world of fiction. Determinations of responses to texts come from beyond the text: the actual world shapes the actual ego, and the actual ego determines the receptivity of the fictional ego. Even Potter, who blames the media for their influences, nevertheless grants importance to the way readers and viewers approach a text:

> For example, some viewers seek out graphic horror for excitement and for the opportunity to demonstrate mastery over fear. These viewers report a positive affect both before and after viewing. But viewers who watch because of anger, loneliness, or personal problems report negative feelings after viewing and attribute these feelings to the exposure; however, these people usually have negative feelings before the exposure.[23]

Positive and negative affective responses to texts, which bear on identification and subsequent behaviors, occur independently from the texts. The position of the fictional ego in reaction to the fictional world — the pathway of its identification — depends on the predispositions that make up the actual ego.

In *Pascalian Meditations*, Pierre Bourdieu explains how influence is contingent upon predisposition:

> Produced by the incorporation of a social structure in the form of a quasi-natural disposition that often has all the appearances of innateness, habitus is the *vis insita*, the potential energy, the dormant force, from which symbolic violence, and especially that exercised through performatives, derives its mysterious efficacy. It is also the origin of that particular form of symbolic efficacy, "influence" (that of a person — "a bad influence" — a thought, an author, etc.), which is often invoked as a tautological explanation and which loses all its mystery as soon as its quasi-magical effects are related to the conditions of production of the dispositions which predisposed agents to undergo it.

Perhaps the most salient concept in Bourdieu's sociology, "habitus" describes the system of predispositions, derived from family, education, and other institutions, that define an individual human agent in and as a relation to a specific "field," which is an "institutionalization of a point of view," a system of relations differentiated within the social world by a particular approach to the social world.[24] Understanding the individual habitus as an inscription, or a determination, of "a social structure" gives influence the status of an epiphenomenon of the social: influence occurs because the social predisposes agents to succumb to it.

Arguing that influence is a "tautological explanation," in effect explaining nothing about the action shaped by influence, does not obviate influence's role within action. As in the example of an author or thought's influence, or the example of an influential text, "influence" describes the relation of the individual to the text. Influence occurs when a fictional ego grows within a fictional world, and as Pavel points out, "actors in the fictional system ... retain most of their traits, cultural or biological, displayed by their actual bearers."[25] Combining Pavel's terminology with Bourdieu's, the fictional ego retains much of the habitus of the actual ego, so the habitus that determines the relation of influence, not the influence itself, ultimately explains whatever actions emerge once the fictional ego shares its growth with the actual ego.

Influence in a text *is* the growth of the fictional ego, not the cause of growth. In retrospect, the growth is certainly an inseparable part of subsequent actions, causing the actions to be in the way they historically are. The growth might even have enabled the actions, giving them a shape without which they could not have been. The text in which the growth has occurred is also a retrospective part of subsequent actions. The text contributes to the actions' historical shape by virtue of its historical presence, in a sense causing that shape. It takes no greater part in causality than that. Though the text has provided the site for growth, predispositions stimulate the growth. The text has provided the path of the causal chain that links predisposition to influence and influence to action, causing the final action to be in the way that it is, but it has not provided the chain's impetus or direction. It is part of the chain's being, supplying the raw material for influence, but it has not caused any link in the chain to be. Outside of this vital causality, the text stands beyond any responsibility, culpability, or accountability associated with causal agency. The language of action that often accompanies claims about influence — as in, "the media exert an influence" — is misleading because it almost assumes such an agency. A text can provide the occasion and material for change, but the change itself depends wholly upon a causal agency that lies within predispositions independent of the text.

Predispositions determine the influences and concomitant processes of identification that occur in an individual's relationships with a text. Identifications shift and multiply according to the habitus of the identifier. Just as the text does not actively participate in the vital causal chain that links predisposition to influence and influence to action, it also stands outside the retrospective process of subject formation. Slavoj Žižek, expounding on Lacanian psychoanalysis, argues that "identity as such is a 'reflective determination,' an inverted presentation of its opposite."[26] A subject identifies with an object, which could be a fictional or real model of some kind, through differentiation. The self must relate to an other as different, as other, in order to imitate it. In Žižek's formulation, both "reflective" and "determination" bear double meanings. Identity is reflective first in that it involves mirror-like reflection; only the inverted difference of the reflection in the mirror can afford the recognition that constitutes selfhood. "Recognition" gestures toward the second sense in which identity is reflective: only through cognitive reflection can the subject ascertain difference and begin the process of imitation that incorporates the other into the self. The double meaning of "determination" works similarly. The other first determines the self through the mirror's presentation of inverse correspondences, and the self then determines, or judges, that it is the other because it is so determined. The judgment and cognitive reflection that constitute selfhood do so only in retrospect. Looking at the self is always looking backward. The site of the initial reflection and determination—the mirror or the text—plays no active role in this retrospection. The mirror and the text are alike occasions for influence, providers of raw material for the shaping of the self. The process of looking back is the process that allows the fictional ego to melt into the actual ego; predisposition, not the text, motivates both the growth and its transference. Retrospection allows for identification, the transference of influence from the site of its birth, the text, to the true site and agent of social action, the human body.

The Body and the Temporality of Freedom

Predispositions determine influences, and influences, in turn, determine new predispositions. Texts, like all other sources for role models, are parts of a social field, and as such they can contribute to the formations of habitus. As a process of growth that augments and changes identity, influence participates in the cycle of determinations through which individual human agents move in the social world. If the agent exists only through such determinations, how is s/he an "agent" at all? Bourdieu uses the concept of habitus to argue that determinism and agency are not mutually exclusive, that the ancient opposition of determinism to free will is as false a dilemma as Potter and others would have it be. Bourdieu effectively argues that humans are agents not despite but because of determinism.

Developing his argument from a reading of Pascal, Bourdieu explains:

> The world encompasses me, comprehends me as a thing among things, but I, as a thing for which there are things, comprehend this world. And I do so (must it be added?) *because* it encompasses and comprehends me; it is through this material inclusion — often unnoticed or repressed — and what follows from it, the incorporation of social structures in the form of dispositional structures, of objective chances in the form of expectations or anticipations, that I acquire a practical knowledge and control of the encompassing space (I know confusedly what depends on me and what does not, what is "for me" or "not for me" or "not for people like me," what it is "reasonable" for me to do, to hope for and ask for). But I cannot comprehend this practical comprehension unless I comprehend both what distinctively defines it, as opposed to conscious, intellectual comprehension, and also the conditions (linked to positions in social space) of these two forms of comprehension.

The relations "for me" and "not for me" are relations of positive and negative identity, and the incorporation of these social relations literally create the "I." "Incorporation" is especially apt because the position that comprehends these relations is a bodily position:

> Having the (biological) property of being open to the world, and therefore exposed to the world, and so capable of being conditioned by the world, shaped by the material and cultural conditions of existence in which it is placed from the beginning, it [the body] is subject to a process of socialization of which individuation is itself the product, with the singularity of the "self" being fashioned in and by social relations.[27]

The body receives the world, and this reception results in socialization, the inscription of habitus, that creates the individual self. "I" am the predispositions of the incorporated social acting within the social. In this sense, as Bourdieu claims, the social's comprehension of me as a permeable body results in my practical comprehension of the social. I relate because I am related, and my body is the intersection of relations where comprehension erupts in present action.

Bourdieu's distinction between "practical comprehension" and "conscious, intellectual comprehension" is crucial. It makes way for a kind of agency very different from traditional conceptions of a free, deliberate will: the knowledge of the subject, of "me," is a bodily knowledge of practice, of the possibilities of action, a "knowledge and control" derived directly from the bodily position of the subject in social space. Habitus

> restores to the agent a generating, unifying, constructing, classifying power, while recalling that this capacity to construct social reality, itself socially constructed, is not that of a transcendental subject but of a socialized body, investing in its practice socially constructed organizing principles that are acquired in the course of a situated and dated social experience.

The power of the embodied agent is not "transcendental" but determined; the agent can construct because s/he is constructed. Action is not "conscious" in the traditional sense because habitus provides the structures of cognition and the predispositions that combine with the possibilities offered by the social field "in determining the things done, or not to be done." Drawing on a common parallel, Bourdieu compares this combination of predispositions with possibilities to the combination of a composer with a piano, which offers "apparently unlimited possibilities" even though the composer's actions are "doubly determined" by the "dispositions of the artist" and the "possibilities of the instrument."[28] Action does not result from a deliberate choice stemming from transcendent selfhood, but it does result from the unique combination of the acting agent and the social field.

The bodily actions that result from the combinations of predispositions and possibilities with the social world belong to no one other than the perpetrator of those actions. The socialization of the body results in individuation, in selfhood, and the movement of the embodied self within the social results in action: the selfhood determined by the social has discrete causal agency. The idea of a self that depends on determining forces for its existence and for its ability to act reconciles determinism with individual causal agency. The causal agent, the body individuated through socialization, is the combination of all of the social and socialized factors that contribute to action. That combination is unique and solely responsible for causing the action. Though the actions stemming from habitus do implicate the social world that has inscribed predispositions, the combination of predispositions is no less individual and no less responsible for its actions for that implication. The social world participates in the causal chain that leads to action. It causes predispositions, predispositions cause influences, and influences can cause something to be that would not have been otherwise. Unlike texts, influences do participate in causal chains that end with crime, but they are just determinations among determinations. No subset of determinations bears responsibility: all determinations together bear responsibility, and the causal agent, the individual criminal, is an embodiment of that totality.

Bourdieu claims that there is freedom within determination, freedom that comes from the bodily knowledge of determination. He calls for a "critical reflexivity," "thought about the social conditions of thought which offers thought the possibility of a genuine *freedom* with respect to these conditions."[29] Freedom, like identity, is reflective, or retrospective. Reflection is an engagement with the self as an object, as a text of predispositions, maintained through the cognitive mechanisms of habitus. Such an engagement is capable of producing an influence, a growth that leads to new predispositions. These new predispositions change the conditions of determination, and this capacity for change looks a lot like traditional accounts of conscious free will.

While Bourdieu and Žižek's approaches to the problem of consciousness differ significantly, Žižek nonetheless offers insight into retrospective freedom that illuminates the temporal dimensions of Bourdieu's concept of agency:

> The common wisdom about how history *in actu* is experienced as the domain of freedom, whereas retroactively we are able to perceive its causal determination... should be reversed: when we are caught in the flow of events, we act "automatically," as if under the impression that it is not possible to do otherwise, there is really no choice; whereas the retrospective view displays how the events could have taken a radically different turn — how what we perceived as necessity was actually a free decision of ours. In other words, what we encounter here is another confirmation of the fact that the time of the subject is never "present" — the subject never "is," it only "will have been": we never *are* free, it is only afterwards that we discover how we *have been* free.[30]

For both Bourdieu and Žižek, the self knows its position within the field of social determinations when it reflects, and that self-recognition creates the possibility of freedom. Žižek inverts the retrospective approach to causality that blames Gothic influences for real-world violence. His reasoning suggests how, looking back, those who blame Gothic influences should be able to see how things that now seem like historical necessities could have happened differently. The criminal, with different predispositions, could have identified with a Gothic text differently. The criminal, if self-reflective, could have produced the predispositions necessary to identify harmlessly. At the present time of bodily action, the criminal has no freedom because predispositions start the causal chain. Retrospectively, the criminal has had freedom and the responsibility and culpability that go with it.

Gothic Realities

Gothic fictions give form to social phenomena, causing them to be in the way that they historically are, but they are not the culpable cause for the phenomena's reality. The definition of objective "reality" is unstable and slippery, but it has a distinct temporality. Noting that "objective reality" derives from the field of science, Bourdieu explains, "This 'objective reality' to which everyone explicitly or tacitly refers is ultimately no more than what the researchers engaged in the field at a given moment agree to consider as such, and it only ever manifests itself in the field through the *representations* given of it by those who invoke its arbitration."[31] Objective reality is only accessible as a consensus of subjectivities; the scientific field produces both the consensus and the subjectivities. The consensus "manifests itself" in "representations," representations that occasion reflections on the consensus. Identity and freedom rely on representations of the self to the self, and reality relies upon representations of a field of selves to the field of selves. Reality, like freedom and identity, is retrospective. All realities come from reflections on representations.

Reality has the power of arbitration because it is a marker of status by which (in terms derived from both Bourdieu and Foucault) an object of knowledge can gain admittance into a field's domain of truth and validity. As the section of this book entitled "Gothic Ghosts" suggests, mainstream science uses its consensus of reality to disqualify ghosts from the domain of truth, but parapsychology uses its consensus to give ghosts the status of possible reality. For parapsychologists, Gothic representations are among the representations that give rise to the reality that allows arbitration and judgment. The power of Gothic fictions to give rise to realities is not unique, but critics' awareness of it is. As the section of this book entitled "Gothic Threats" demonstrates, volatile attacks on the Gothic's formative potential have accompanied Gothic representations since the eighteenth century. These attacks have shaped the Gothic's place in critical discourse, making the Gothic both low culture and a focus for cultural anxieties about art's influences. The section of this book entitled "Gothic Violence" goes further, showing ways that fear of an influence's power actually gives that influence power, so the cultural predisposition is complicit with the influence's outcome.

Žižek generalizes about how presupposition of an object's power serves to give that object power. When the subject blames the object for having power over him,

> the subject fails to notice how he himself *posits* the Other: by means of the very act of recognizing myself as the addressee of an ideological call, I (presup)posit the Other as the agency which confers meaning upon the contingency of the Real; by means of the very act of perceiving myself as the impotent, negligible, insignificant witness of the spectacle of the Other, I constitute its mysterious, transcendent character.[32]

The big O in Žižek's "Other" identifies that Other with the entire symbolic order that structures and determines thought, but his analysis of the Other applies to any specimen of that order that has the same structuring potential. A reader brings predispositions into a Gothic text, and the predispositions determine the Gothic's structuring influence. If the reader is predisposed toward the Gothic influence, s/he effects that influence. The reader is the source of and is responsible for the Gothic's power. Žižek describes the Other as an "illusion" that derives its power from the subject, but his "crucial point is that this 'illusion' structures our (social) reality itself."[33] The agency of the Gothic is illusory, derived from human agents, but as an illusion, its formative potential is vast.

Social reality differs from "the Real" in Žižek's Lacanian reasoning. While reality is the symbolic, that which "serves as the external boundary which enables us to totalize language," the Real is "its inherent limit, the unfathomable fold which prevents it from achieving its identity with itself." Reality is the condition of thought, the consensus that allows for meaningful discourse, but the Real is that which disrupts that consensus, the kernel of the irrational against which reason defines itself. The Gothic, born during the heyday of the Enlightenment, is the intrusion of irrationality on the rational: Žižek even posits that "the Gothic novel is a kind of critique *avant la lettre*" of Enlightenment philosophy.[34] Gothic representations of unreality are representations of what Žižek calls "the Real." As representations within the symbolic they have the power to structure social reality, but by introducing the Real into reality, they threaten the coherence of the reality they help constitute. Žižek warns that "'madness' (psychosis) sets in... when the [R]eal overflows reality... or when it is itself included in reality."[35] One form of this madness is what Foucault calls the madness of romantic identification: when the subject identifies within the Gothic, the subject includes irrationality within rationality, the Real in reality. The subject is culpable for this inclusion, for being predisposed to succumb to the Gothic's irrational influence. The subject is tainted by unreason but nevertheless free in her or his incorporation of the irrational into her or his rational self. To frame the issue in the terms of criminal justice, the subject is sane and guilty, but the Gothic is not guilty by reason of insanity.

Part One
Gothic Threats

1

The Threat in the Gothic's Foundation
From John Locke to Horace Walpole

Since the first Gothic novels appeared in the eighteenth century, the Gothic has been on trial for creating unsettling realities. At the time of the Gothic's birth, the novel itself was still a fairly new phenomenon. Because it could use exciting stories to communicate almost anything to newly literate masses of women and members of the lower classes, the novel made many people uneasy. Critics worried that communicable ideas, when bad, could function like communicable diseases, infecting all who encounter them. Gothic fictions center on representations of the outré, the violent, and the horrible, so critics often treated them as the worst of a bad form, destined to communicate bad ideas. Any writing had the potential to be a bad influence, but Gothic writing seemed to realize that potential just by being Gothic. This chapter examines how being Gothic became synonymous with being bad, and it turns to eighteenth-century philosophy for an explanation of why critics regarded dark fiction as dangerously infectious. The idea that Gothic fictions are responsible for reshaping readers in their own horrific images stems from a translation of a philosophy of mind into moral and aesthetic imperatives for the governance of both writing and criticism. Enlightenment thinkers nurtured this idea, endowing it with the quality of truth that it still has today.

Horace Walpole's Anti-Enlightenment Agenda

Widely regarded as the first Gothic novel, Horace Walpole's *The Castle of Otranto* appeared in December 1764 not as a novel but, according to its preface, as a translation of a recently rediscovered Italian manuscript of a medieval romance. In 1765 Walpole published a second edition, appended the subtitle "A Gothic Story," and included a new preface that confesses his authorship. Walpole excuses his dissimulation by pleading that, since "diffidence of his own abilities, and the novelty of the attempt, were his sole inducements to assume that disguise, he flatters himself he shall appear excusable."[1] Though he appears to tell the truth about the novel in the second preface, his claim about his modest motives is another lie. Walpole writes of *Otranto* in a letter to his friend Madame du Deffand, "j'ai voulu qu'elle passât pour ancienne, et presque tout le monde en fut la dupe."[2] Walpole glories in having tricked the world into believing his work is something it is not — a "real" tale from "Gothic" times. He suggests that his motive for writing the first so-called "Gothic Story" — his motive for creating the Gothic itself — was a desire to lead readers astray.

Framing a novel in a way that tricks its audience was common practice in the eighteenth century. Lennard Davis's study *Factual Fictions* discusses how early eighteenth-century novels trick people by using an "overt" frame of truth to mask a "covert" frame of fictionality.[3] For readers, this trick produces "a characteristic uncertainty or ambivalence as to whether they were reading something true or false."[4] A play of overt and covert frames pertaining to the "truth" of a work produces uncertainty about the boundary between fiction and reality. The aim of the "trick" is a state of epistemological uncertainty that destabilizes the perception of "reality" itself.

Walpole's trick differs from the standard trick of authors who, like Daniel Defoe, frame their fictions as true stories. The uncertainty created by *Otranto* is not about whether the events related in the story actually occurred: it is about whether the text itself is "real," a product of an era when a story involving gigantic ghosts, moving portraits, and walking skeletons could be believable. A reviewer, angry at being one of Walpole's dupes, explains his distress in *The Monthly Review* of May 1765:

> But when, as in this edition, the Castle of Otranto is declared to be a modern performance, that indulgence we afforded to the foibles of a supposed antiquity, we can by no means extend to the singularity of a false taste in a cultivated

1. The Threat in the Gothic's Foundation

period of learning. It is, indeed, more than strange, that an Author, of a refined and polished genius, should be an advocate for re-establishing the barbarous superstitions of Gothic devilism![5]

While *Otranto* would be acceptable as a specimen framed by its origin in "barbarous" times, the "cultivated period of learning" that is the eighteenth century should not produce such "devilism." Proponents of so-called Enlightenment sought to distance the era from the barbarism and superstition perceived in *Otranto*'s medieval setting and supposed origin. The *Monthly* reviewer suggests he could excuse the barbarism of the first edition because it seemed naturally to reflect the acknowledged barbarism of its alleged origins. The barbarism of the first text was not a threat because it confirmed widespread assumptions about the Middle Ages, the dark times before the Enlightenment's light. The second edition situates the text's darkness firmly within that light, revealing the fragility of the reviewer's assumptions. If Walpole's text could be written and published in the 1760s, then the definitional opposition of this "cultivated period" to Gothic barbarism collapses. Walpole's fiction about his text's reality threatens to expose the "cultivated" reality of the eighteenth century as a fiction.

Otranto's story, when read alongside its inveigling prefaces, suggests that Walpole intended his trick to create an uncertainty beyond mere confusion about when the text was written. Walpole's first preface deceived the world about the origin of his novel. Similarly, the family of Manfred, who is *Otranto's* archetypal Gothic villain, deceives the world about the origin of its claim to the titular castle, and the novel's plot focuses on the supernatural repercussions of this deceit. In "The Gothic Ghost of the Counterfeit and the Progress of Abjection," Jerrold Hogle exposes a pattern of deceptions and counterfeits throughout the novel. The ghost who exposes Manfred's deception, Alfonso, comes from a statue, and a second ghost, Ricardo, comes from a portrait. Virtually every origin in the novel is some kind of artifice, and characters throughout the novel, confronted by ghosts of counterfeits, can never be certain about what they see.[6] Fakery within *Otranto* causes violent, unnatural disturbances in the lives of its characters. Fakery surrounding the novel disturbed critics because it disrupted the sense of cultivation with which they defined and regulated their cultural lives. Disturbances within the text anticipate the disturbance created by the text, making *Otranto* seem calculated to transfer the chaos of a Gothic fiction into an unready cultural reality. The reviewer for *The Monthly* who calls Walpole an "advocate" for the instability that his text could cause can justify the claim by pointing at the text itself.

The most disturbing thing for the *Monthly* reviewer of *Otranto* is not that the novel confuses enlightened beliefs but that it might have the ability to "re-establish" the wrong kind of beliefs. Walpole supposedly advocates darkness in the Enlightenment, creating with his "Gothic Story" a new form, the Gothic, that provides images, tropes, and vocabulary that resist the cultural establishment's regulating definitions. While an anti-establishment agenda might seem odd in the hands of Horace Walpole, a wealthy son of a prime minister and "a refined and polished genius," his work exhibits such perverse "devilism" nonetheless. Walpole's politics are slippery, but Crystal Lake compellingly argues that Walpole's misleading first preface to *Otranto* satirizes royalist antiquarianism in ways that reveal his "Whiggish political agenda."[7] Progressive and even subversive in its very form, the Gothic as Walpole fashioned it intrinsically challenges the reigning social order. Analyzing the *Monthly*'s reaction to *Otranto*, E.J. Clery argues that no reviewer could "countenance" a work that would taint "an age of reason" with an interest in the supernatural.[8] Perceiving how such an interest threatens the establishment's interest in natural, stable, rational order, critics must declare it "a false taste" and condemn it.

This *Monthly* review models a derisive attitude toward the Gothic that became a norm for the Gothic's critics. Critics could label writers who followed in Walpole's footsteps as guilty by association alone. In her 1778 preface to *The Old English Baron*, the second major Gothic novel, Clara Reeve claims she has followed Walpole's design for *Otranto* in creating her own "Gothic Story," but she also explains that she has modified it to exclude her forebear's "redundancy" of the "marvelous" because it "palls upon the mind."[9] Reeve's novel backs away from the rampant supernaturalism of Walpole's tale — its excess of superstitious devilism — and adds strong and overt moralizing where Walpole only offers vague (and generally unconvincing) moral insights. Reeve's revision of Walpole's plan suggests a familiarity with the critics who immediately condemned Walpole after he unmasked *Otranto* as a modern production; moreover, the impulse to revise it at all suggests acceptance of the idea that there is simply something wrong with the Gothic that must be corrected.

Despite Reeve's efforts to fix the Gothic, *The Old English Baron* appears alongside Walpole's work in later reviews of Gothic novels that condemn the Gothic for its erroneous reflection of the times that produce it. In its November 1792 issue, the *Monthly* condemns *The Castle of St. Vallery, an Ancient Story*:

This story is an imitation of the Castle of Otranto, Sir Bertrand, and the Old English Baron, and others, in which the chief passion intended to be excited is fear. Of all the resources of invention, this, perhaps, is the most puerile, as it is certainly among the most unphilosophic. It contributes to keep alive that superstition which debilitates the mind, that ignorance which propagates error, and that dread of invisible agency which makes inquiry criminal.[10]

The Castle of St. Vallery is guilty by association with Walpole and his imitators of being "puerile," or immature (undeveloped — even barbaric), and "unphilosophic," or outside the normative discourses of reason. Instead of addressing the specific flaws of *The Castle of St. Vallery*, the critic just enumerates the flaws of the Gothic. With recourse to the well-established failings of Walpole, the reviewer can dismiss this new novel summarily. The next chapter analyzes other critics' more specific complaints and the effects of those complaints on the Gothic. The generality of this complaint, however, reflects how critics perceived texts built on Walpole's foundation as intrinsically dangerous.

The Gothic's Dangerous Impressions

The Gothic poses a dangerous challenge to claims about the eighteenth century's enlightenment, but concern about how *St. Vallery* "debilitates the mind" points to an even deeper threat in the Gothic's foundation. The philosophies of John Locke and his eighteenth-century successors created an intellectual environment where concerns about literature's connection to the maintenance of a healthy mind were paramount. Locke's first and most devastating point in *An Essay Concerning Human Understanding*, first published in 1690, is that there are "no innate principles in the mind." He begins, "It is the established opinion amongst some men that there are in the *understanding* certain *innate principles*...which the soul receives in its very first being and brings into the world with it." Locke overturns "established opinion" when he describes how "the senses at first let in particular *ideas* and furnish the yet empty cabinet" of the mind, and though "some truths" appear "very early," even "infants" owe them to "impressions on their senses" rather than innate principles.[11] The initial shock of abandoning the notion of innate principles reverberates throughout eighteenth-century moral and aesthetic discourses. Shifting to a belief in the mind's dependence on sense-impressions for all its ideas renders the mind newly vulnerable: without an innate core to structure it, the mind looks like clay in the hands of innumerable influences.

The idea of a uniform or universal morality is one of the first concepts to fall before Locke's conception of a mind without innate principles. Though Locke contends that "morality [might be placed] amongst the sciences capable of demonstration," he nevertheless argues that morality is not universal. He treats the lack of uniformity as self-evident, stating, "Whether there be any such moral principles wherein all men do agree, I appeal to any who have been but moderately conversant in the history of mankind, and looked abroad beyond the smoke of their own chimneys."[12] Locke maintains that even the most cursory glance at the varying moral systems in the world would support his dismissal of the idea of a natural morality that binds humankind together. David Hume, making an argument similar to Locke's in *A Treatise of Human Nature*, first published in 1739 and 1740, concludes that the category of the "natural" when applied to human behavior is highly vexed: "'Tis impossible... that the character of natural and unnatural can ever, in any sense, mark the boundaries of vice and virtue." Hume explains:

> So that when you pronounce any action or character to be vicious, you mean nothing, but that from the constitution of your nature you have a feeling or sentiment of blame from the contemplation of it. Vice and virtue, therefore, may be compar'd to sounds, colours, heat and cold, which, according to modern philosophy, are not qualities in objects, but perceptions in the mind.[13]

Vice and virtue are matters of perception, perception, moreover, that is contingent on a changeable "feeling or sentiment" rather than fixed laws or principles. Neither Locke nor Hume is an amoral philosopher — quite the contrary — but their ideas, by challenging the innateness of morality, create the possibility of a highly dangerous moral vacuum.

According to Hume and Locke, ideas that moralists feel ought to be connected to one another will not necessarily be connected. Hume argues that ideas that seem to be connected by necessity in actuality share only a "customary" link.[14] Because only custom connects one idea to another, people's impressions might cause them to make the wrong connections. Locke explains the consequence:

> This wrong connexion in our minds of ideas, in themselves loose and independent one of another, has such an influence and is of so great force to set us awry in our actions as well moral as natural, passions, reasonings, and notions themselves, that perhaps there is not any one thing that deserves to be more looked after.[15]

Though Locke denies the existence of an innate and universal morality, his sense that moral principles are objectively demonstrable allows him

1. The Threat in the Gothic's Foundation

to judge actions and other results from the connection of ideas as right or wrong. To prevent actions that are morally wrong, Locke recommends "looking after" the discourses that might create faulty or even uncertain moral connections. He argues that "it is a great negligence and perverseness to discourse of moral things with uncertainty and obscurity."[16] Locke suggests that every source of moral impressions needs policing: those who contribute to or allow bad discourses are guilty of being negligent and perverse.

When Locke considers how obscure moral discourses can lead to erroneous connections of ideas, he implicitly grants literature the power to shape readers in its own image. Locke suggests "that those who have children or the charge of their education would think it worth their while diligently to watch and carefully to prevent the undue connexion of *ideas* in the minds of young people."[17] The minds of the young, which are not yet furnished with a full stock of ideas, are especially impressionable. Any discourse that could reach the ears or eyes of the young requires the strictest policing: potential for education is potential for harm. Either directly or indirectly, eighteenth-century reviews of literature act on Locke's warnings when they treat literature as a potent source of moral impressions and take on the task of policing it.

Providing reviewers with direct fodder for their attacks on the Gothic, Locke singles out discourses of the supernatural for making particularly undesirable impressions on the young. Describing a frightening walk around the ruins of an old abbey on a dark night, Joseph Addison, in issue 110 of *The Spectator*, cites Locke to explain why the combination of this setting's features with darkness produce fear:

> These Objects naturally raise Seriousness and Attention; and when Night heightens the Awfulness of the Place, and pours out her supernumerary Horrours upon every thing in it, I do not at all wonder that weak Minds fill it with Spectres and Apparitions.
> Mr. *Lock*, in his Chapter of the Association of Ideas, has very curious Remarks to shew how by the Prejudice of Education one Idea often introduces into the Mind a whole Set that bear no Resemblance to one another in the Nature of things. Among several examples of this Kind he produces the following instance. *The Ideas of Goblins and Sprights have really no more to do with Darkness than Light; yet let but a foolish Maid inculcate these often on the Mind of a Child, and raise them there together, possibly he shall never be able to separate them again so long as he lives, but Darkness shall ever afterwards bring with it those frightful Ideas, and they shall be so joyned that he can no more bear the one than the other.*[18]

Locke attributes the erroneous connection between darkness and unreal, supernatural beings to the foolish maids of the world who "inculcate" this connection through fantastic stories, and Addison demonstrates the practical application of Locke's view. Addison's Lockean attack on the "Prejudice of Education" suggests that some people, on some subjects, should remain uneducated: some stories should not be told. Addison shows how Locke's philosophy taboos literature focused on supernatural exploits, and that taboo falls squarely on Walpole's version of the Gothic.

Gothic literature might offer dangerous impressions in an even more fundamental way. Locke argues that a complex idea is made up of simple ideas, and a person can grasp a complex idea merely by grasping the simple ideas that constitute it; "[t]hus a man may come to have the *idea* of *sacrilege* or *murder*, by enumerating to him the simple *ideas* which these words stand for, without ever seeing either of them committed." On the surface, this concept is very plain: most people know what murder is but are lucky enough never to have seen it. Conjoined with Locke's notion that many "complex ideas… must needs have been in the minds of men before they existed anywhere else," it has profound implications.[19] Locke argues that many actions owe their existence to precedent ideas. Because ideas are often necessary conditions for action, ideas seem to have causal potential. Apprehending a complex idea like sacrilege or murder might appear, then, to be one step in the direction of committing an actual sacrilege or murder. Encountering the sacrileges and murders of a fictional character like Walpole's Manfred, who murders his own daughter in a church, might be particularly hazardous for impressionable young people. Fictions that depict the horrible might enable impressionable people to enact the horrible. The philosophy of Locke and his successors grants literature the power to communicate ideas that cause things to happen in the real world. Literature dedicated to the expression of horrifying ideas might cause — and be responsible for — horrifying realities. Gothic fictions might even have the power to kill.

The Gothic's Infernal Instructions

Locke's philosophy informs eighteenth-century aesthetic theories that make the morally instructive dimension of literature — its capacity to provide formative impressions — central to consideration of literature's purpose and merit. In his 1765 "Preface" to *The Plays of William Shakespeare*, Samuel

1. The Threat in the Gothic's Foundation

Johnson states unequivocally, "The end of writing is to instruct; the end of poetry to instruct by pleasing." This maxim, more or less accepted by the vast majority of literary critics in Johnson's age, provides a tool that makes matters of aesthetic judgment relatively simple. Does the work instruct? How well does it instruct? Answering these questions will go a long way toward indicating a work's merit. Johnson's assessment of Shakespeare exemplifies this procedure. "Nothing can please many, and please long, but just representations of general nature," Johnson asserts, and since Shakespeare is "the poet of nature" who excels all others in providing "practical axioms and domestic wisdom," he passes the test of instruction.[20] James Beattie, in his *Essay on Poetry and Music, as they Affect the Mind*, written in 1762, claims that, though instruction is not absolutely necessary, "instruction... is necessary to [poems'] *perfection*, because they would not be *perfectly agreeable* without it." Beattie asks, "Verses, that give pleasure only, without profit,—what are they but chiming trifles?"[21] For a work to have true merit, for it to be more than a trifle, it must both please and instruct. A work that lacks instruction is, at the very least, imperfect, and it is more likely to be grievously flawed. A work's instructive capacity determines whether critics will declare it fit for reading.

For many who adopt Locke's view of literature's capacity to produce mind-shaping impressions, literary works seem to have a moral responsibility for their readers. Beattie asserts, "Whatever tends to raise those human affections that are favourable to truth and virtue, or to repress the opposite passions, will always gratify and improve our moral and intellectual powers, and may properly enough be called *instructive*."[22] Beattie makes moral improvement synonymous with "proper" instruction. Beattie and others who emphasize "our" need for improvement cast readers in the roles of students and children, undiscerning people in need of moral guidance placed delicately in the hands of an author working through the medium of a literary work. The hands can raise and repress passions, molding the clay of the mind. When the reader leaves those hands, the author and the work deserve the credit or the blame for what emerges.

A work that pleases but does not provide moral improvement could ultimately be far worse than a mere trifle with low aesthetic value. Though the greatest pleasure might accompany proper instruction, there are other, darker pleasures that literature might provide. Beattie poses a compelling question: "And if a poem were to please, and at the same time, instead of improving, to corrupt the mind, would it not deserve to be considered as a poison rendered doubly dangerous and detestable by its alluring qualities?"²³ In her *Strictures on the Modern System of Female Education*, Hannah More considers the advantage of knowing that an author writes from the perspective of "sound Christian principles":

> It is at least a comfort to the reader, to feel that honest confidence which results from knowing that he has put himself into safe hands; that he has committed himself to an author, whose known principles are a pledge that his reader need not be driven to watch himself at every step with anxious circumspection; that he need not be looking on the right hand and on the left, as if he knew there were pitfalls under the flowers which are delighting him. And it is no small point gained, that on subjects in which you do not look to *improve your* religion, it is at least secured from deterioration.²⁴

A good author is one who takes on the role of a pious protector, for only with such an author can a reader feel safe from the alluring poison, the pitfall that is the delight of impious pleasures. A work might use pleasure to conduct readers to bad ends, and thus it could become "a manual for misconduct."²⁵ A reader risks misdirection every time she or he picks up a book.

The idea that fiction could become a manual for misconduct suggests that good literature will observe strict limits on the aspects of life that it represents. Samuel Johnson justifies placing limits on novelistic representations in the fourth issue of *The Rambler*:

> But the fear of not being approved as just copyers of human manners, is not the most important concern that an author of this sort ought to have before him. These books are written chiefly to the young, the ignorant, and the idle, to whom they serve as lectures of conduct, and introductions into life. They are the entertainment of minds unfurnished with ideas, and therefore easily susceptible of impressions.

Johnson's concern about impressionable minds echoes Locke, not only using Locke's vocabulary of impressions and ideas but also his metaphorical image of the mind as a place that wants furnishing. Providing good impressions, or good moral instruction, requires something other than providing just copies of human manners. Johnson explains:

> It is therefore not a sufficient vindication of a character, that it is drawn as it appears, for many characters ought never to be drawn; nor of a narrative, that the train of events is agreeable to observation and experience, for that observation which is called knowledge of the world, will be found much more frequently to make men cunning than good.²⁶

In accord with Addison's application of Locke, Johnson suggests that some characters should never be represented, and some stories should never be

1. The Threat in the Gothic's Foundation 35

told. Faithful representations of the impure parts of life have the power to corrupt as well as the unfaithful, so authors should avoid such representations, and readers should avoid the authors who don't.

Surveying authors who ignore this imperative, Johnson laments:

> Many writers, for the sake of following nature, so mingle good and bad qualities in their principle personages, that they are equally conspicuous; and as we accompany them through their adventures with delight, and are led by degrees to interest ourselves in their favour, we lose the abhorrence of their faults, because they do not hinder our pleasure, or, perhaps, regard them with some kindness for being united with so much merit.[27]

A mixed character, because she or he has admirable qualities as well as condemnable, could be even more dangerous than a purely bad character because the good mitigates the bad and makes it seem more acceptable. A mixed character offers what Locke might call an erroneous connection of good and bad qualities. On this ground Clara Reeve, in *The Progress of Romance*, disapproves of mixed characters such as Henry Fielding's Tom Jones, who is "capable of doing much mischief," while "[o]n the contrary no harm can possibly arise from the imitation of perfect character, though the attempt should fall short of the original."[28] Realism is not enough for a work to be properly instructive. For fictions to make the proper impressions, they must present an uncommon degree of perfection.

The end of the instruction that writing ought to provide, then, is not just a maintenance but a strengthening of the norms of the status quo. Even if the reader "should fall short" of the model a perfected representation offers, she or he is less likely to fall beneath the moral standards of the time. Fiction should not present the real, but the ideal. For his failure to do so Johnson faults even Shakespeare:

> His first defect is that to which may be imputed most of the evil in books or in men. He sacrifices virtue to convenience, and is so much more careful to please than to instruct that he seems to write without any moral purpose. From his writings indeed a system of social duty may be selected, for he that thinks reasonably must think morally; but his precepts and axioms drop casually from him; he makes no just distribution of good or evil, nor is always careful to show in the virtuous a disapprobation of the wicked; he carries his persons indifferently through right and wrong, and at the close dismisses them without further care, and leaves their examples to operate by chance. This fault the barbarity of his age cannot extenuate; for it is always a writer's duty to make the world better, and justice is a virtue independent on time or place.[29]

Representing a world where justice does not always function ideally, Shakespeare makes the moral impressions left by his works unpredictable and therefore dangerous. In the name of morality, Johnson makes idealization an aesthetic imperative.

Johnson elaborates on this imperative in *The Rambler*, stating that, since wickedness might otherwise have some appeal, "it is therefore to be steadily inculcated, that virtue is the highest proof of understanding, and the only solid basis of greatness; and that vice is the natural consequence of narrow thoughts, that it begins in mistake, and ends in ignominy."[30] Johnson knows that, outside of fiction, virtue is not always rewarded, and vice sometimes triumphs. His praise of naturalness in art, of Shakespeare as the poet of nature, might seem to contradict his aesthetic imperative of idealization. Johnson credits Shakespeare's naturalness for his ability to be so instructive, but he also criticizes Shakespeare for showing things how they are. Davis observes this apparent contradiction in eighteenth-century aesthetic standards and explains, "We are dealing with types or varieties of truth... for a work to be morally verisimilar it has to be actually *un*verisimilar."[31] To maintain natural morals — morality as it really ought to be — representations of life must be unreal. Moral truth takes precedence over literary verisimilitude.

While the tension between natural morals and human nature that arises from the aesthetic imperative of idealization might dissolve with recourse to "varieties of truth" in theory, in practice the imperative produces blatant hypocrisy. In the *Critical Review* for January 1789, a reviewer blasts Clara Reeve, whose *Progress of Romance* numbers her among the champions of moral verisimilitude, for representing the efficacy of deceit in her novel *The Exiles*: "In a moral view, we must, however, object to the necessity which there appears to be for so much deceit: it should be carefully concealed that deceit can ever become necessary."[32] This reviewer states that Reeve needs to conceal, or lie about, the necessity of lying, doing the very thing she or he condemns. The critic's hypocrisy gestures toward the purpose behind the play of multiple truths inherent in the aesthetic imperative of idealization. Locke's philosophy of mind does away with universal morality, creating new anxieties about morals that lead to mandates for the stronger policing of moral influences. Encouraging writers to do things like lying about lying, the aesthetic imperative of idealization would ensure the purity of moral influences by creating the illusion of fixed and reliable morality — a morality in which the horrors of vice and the triumph of virtue make moral distinctions clear and consistent. With no innate morality, lying about lying can be moral. The lie fills the vacuum left in the absence of innate ideas; it is a relativistic instantiation of the higher morality of absolutes.

1. The Threat in the Gothic's Foundation

Gothic novels fail to conform to the aesthetic imperative of idealization: their unrealistic representations increase the uncertainty that the imperative would diminish. Gothic novels of the eighteenth century often do end with rewards for the virtuous and punishments for the vicious, but their dedication to exhibiting illicit behaviors and unreal horrors connects the pleasures of reading them with things far from ideal. Though Johnson never makes any direct comment on the Gothic, his thoughts in *The Rambler* on why the modern novel is more pernicious than the ancient romance provide insight into how the heirs of his ideas might apply them to Walpole's innovation:

> In the romances formerly written, every transaction and sentiment was so remote from all that passes among men, that the reader was in very little danger of making any applications to himself; the virtues and crimes were equally beyond his sphere of activity; and he amused himself with heroes and with traitors, deliverers and persecutors, as with beings of another species, whose actions were regulated upon motives of their own, and who had neither faults nor excellencies in common with himself.
> But when an adventurer is leveled with the rest of the world, and acts in such scenes of the universal drama, as may be the lot of any other man; young spectators fix their eyes upon him with closer attention, and hope by observing his behaviour and success to regulate their own practices, when they shall be engaged in the like part.[33]

Johnson approves the improbabilities of ancient romance because they are too "remote" from eighteenth-century reality to be practically instructive, but because modern romances lack this remoteness, they have a greater potential for bad instruction.

In his second preface to *Otranto*, Walpole explains that his creation of the Gothic "was an attempt to blend the two kinds of romance, the ancient and the modern," combining the "imagination and improbability" of the ancient romance with the "strict adherence to modern life" in modern fictions.[34] This blend of kinds makes unrealistic evils appear to be a part of the "universal drama"; it allows Walpole to present a character, Manfred, who behaves like the most extravagant persecutor in an ancient romance without seeming to belong to "another species." Manfred's combination of inhuman ambition and cruelty with glimmers of compassion and other human feelings sets a precedent for excessively evil characters with whom a reader might nonetheless identify, making "applications to himself" from a Gothic villain. Even though many Gothic novels set their stories in the remote past, the manners of their characters are almost always decidedly modern. The Gothic eliminates the remoteness that made ancient romances safe and adds in its place the verisimilitude that makes modern novels dangerous. Clery notes that *Otranto*'s combination of kinds offers "a possibility unforeseen by Johnson" that amounts to "a peculiarly dangerous threat."[35] From the perspective of Johnson's heirs, the Gothic might seem like the worst of both worlds.

The dangerous, subversive elements in Walpole's formula for the Gothic fail to meet the standards of the aesthetic imperative of idealization. The Gothic is an inherently dangerous combination of the un-ideal elements from ancient romances and modern novels. Instead of masking the uncertainties that surround virtue and vice in life beyond fiction, it magnifies them to unrealistic extremes. In doing so, it threatens to open up the moral vacuum created by the absence of innate ideas that the imperative would close. Adopting the imperative as an equation of aesthetic and moral principles, a critic could condemn the Gothic for the very terms that Walpole uses to define it. Creating more than a threat to Enlightenment's self-definition, Walpole appears to have forged the Gothic as a forum for bad instruction, a tool for misshaping minds. Knowing Walpole's formula and armed with the philosophy of Locke as applied by Addison, Johnson, and others, a literary critic could condemn any self-proclaimed "Gothic Story" without even turning a page.

2

Gothic Threats and Cultural Hierarchy
The Critical Evaluation of The Monk *and* The Mysteries *of* Udolpho

Most eighteenth-century literary critics did not condemn the Gothic blindly. They performed their duties as literary police, duties derived from and justified by Locke's philosophy of mind, quite thoroughly, examining Gothic novels for erroneous moral connections and any other threats they might pose to the social order. Critics' scathing reviews use their powers of condemnation and approval to weed out the most dangerous Gothic texts. The society that the reviews defend is their own: the critics' aesthetic ideal is fiction that acts as a bulwark for the status quo that gives them the power to criticize. A political agenda either overtly or covertly informs the judgments they pass in the name of the aesthetic imperative of idealization. As Peter Stallybrass and Allon White state in *The Politics and Poetics of Transgression*, "because the higher discourses are normally associated with the most powerful socio-economic groups existing at the centre of cultural power, it is they which generally gain the authority to designate what is to be taken as high and low in the society."[1] Critics operating within the "higher discourses" divide the field of culture into high and low aesthetic categories, and the aesthetic merits or demerits they applaud or denounce correlate predictably with their perceptions of how artworks support or erode the social order and their own privileged positions within it.

After explaining the specific threats that eighteenth-century critics found within the Gothic's pages, this chapter demonstrates how critics' responses to Matthew Lewis's *The Monk* and Ann Radcliffe's *The Mysteries of Udolpho* exemplify the relation between perceptions of threat and proclamations of merit. The belief in and fear of Gothic fiction's potential to create Gothic realities provided the basis for the Gothic's critical evaluation in the eighteenth century. Belief in that power shaped the criticism, and the criticism, in turn, shaped the Gothic.

A Taxonomy of Gothic Threats

Though David Richter provides an accurate generalization when he claims, "Reviewers for both highbrow and popular publications generally gave the back of their hand to the Gothic," the exceptions to the back-hand rule reveal as much about critics' habits as the adherents do.[2] In an April 1794 review of Regina Maria Roche's *The Maid of the Hamlet* from the *Critical Review*, a reviewer writes that for those who enjoy this sort of novel, "it is an amusement they may be allowed to take without scruple, provided only they forget [it] again the next day; for as there is nothing in the story of the *Maid of the Hamlet* which will contaminate the mind by passing through it, so neither is there any thing which can possibly improve it by being retained there."[3] With reasoning that echoes Hannah More's, this cool but not condemning review approves *The Maid of the Hamlet* for *not* contaminating its readers. The review reads as if the novel has passed an inspection; having examined the work, the reviewer announces that it is contaminant-free.

Eighteenth-century literary critics didn't actually have a universal rubric for assessing the threats posed by Gothic novels, but the trends that emerge in a study of the period's reviews conjure a sort of checklist. A critic might range far from this imaginary list, but in a typical review a typical critic searches for threats that fall into one or more of four categories. First, the critic considers what effects the novel might have on its young readers. Second, the critic checks to see whether the novel subverts normative gender roles. Third, the critic considers the potential the novel might have for inspiring heretical supernatural belief. Finally, the 1790s British critic, aware of the horrors faced by her or his counterparts at the hands of French revolutionaries, determines whether the novel might inspire violent feelings or actions opposed to the ruling order. If, like *The Maid of the Hamlet*, a novel does not exhibit any of these types of threats, critics might assign it a relatively decent, but still low, place in the artistic hierarchy. If, like the work of Ann Radcliffe discussed below, a novel seems

1. Threats to the Young

The *Monthly Review* for March 1793, using a positive evaluation of Robert Bage's novel *Man As He Is* as an opportunity to discuss the potential merits of novels more generally, observes of the role novels play for the young:

> When we consider the influence that novels have over the manners, sentiments, and passions, of the rising generation,—instead of holding them in contempt which, as reviewers, we are without exception said to do,—we may esteem them, on the contrary, as forming a very essential branch of literature. That the majority of novels merit our contempt, is but too true; and, for the reason above given, it is a truth of a serious and painful nature.[4]

This reviewer finds the fact that novels usually deserve the contempt they customarily receive "serious and painful" because novels will shape the young, whom Locke describes as particularly impressionable, in the image of the "manners, sentiments, and passions" they represent. This reviewer implies that parents who are unsatisfied with the shape of their children's minds can justly blame contemptible novels. An anonymous piece called "Terrorist Novel Writing," published in 1798, considers the impractical content of Gothic novels and asks, "Are the duties of life so changed, that all the instructions necessary for a young person is to learn to walk at night upon the battlements of an old castle, to creep hands and feet along a narrow passage, and meet the devil at the end of it?"[5] If children read only Gothic novels, this writer suggests, they will lack the instruction necessary to function in the modern world. In this view, even *The Maid of the Hamlet* threatens its young readers by offering them nothing practical to improve their minds.

John Tinnon Taylor pinpoints the most alarming way that novels can corrupt the young when he observes, "A point very often raised against this imitation of the standard of conduct found in novels was that it supposedly caused, among other undesirable attitudes, a disregard for the authority of parents."[6] Novels that offer useless instruction about navigating through Gothic structures can nevertheless convey the impression of superior wisdom, which leads to contempt for and ridicule of the wisdom of social obligation that should establish parents as their children's masters. Richter observes of the late eighteenth century:

> There was clearly a growing ideology of affective individualism, a sense that individuals had a right to autonomy, which clashed with residual forms of con-

trol imposed by families, organized religion, and other social institutions. One outgrowth of this was sentimentalism; the Gothic, with its themes of imprisonment and deprivation, control by unnatural beings and forces, was the nightmare underside of the same development.[7]

After reading Gothic fictions, children might see their parents as their captors rather than as their benefactors and, deriving from novels a feeling that they have the right to autonomy, strike out against their parents' authority. This domestic rebellion might lead to more than a weakening of the authority of the family: all other social institutions could fall like dominoes.

2. Threats to Gender Norms

Patriarchy, which requires stable gender roles to survive, could be one of the institutions to fall as a result of Gothic novels' corruptive force. In *The Contested Castle*, Kate Ferguson Ellis argues that Gothic novels of the period offer women "resistance to an ideology that imprisons them."[8] Exposing the restrictions society places on women and suggesting possible alternatives, many Gothic novels at least potentially provide women with the cognitive tools to escape their prescribed roles. In doing so, such novels often represent female subjectivity in dynamic ways that might unsettle the average eighteenth-century man. A critic responds to the representation of women in Clara Reeve's *The School for Fathers* in the *Analytical Review* for October 1788:

> It appears strange that the heroine should so often dwell on the *beauty* of her lover, it is inconsistent with her character; for certainly a woman may love a man who has not white teeth or fine eyes; and to tell him of them is "passing strange," or rather a breach of that decorum which is not artificial but instinctive.[9]

An emphasis on male beauty disconcerts this reviewer where an emphasis on female beauty likely would not. The reviewer's anxiety about the relation of a man's physical appearance to a woman's capacity to love him reflects the position where men find themselves in the late eighteen century perhaps for the first time in history. Many Gothic novels, produced and consumed by the newly literate female portion of the population in unprecedented volumes, bring the desires of women to the forefront, and in them men find themselves frequently portrayed not as the subjects but as the objects of desire. The representation of a woman's active physical desire conflicts with women's "instinctive" roles as passive, pretty objects to be wooed according to laws negotiated solely between men.

The Gothic's frequent "counter-instinctual" reversal of subject and object roles for men and women stretches the boundaries of late eighteenth-century gender roles to the point where the line between male and female threatens to break. In his study *Romanticism and the Gothic,* Michael Gamer points to "what British reviewers and social critics in the next years came to fear most from the popular rise of gothic fiction and drama — that it produced ambiguously gendered and ambiguously desiring reading subjects."[10] Reviewing Joseph Fox's novel *Tancred, or a Tale of Ancient Times* in the August 1791 *English Review,* a critic states, "The character of Marguenta, who had murdered two husbands, and attempted the life of her son, is, however, too horrible, too unnatural — We ever dislike seeing any of the female sex depicted in such odious, such abominable colors."[11] The claim that to murder husbands and threaten sons is "too unnatural" for "the female sex" suggests that it would be more natural (though perhaps still horrible) for the male. The reviewer objects to the way Marguenta sets a masculinizing example for female readers. While this complaint suggests that Gothic novels might masculinize women, other complaints suggest that they might feminize men. Gamer presents an overview of novel-reading's supposedly "feminizing effects," effects "which can transform even the minds of young male readers into a state of pleasured, passive 'ductility.'"[12] Gothic novels encourage women to be too active and men to be too passive, making women behave like men and vice versa. Images of the overly active woman and the overly passive man evoke not just ambiguous gender but also ambiguous desire. The Gothic confounds traditionally gendered binaries like subject/object, active/passive, and man/woman, threatening patriarchal control and the forms of sexual relations that support it.

3. The Threat of Superstition

As the *Monthly* reviewer of *The Castle of Otranto* suggests, by depicting ghosts and other supernatural forces, the Gothic threatens a revival of a superstition that is anathema to the proponents of Enlightenment. This heretical superstition endangers two much-touted forms of social control in the eighteenth century: reason and religion. As Fred Botting states, "Encouraging superstitious beliefs, Gothic narratives subverted rational codes of understanding and, in their presentation of diabolical deeds and supernatural incidents, ventured into the unhallowed ground of necromancy and arcane ritual."[13] Gothic fictions threaten to transform readers into creatures as irreligious and irrational as their storylines, creatures beyond the governance of God and reason. Samuel Taylor Coleridge, in a review from the February 1797 *Critical Review* discussed in more detail below, writes of *The Monk*, "Tales of enchantments and witchcraft can never be *useful*: [Matthew Lewis] has contrived to make them *pernicious*, by blending, with an irreverent negligence, all that is most awfully true in religion with all that is most ridiculously absurd in superstition."[14] Gothic novels typically situate their supernatural events within a Christian context. According to Coleridge, blending elements of "false" superstition with "true" religion blurs the line between the absurdity of the one and the authenticity of the other, and thus the Gothic could impinge on the church's ability and authority to arbitrate truth.

The Gothic threatened to substitute "absurd," irrational superstitions for the socially and politically mandated belief in the supernatural that was Protestant Christianity. The relationship of Protestantism and its other, Catholicism, played a significant role in Britain's struggles to build and maintain power in the late eighteenth century. In "Europhobia: The Catholic Other in Horace Walpole and Charles Maturin," Robert Miles observes the substitution of "religious paradigms" for "nationalist ones" and notes how eighteenth-century Gothic's anti–Catholicism "cues us into some of the sources of internal, Protestant, British unease."[15] The Gothic threatened the state's authority by threatening Protestant authority. As a result, it could accomplish what T.J. Mathias, in his late-eighteenth-century *The Pursuits of Literature*, describes as the Catholic agenda in Protestant England. Mathias claims of Catholics, "That which is true of Christianity, *in itself and by itself alone*, independent of *any* establishment whatsoever, that they assert of their own tyrannical superstition." According to Mathias, Catholics try to create a necessary link between any aspect of Christianity and their own superstitious beliefs, which are inherently "tyrannical." Catholics would use such a link to further their own aims of political domination. The emigration of French priests to England to escape the Terror heightens Mathias's concerns. Though they flee the Revolution, paradoxically, these priests might also bring it with them. In another attack on Catholicism, Mathias writes:

> There is such a connection between superstition and atheism, and their allies, cruelty and tyranny, that the wisest and the most experienced statesmen and moralists have declared it to be indissoluble. In *their* cause, they would unite with any, even with Jacobin, principles.[16]

The threat of a revival of superstition is also the threat of a revolution's reign of tyranny.

4. The Threat of Revolution

All of the Gothic's threats to dominant ideologies are potentially revolutionary. A writer for the *Anti-Jacobin Review* for August 1798 defines Jacobinism with astonishing breadth:

> By Jacobinism I understand principles, doctrines, and conduct, similar to those which have proceeded from the Jacobin clubs in France, their imitators, and coadjutors in other countries. These may be reduced to three general classes — hostility to religion, hostility to monarchy, and hostility to social order, property, and virtue. Whoever is the enemy of Christianity and natural religion, I call a Jacobin.[17]

Opposition to almost any norm of the "social order" could be construed as a Jacobin, revolutionary impulse in the tense political climate of the 1790s. Richter offers an apt comparison: "What ... happened between June 1794 and February 1797 was a temporary accession of political paranoia like the McCarthy era in the United States."[18] This political paranoia had a deep impact on the reception of Gothic literature. The anonymous author of a complaint called "The Terrorist System of Novel-Writing" (1797) explicitly links terror in fiction to the Terror in France, attributing the same impulse to both:

> and just at the time when we were threatened with a stagnation of fancy, arose Maximilian Robespierre, with his system of terror, and taught our novelists that *fear* is the only passion they ought to cultivate, that to frighten and instruct were one and the same thing.[19]

In this view, the literature of terror becomes a kind of terrorism, which suggests another apt comparison with political paranoia in the United States, the climate of fear in the twenty-first century. This author frames Gothic novels as a breeding ground for terrorists.

Writers and critics such as Mathias, then, were ideological soldiers on a mission to rescue society from the ravages of bloody conflict by stopping the subversion of dominant ideologies. Mathias rallies his readers with the assurance, "All the minor powers of infidelity, of anarchy, of sedition, of rebellion, and of democracy, may *yet* be dispersed *in England*"; all they have to do is stamp out things like "the vulgar and illiterate blasphemy of Thomas Paine, and the contemptible nonsense of William Godwin." Identifying and condemning the literary works that could have a subversive, revolutionary influence becomes the critic's primary cause. Mathias lists Lewis's *The Monk*, John Moore's *Zeluco*, and William Godwin's *Caleb Williams*, all of which contain gothic elements, as dangerous, revolutionary texts.[20] The *British Critic* provides many reviews that join in Mathias's cause. In June 1793, this journal warns that Charlotte Smith's *Old Manor House* contains "Political Reflections" that "favour in the slightest degree of those erroneous and pernicious principles which have been recently promulgated with such fatal effect." Similarly, the July 1794 issue announces that *Caleb Williams* is "directly pointed at every band which connects society," November 1795 warns that Eliza Fenwick's *Secresy; or, The Ruin on the Rock* contains "a morality, worthy enough of modern France," April 1796 accuses *Hermsprong*'s author Robert Bage of being "a friend to many principles which, having been tried, have been found destructive," and January 1800 attacks Godwin yet again for the way *St. Leon* shows "a distrust and contempt for all laws."[21] These reviews imagine a horde of Gothic novels set to destroy civilized society. They hint that, in the wake of the French Revolution, to be Gothic is to be inherently revolutionary.

The Failure of Matthew Lewis's The Monk

By far the most controversial Gothic novel of the eighteenth century, *The Monk* seems to be as systematic in the way it threatens the social order as critics are systematic in their assessments of Gothic threats. W.W.'s "On Novels and Romances" concisely summarizes the evils of Lewis's novel:

> All the faults and immoralities ascribed to novels will be found realized in the Monk: murders, incest, and all the horrid and aggravated crimes which it is possible to conceive, appear in every chapter, and are dwelt on with seeming complacency, without any apparent intention of advantage to the reader from such a recital.[22]

In this exaggerated view of Lewis's work, *The Monk* portrays every conceivable evil, so it could also be held responsible for every conceivable evil. Though *The Monk* does not deliver such excitement in every chapter, and though the intention of its nineteen-year-old author is a vexed issue, it does manage to score checks in each of the four main categories of Gothic threats. Mathias was not the only critic to find a revolutionary agenda in Lewis's novel. The *European Magazine and London Review* of February 1797 writes of *The Monk*:

> What good purpose is to be answered by an *oblique attack* upon *venerable establishments*, we are at a loss to conjecture. We know that the presses of the Continent teemed with compositions of this character while the Revolution was preparing in France; yet what have the *infidels* who produced it substituted in the place of the *religion* they have banished?[23]

Detecting in Lewis's novel an anti-establishment agenda, this reviewer pronounces it revolutionary. That, as Andre Parreaux notes in his study *The Publication of The Monk*, "Mat Lewis, of course, was not a democrat—let alone a Jacobin" was unimportant to the paranoid critic: Lewis's work expresses hostility to the social order, so it must be condemned for encouraging a violent revolt.[24]

As this review indicates, Lewis's story of a corrupt clergyman is openly hostile to religion. Though the religion it lampoons appears to be Catholicism, conjoining a critique of Catholicism with other transgressions serves to identify Lewis not as a good English anti–Catholic Protestant but as an "infidel." In a passage already cited from his attack on *The Monk* in the February 1797 *Critical Review*, Coleridge links the novel's superstition-encouraging depiction of the supernatural with an irreligious agenda. Coleridge sees the novel's aesthetic error of implicitly revolutionary irreligiousness compounded by the "shameless harlotry" of Matilda, *The Monk*'s primary villainess, and "the most voluptuous images."[25] The *Monthly Review* also laments, "A vein of obscenity ... pervades and deforms the whole [novel] ... which renders the work totally unfit for general circulation."[26] Because of its threats of superstition and transgressions of sex and gender norms, Coleridge declares that the novel is "a poison for youth, and a provocative for the debauchee."[27] These reviews indict *The Monk* for containing elements from all four of the major interrelated categories of threats.

While in hindsight the idea that Lewis intended his novel to bring about radical social upheaval might seem a little far-fetched, the work does offer ample fodder for critical paranoia. Its transgression of gender norms goes beyond the portrayal of a wanton woman who delights in murder and promiscuity, which alone would be enough to discomfit the *English* reviewer of *Tancred*. Not solely masculinized by her wantonness, Matilda first appears in the novel dressed as a boy, Rosario, of whom the title character, Ambrosio, is inordinately fond. The use of masculine pronouns for the character until Rosario/Matilda shockingly proclaims to his/her *very* close friend, "'I am a Woman,'" exposes the ambiguity of the signs by which characters and readers alike attribute gender to bodies, implicitly destabilizing the fixed gender-identities required by patriarchy.[28] Even after this revelation, Matilda's cross-dressing continues to create what Judith Butler calls "gender trouble" because Matilda's behavior, like the costume she has shed, suggests a manliness that clashes with her putative female sex.[29] Ambrosio, after his relationship with Matilda has become explicitly sexual, "grieve[s], that Matilda prefer[s] the virtues of his sex to those of her own," and thus he "regret[s] Rosario, the fond, the gentle, and submissive."[30] Instead of wanting a manly woman for his sexual pleasure, Ambrosio seems to want a womanly man, and with the expression of this simple wish, filled with barely latent homoeroticism, *The Monk* transgresses almost every rule for sex and gender.

Lewis's novel presents a literal image of upheaval in the mob-driven violence of its conclusion. Revelations about the evil Prioress of the Convent of St. Clare prompt "the Mob" to attack, and the violent results resonate loudly with then-recent uprisings against ecclesiastical and other authorities in France.[31] The resonance of this scene and others with the Revolution is so clear that the Marquis de Sade, in his *Idee sur les Romans*, calls *The Monk* "'the inevitable outcome of the revolutionary upheaval which had been felt all over Europe.'"[32] That Lewis depicts the Mob's "barbarous vengeance" in an unsympathetic light is unimportant to most eighteenth-century critics: the typical critic would be incensed because Lewis dares to represent such violence at all.[33] The scene not only resonates with the Revolution, it also partly justifies revolt by portraying the Mob's target as truly corrupt and allowing the Mob's ravages to facilitate a happy ending. Jacobin or not, Lewis infuses his work with ambivalent revolutionary tendencies, and for English critics such tendencies, no matter how obscure, were intolerable.

In addition to condemning it for its general aura of subversiveness, Coleridge and Mathias fault *The Monk* for one passage in particular. The passage describes how Elvira, mother of Ambrosio's angelic lust-object Antonia, censors the Bible because she believes "no reading more improper could be permitted a young Woman."[34] Mathias quotes the passage in full and rants about its blasphemy:

> Whether the passages, which I have cited in a *popular* novel, have not a *tendency* to corrupt the minds of the people, and of the younger unsuspecting part of the female sex, by *traducing and discrediting* THE HOLY SCRIPTURES, is a matter of publick consideration. ... Religion is *part of the common law*, and therefore *whatever is an offence* against that, is an offence *against* THE COMMON LAW.[35]

Mathias suggests that this textual moment alone contains elements from all four of the major categories of Gothic threats. It corrupts minds — particularly young ones — and is unsafe for women. It discredits the scriptures, which are a Protestant's only true guide to proper belief in the supernatural. Finally, it violates common law and is therefore legally punishable; as Parreaux observes, "blasphemy was considered punishable mainly because it was seditious," and sedition, taken to the greatest extreme, is revolution.[36]

The passage that Mathias finds so blasphemous challenges not only the authority of the scriptures but also the authority of critics. Critics wield their power to protect the public from the dangers of reading, and, as Ellis argues, "it is this very attitude toward the danger of popular reading that is the object of Lewis's attack, using Elvira, the apparently perfect mother, as an example of it."[37] Elvira's censorship of the Bible, her belief that it has corruptive power, is the object of Lewis's attack, not the Bible itself. Elvira stands in for the critic, and, choosing the Bible as the object of her paranoid attack, she makes critical posturing about protecting naïve readers seem ridiculous. Lewis turns the tables on critics, suggesting that they endanger readers by promoting ignorance.[38]

Anti-critical sentiment appears elsewhere in the novel. The character Raymond, talking to his young poet protégé, explains:

> "An Author, whether good or bad, or between both, is an Animal whom every body is privileged to attack; For though All are not able to write books, all conceive themselves able to judge them. A bad composition carries with it its own punishment, contempt and ridicule. A good one excites envy, and entails upon its Author a thousand mortifications."[39]

Raymond's advice attacks the authority and status of critics by suggesting both that they are a common lot and that they act from the base motivation of jealousy. Criticism, Lewis suggests via Raymond, is neither venerable nor objective. Lewis attacks the highness of the high and exposes the degree of self-interest that might be involved in critical condemnations of his and other Gothic novels as low.

Whether fueled by this blasphemy against critics or not, Mathias makes clear that he expects the law to help him protect the public by suppressing such despicable literature. In the poetic portion of the *Pursuits*, Mathias looks upon *The Monk* and asks, "Why sleep the ministers of truth and law? / Has the State no control, no decent awe...?"[40] The power of suppression that Mathias would awaken was a formidable power indeed. Even if prosecution for obscene libel, which seems to have been Mathias's goal, did not occur, the threat alone of legal action was a powerful tool of censorship. Lewis eventually agreed to censor himself for fear of attracting too much attention. Considering the possible motives for Lewis's assent to censorship, Parreaux conjectures, "Another reason for his compliance may have been that Lewis, who was a homosexual, disliked the idea of attracting upon himself the attention of the courts [because] sodomy was still a capital offence."[41] Indirectly, Lewis's authorship could have been punished by death, so he had little choice but to obey the critics who would contain the subversive potential of his work with their condemnations.

That most of *The Monk*'s detractors praise Lewis's talents as a writer while trying to contain his influence with their legal and aesthetic condemnations underscores the precedence of the political and the moral over the artistic in "aesthetic" evaluations of Gothic novels and of novels more generally. Even Coleridge, whose attack on Lewis stands second only to Mathias's for its virulence, remarks that it is a work "of no common genius," but he calls the general offensiveness of the novel "a fault which all other excellence does but aggravate, as adding subtlety to a poison by the elegance of its preparation."[42] Coleridge employs the same reasoning that James Beattie uses when he explains that conjoining pleasure with bad instruction renders the "poison ... doubly dangerous."[43] Lewis misapplies his skills when he uses them to render the Gothic pleasing; his literary production is comparable to the mixed characters derided by Samuel Johnson for making bad behavior seem more acceptable.

The sense that Lewis has misapplied his skills shifts the focus from the idea of Lewis as a social agitator to the idea of a certain type of Gothic novel as a social agitation. This type of Gothic is a poisonous, low form to which good talents should simply not be applied. Coleridge broadens the scope of his attack on offensive Gothic writing when he claims, "Figures that shock the imagination, and narratives that mangle the feelings, rarely discover *genius*, and always betray a low and vulgar *taste*."[44] Associating the Gothic with vulgar taste condemns not only writers but also readers who exhibit such a lack of discernment in their choice of subjects. Labeling a work as vulgar or low steers readers away by suggesting that readers must share in the stigma of art not approved by those who represent the interests of the powerful.

The Success of Ann Radcliffe's The Mysteries of Udolpho

A claim that these attacks on *The Monk* in the late 1790s ultimately condemn all Gothic novels and their readers would be a gross overstatement. By the time Lewis wrote, "Gothic" had evolved from the form of fictional narratives driven by supernatural incidents that began with Walpole. Thanks in large part to Ann Radcliffe, a work no longer needed the supernatural elements that Coleridge found so vulgar to be called "Gothic." Radcliffe's most important works substitute the suggestion of the supernatural for the depiction of "actual" supernatural events. Coleridge praises *The Mysteries of Udolpho* in the *Critical Review* of August 1794 for the fact that "mysterious terrors are continually exciting in the mind the idea of a supernatural appearance, keeping us, as it were, upon the very edge and confines of the world of spirits, and yet are ingeniously explained by familiar causes."[45] While Coleridge's review of *The Monk* indicates how he responds to a work that crosses *over* the edge into the spirit world, this review attributes genius to Radcliffe's art of keeping the reader *on* that edge with the device of the explained supernatural.

Not everyone adored Radcliffe. Anna Maria Mackenzie attacks Radcliffe for using terror as the driving force in her novels: "if the spirit of description can only be kept up by a succession of bold and horrible images, there is some reason to fear the unhappy effects on the young and ductile mind."[46] Even without supernatural incidents, Radcliffe's work still contains Gothic threats that could leave a bad impression on the "ductile" minds of the young. In a tone somewhere between commendation and lament, the *British Critic* of September 1797 reports in a review of Radcliffe's *The Italian*, "the exuberance of her imagination, added to the elegance of her style, would have formed materials, in our apprehension, for a species of fame not usually annexed to works of romance."[47] Radcliffe's work shows talent, but its undeserving "species" does not deserve the approbation of high culture. Her talents, like Lewis's, should not be applied to the foundationally flawed Gothic romance.

With these and a few other exceptions, the vast majority of critical responses to Radcliffe in her own time were overwhelmingly positive. In his review of *Udolpho*, Coleridge claims that "the Muse" lavished the same "gifts" on Radcliffe as on Shakespeare; Nathan Drake simply calls Radcliffe "the Shakespeare of Romance Writers."[48] The Irish journal *Walker's Hibern-*

ian for April 1797 states that Radcliffe "has written with such a singular fancy, such acute perceptions of the grand, the delicate, the beautiful and the dreadful in life and nature, and such descriptive powers, as must not only command the praise of present times, but probably consign to immortality 'The Mysteries of Udolpho.'"[49] In the estimation of many of the critics who are usually hostile to the Gothic, Radcliffe's masterpiece stands among the immortals of high culture.

Since little information survives about Radcliffe's life and personal opinions, twenty-first-century readers can only speculate about the political intentions behind her works. Traditional Radcliffe scholarship depicts her as conservative, but Rictor Norton's biography *Mistress of Udolopho: The Life of Ann Radcliffe* argues that in part because "she emerged from a radical Unitarian, rather than a conventional Anglican, background, ... she fully merits consideration as part of that circle of radical Dissenters that included Anna Laetitia Barbauld, Elizabeth Inchbald, Mary Hays and Mary Wollstonecraft."[50] Norton's arguments are compelling, but the relative lack of direct evidence for Radcliffe's radicalism, evidence of the kind found copiously in the writings of radicals such as Wollstonecraft, renders any absolute claim about Radcliffe's political orientation assailable. Whether Radcliffe's political motivations harmonized with her critics' conservatism remains a question without a definitive answer.

Though definitive evidence of Radcliffe's political motivations may be lacking, there is evidence that Radcliffe was at least attentive to the demands of her conservative critics. Mackenzie's complaints about Radcliffe's threatening potential apply mostly to the novels that preceded *Udolpho*. In those novels, Mackenzie claims, "Dreams and apparitions favour too much of the superstition which ought never to be encouraged," but she sees "an amendment of this error" in *Udolpho*.[51] *Udolpho* presents the most fully developed instance of the explained supernatural in all of Radcliffe's novels; Mackenzie's claim suggests that this development was an "amendment" made according to critical precepts. Like Clara Reeve's *The Old English Baron*, *Udolpho* attempts to fix the fault in the Gothic's foundation. Just as *The Monk* seems calculated to be as threatening as a Gothic novel could be, *Udolpho* seems calculated to be contaminant-free in the eyes of critics. *Udolpho*, Radcliffe's greatest critical and popular success, works against the typical threats of the Gothic, using the explained supernatural, a critique of sensibility, and warnings against the influences of other kinds of Gothic romance in ways that reaffirm eighteenth-century critics' assumptions. Though Radcliffe's talents might have won her respect under any circumstances, shaping her work according to critical precepts almost guaranteed her warm reviews.

Udolpho's narrator and protagonists shun superstition, calling it "lamentable," a "misery," and a "weakness." *Udolpho* marks superstition as a threat, dampening its own capacity for encouraging wayward belief and warning against the threats of superstition that might come from elsewhere. A father figure warns the novel's heroine, Emily, that an abbess in a convent she frequents "'will teach [her] to expect a ghost in every dark room,'" and the end of the novel reveals that Emily's perception of a wax figure as a mangled corpse should be blamed on "monkish superstition."[52] The novel's attacks on superstitious Catholicism align Anglican religious authority with parental authority, safeguarding both. Since, as Mathias points out, "Religion is *part of the common law*," *Udolpho*'s warnings about heretical superstition inherently support the rule of law, avoiding the revolutionary antagonism that Mathias and others see in the Gothic works of Lewis and Godwin. *Udolpho* internalizes the interdependent authorities of religion and law by making their control a matter of self-control. Robert Miles argues that "the contagion of superstition amounts to a loss of self-control," and since "this lack of self-control is linked to sexual desire and criminality," the novel's rational explanations of apparently supernatural events "return Emily, not just to 'reason,' but to cultural and gender norms."[53] Radcliffe's treatment of the supernatural at least superficially supports England's patriarchal Protestant order, working against all four categories of Gothic threats.

What Mary Poovey identifies as a "critique of sensibility" running throughout *Udolpho* also buttresses the social establishment by working against the Gothic's typical threats.[54] *Udolpho*'s narrator claims that sensibility, or the capacity to receive and express profound aesthetic and emotional impressions, "render[s the mind] more liable to the influence of superstition," thereby aligning sensibility with the threat of superstition and condemning both.[55] Relating sensibility to gender norms, Poovey suggests that sensibility and the corresponding "sentimental virtues ... constituted virtually [women's] only source of social power" in the eighteenth century; Radcliffe, however, "is quick to note [that] sensibility itself is inherently unstable," and thus she "is only willing to elaborate the feminine potential for power within definite bounds."[56] In this view, though Radcliffe does not work to disempower women, she does appear to keep women's power within limits acceptable to patriarchy.

Poovey also shows how Radcliffe's depiction of sensibility demonstrates that "sensibility needs ... external governance," governance supplied by Emily's parental figures, most notably her father, and when at the end of the novel Emily "resolutely follows her father's advice, subduing her implicitly sexual passion by means of principled feeling, she proves herself capable of managing her own sensibility."[57] Radcliffe's treatment of sensibility as something requiring control supports patriarchy and parental authority. Miles summarizes the threats of sensibility perceived by the cultural establishment in the wake of the French Revolution: "Sensibility was attacked for being implicitly anti-hierarchical, for presupposing a democracy of feeling hearts; moreover, it was perceived to empower women while dis-empowering men (by encouraging them to be teary, uxorious and weak)."[58] By critiquing sensibility, Radcliffe's novel appears to critique all revolutionary anti-hierarchical tendencies, making itself safe for the guardians of culture and therefore, in the eyes of those guardians, safe for the masses to consume.

Radcliffe's critique of sensibility goes hand in hand with a critique of the dangers of the imagination. The terrors in Radcliffe's fiction stem largely from a failure to "distinguish fact from fantasy"— to separate Gothic fiction from reality.[59] *Udolpho* shows not only the dangers of the Gothic's particular threats but the dangers of the Gothic's influential power as such. A critique of the dangers of the imagination implicitly involves a critique of the dangers of imaginative fiction, and the Gothic was one of the most popular forms of imaginative fiction in Radcliffe's day. Michael Taylor argues that Radcliffe's "insistent didacticism about the duplicity of romance ... enables [her] to appear to have no qualms about her undertaking."[60] In short, Radcliffe's didacticism about the Gothic's threats enlists her in the critical mission to conserve the status quo, announcing her work as the critics' ally.

That Radcliffe's work apparently serves a conservative end does not, however, mean that she was herself conservative or that her work is definitively reactionary. Miles calls the question "How conservative was Radcliffe?" "a central, troubling question in Radcliffe criticism." Miles claims that there is a radical component in Radcliffe's fiction, "but to get at it the modern critic has to read against the grain of Radcliffe's apparent intentions," and he concludes, "The tension between Radcliffe's surface narrative, which appears to go in a conservative direction, and her subtext, which moves in quite other ways, is the source of Radcliffe's aesthetic dynamism." [61] More than a source of aesthetic dynamism, Radcliffe's conservative appearance was a source of critical applause. Without it, her works, like *The Monk*, might be better remembered for the scandal they caused than for their artistic merit — if they were remembered at all. The conservatism of eighteenth-century critics shaped the surface narrative of *Udolpho*, and that surface, in turn, shaped the critics' responses in the novel's favor.

The critical strategy that would contain the dangers of the Gothic with condemnations relies on the idea that readers will actually heed critics' warnings. Though this strategy is imperfect, it has had lasting results. The literary establishment has only recently (on the scale of centuries) accepted the notion that the Gothic is a form of literature worthy of serious study. Disparagement of Gothic fiction is common in critical writings from the eighteenth century to the present. In academic and other arenas where these critical writings hold sway, condemnation has succeeded in containing the Gothic's subversive potential. In other arenas, however, it has failed: the Gothic's popularity has never entirely faded. If critics' conclusions have any claim to validity, the Gothic has shaped many generations of eager readers. As long as Gothic fictions have circulated, critics have accused them of corrupting readers and creating horrific new realities. Those accusations, by prompting Gothic writers such as Reeve and Radcliffe to adjust their work, have had a formative influence of their own. Eighteenth-century critics began a prosecution that has continued for centuries, and the trial has altered both the accusations and the accused.

PART TWO
Gothic Sexualities

3

Pathological Reproduction
The Emergence of Homosexuality through Nineteenth Century Gothic Fiction

One of the threats that eighteenth-century critics attributed to the Gothic was a threat to inculcate non-normative gender behaviors, and the ways Matthew Lewis's *The Monk* flirts with a behavior so subversive it was a capital offense — the choice of a same-sex sexual partner — helped make it one of the most threatening Gothic novels of all. This chapter examines how certain tropes, and one trope in particular, developed through some of the nineteenth century's best-known Gothic novels in ways that, when they appeared in Oscar Wilde's 1891 novel *The Picture of Dorian Gray*, helped homosexuality to emerge as a category of identity with specific pejorative attributes, a category that allowed defenders of the status quo to identify and attack communities that threatened to destroy established norms with their illicit sexual behavior.

A great deal of criticism has already been written about *The Picture of Dorian Gray*'s implications for the history of sexuality; the novel has been a central text for the literary study of homosexuality not only because it is a major work written by an influential author now perceived (by some) as homosexual, but also because Wilde and his novel were at the center of a controversy that helped to define "homosexuality" as a category of identity in the popular consciousness. During the trials in 1895 that led to Wilde's conviction and imprisonment for acts of "gross indecency" with other men, attorneys read passages from *Dorian Gray* into evidence and debated their sexual implications. To secure legal victories, Wilde's enemies tried to prove that the sexuality they saw in Wilde's fiction matched Wilde's real-life sexuality and that real-life sexuality corresponded with Wilde's fiction. As they characterized Wilde as a criminal type like the ones found in *Dorian Gray*, they also characterized "the homosexual" more generally. Thus, Wilde's putative character and his fictional characters helped to shape the threatening, criminal image of "the homosexual" handed down to the twentieth and twenty-first centuries.

Menacing attributes of "the homosexual" that emerged from Wilde's trials derive from Gothic fiction. The characters and scenarios of *Dorian Gray* develop tropes that run through many of the nineteenth century's most famous Gothic works; as Donald Lawler attests, "gothic informs every important aspect of the novel."[1] After Wilde's trials, "the homosexual" appeared to be a kind of Gothic monster. I argue not, as many critics maintain, that the Gothic is in some ways homosexual. Rather, I argue that "the homosexual" is, in a crucial way, Gothic. As George Haggerty unambiguously asserts in *Queer Gothic*, "gothic fiction gave sexuality a history in the first place."[2] The use of Wilde's novel as evidence in his trials was only part of the Gothic's participation in the emergence of homosexuality, but in pivotal ways it grafted ideas and images that *Dorian Gray* adapts from the Gothic tradition onto the "homosexual" that was emerging from other legal, medical, and cultural discourses during the Victorian age. When Wilde's enemies attributed Gothic characteristics from *Dorian Gray* to the figure of the homosexual, they helped fashion homosexuality in a Gothic image.

A Gothic Birth

Arguments about homosexuality's emergence have proliferated since Michel Foucault's *History of Sexuality* hit the academy. Foucault states, "Homosexuality appeared as one of the forms of sexuality when it was transposed from the practice of sodomy onto a kind of interior androgyny," and dating the "birth" of homosexuality around 1870, he pronounces, "the homosexual was now a species."[3] Foucault investigates the normative impact of approaching sex in terms of "sexuality." In the opening pages of his *History*'s second volume, he cautions that, though the conceptualization involved in these terms is more than "a simple recasting of vocabulary," it should "neither be underestimated nor overinterpreted."[4] Correcting a common misunderstanding, David Halperin urges that "Foucault ... should not be invoked to justify the claim ... that before the cultural constitution of homosexuality and heterosexuality in the modern period there were no such things as sexual identities, only sexual acts."[5] The sexualities that gradually emerged in the late nineteenth century were not the beginning of sexual identity itself; they were part of a new normative paradigm.

The birth of the homosexual species did not occur instantaneously with the coinage of "homosexual," which Ed Cohen dates to 1869. Even though Krafft-Ebing's *Psychopathia Sexualis* introduced "homosexuality" as a pathological condition to English-speaking audiences in 1892, the trials of Oscar Wilde were largely responsible for giving the pathologized category life in the popular consciousness: "Wilde's trials and conviction were the most widely publicized events of their kind in the nineteenth century [, and as] such they were instrumental in disseminating new representations of sexual behavior between men." Because of the trials' publicity, Wilde became "the paradigmatic example for an emerging public definition of a new 'type' of male sexual actor: 'the homosexual.'" Wilde's trials were therefore pivotal in "the emergence in England of 'the male homosexual' as a distinctly counternormative category, signifying not only the presence of sexual and/or emotional bonds between men *but also* the absence of (re)productive male (hetero)sexuality." [6] Given Wilde's marriage and children, calling Wilde homosexual might miscast his sexuality, but whether or not Wilde was *truly* homosexual (which assumes "homosexuality" or "heterosexuality" could ever be *true*— a problematic assumption), the representations of him and his trials nevertheless contributed to the construction of homosexuality that Cohen describes.

Cohen focuses on the male homosexual, but in *Epistemology of the Closet*, Eve Sedgwick notes that "from the turn of the [twentieth] century ... every given person, just as he or she was necessarily assignable to a male or a female gender, was now considered necessarily assignable as well to a homo- or hetero-sexuality, a binarized identity."[7] What emerged at the end of the nineteenth century was a binary conception of the normal reproductive human and the dangerous, diseased class against which the "normal" defined itself. The universality, the totalizing assignability to which Sedgwick refers, is an assumption embedded within the construction. Again, it, like the other assumptions that this chapter addresses, is not necessarily *true* and is indeed much more likely to be false. The truth or falsity — or the real reality, for lack of a better term — isn't a concern here. The discursive assignation of reality, and how that assignation relates to the Gothic, is this chapter's primary concern.

Gothic language renders the contours of the homosexual threat intelligible. In *Between Men*, Sedgwick observes that the Gothic provided the clearest picture of "the homosexual" in the popular imagination:

> It was part of the strange fate of the early Gothic that the genre as a whole, conflicted as it was, came in the nineteenth century to seem a crystallization of the aristocratic homosexual role, even as the aristocracy was losing its normative force in English society more generally. And by the turn of the twentieth century, after the trials of Oscar Wilde, the "aristocratic" role had become the dominant one available for homosexual men of both the upper and middle classes.[8]

Many early Gothic novels, such as Horace Walpole's 1764 *The Castle of Otranto*, focus on the excesses of aristocrats whose appetites for money and sex imperil normal domesticity.[9] Wilde, though not an aristocrat, indulged in similar excesses, which facilitated the transposition of a Gothic syndrome of economic and sexual practices onto the pathologized interiority of the homosexual. To the denizens of normality who felt threatened by Wilde's proclivities, Wilde looked like a Gothic villain. This resemblance enabled "the normal" to equate Gothic characterizations with same-sex desire.

As Sedgwick's consideration of the intersection of class and sexuality indicates, the Gothic never represents sexuality in a vacuum: sexual aberrance almost always appears alongside other counternormative economic, gender, and racial characteristics. Judith Halberstam credits nineteenth-century Gothic novels about monsters for helping to articulate the broad category of "the human" in very specific terms: "these novels make way for the invention of human as white, male, middle class, and heterosexual."[10] By characterizing creatures not white, not male, not middle-class, and not heterosexual as monsters, Gothic fictions provided a very narrow definition of non-monstrous, normal "humanity." Focusing on the Gothic contribution to "homosexuality" without equal attention to other identity categories risks obscuring intersectional distinctions within "homosexuality," particularly distinctions based on gender. The laws under which Wilde was prosecuted applied only to men, and as Jeffrey Weeks notes, while *Dorian Gray* and Wilde's trials had a profound impact on male homosexuality, no collision of literature with law had a similar impact on female sexuality until the obscenity trial of Radclyffe Hall's 1928 novel *The Well of Loneliness*.[11] Nevertheless, in the Gothic imagination, both male and female homosexuals dwell within the realm of the abnormal and inhuman, and both often receive the same horrific attributes.

3. Pathological Reproduction

Though their approaches to the intersections of identities differ, Sedgwick and Halberstam both demonstrate that the Gothic helped produce homosexual identities in the nineteenth century. Given that Gothic fiction and Wilde's trials contributed attributes to the emerging concept "homosexuality," the argument that follows considers what attributes the fiction contributed and, as a key factor in Wilde's trials themselves, how it made such contributions. Sedgwick provides one example of a Gothic contribution to homosexuality in her exploration of the Gothic trope of "the unspeakable." Same-sex sexual contact had, as Sedgwick notes, been considered unspeakable "throughout the Judeo-Christian tradition," but the Gothic representation of the unspeakable had special significance for Wilde. Identifying himself with the titular monster of Charles Maturin's Gothic novel *Melmoth the Wanderer*, who offers his victims an unspeakable bargain, Wilde changed his name to Melmoth after his conviction for same-sex sexual offenses.[12] Thus Wilde rendered the unspeakable monstrosity attributed to him intelligible by giving it a Gothic name.

Later, the monstrous name that would replace Melmoth's would be Wilde's own. In the early twentieth century, "'an unspeakable of the Oscar Wilde sort,' as E.M. Forster's Maurice presents himself, became the commonest name" for a homosexual.[13] Maurice is not a Gothic villain, and *Maurice* is not a Gothic novel, but when Maurice, like Wilde, tries to make sense of the horror associated with his desires, he resorts to a Gothic trope. Maurice's maleness puts him closer to the "Wilde sort" than a female would be, but *The Well of Loneliness* exemplifies how the trope of the unspeakable also applies to women when a male character, horrified by his discovery that Hall's female protagonist is attracted to women, resorts to referring to her as unspeakable.[14] The Gothic did not invent the association between same-sex attraction and unspeakability, but the trope of the unspeakable amplified and popularized it, making it a common attribute of the category "homosexual."

Another Gothic trope helped to delineate an attribute of homosexuality that has had even deeper ramifications than "the unspeakable." Though cultural discourses define homosexuality as the absence of normal reproductive desire, the Gothic trope of pathological reproduction allows the homophobic imagination to conceive of how monstrous homosexuals can nevertheless reproduce. Attributing Gothic, pathological reproduction to homosexuals deepens the division in the heterosexual/homosexual binary, providing heterosexuality's opposed other with a means of proliferation radically different from its own.

Pathological Reproduction

On its website, in an article entitled "Homosexuals Recruit Public School Children," the Traditional Values Coalition (TVC) publishes a strong warning: "since homosexual couples can't reproduce, they will simply go after *your* children for seduction and conversion to homosexuality."[15] This warning indicates that, barred from heterosexual reproduction, homosexuals will proliferate parasitically. Homosexuals, like the military, recruit, building their army via conversion instead of normal breeding. On the website of the American Family Association (AFA), an article entitled "Homosexuality in America: Exposing the Myths" argues that a "legitimate reason for public concern is the harm done to the social order when policies are advanced that would increase the incidence of the gay lifestyle and undermine the normative character of marriage and family life." While the TVC focuses on homosexual "conversion," the AFA sees the threat of increasing homosexual "incidence" stemming less from active recruitment and more from "policies" that favor the existence of a sexuality opposed to the norm. The AFA clarifies, "Since there are good reasons to support the heterosexual norm, since it has been developed with great difficulty, and since it can be maintained only if it is cared for and supported, we cannot be indifferent to attacks upon it."[16] This vision presents heterosexuality as a fragile thing that has undergone difficult development, a thing that requires care, support, and defense to survive. In other words, the AFA figuratively represents the heterosexual norm as the embattled child that the TVC addresses more literally. For homosexual predators, the heterosexual norm is, like a child, easy prey.

Lee Edelman's *No Future: Queer Theory and the Death Drive* examines the roles of literal and figurative children in the political struggles that pervade the history of sexuality. The child, as Edelman explains, is the "telos of the social order," the product that all politics seeks to defend because the figure of the child allows the social order to project a future for itself that constitutes and justifies its present existence. A sexuality defined as the absence of reproductive heterosexuality, then, threatens the heterosexual order with a queer negativity that is "reality's abortion," the refusal of the child, the social order, and the politics of what Edelman brands "reproductive futurism." Edelman is careful to distinguish this queer negativity, which he names "sinthomosexuality," from the people labeled "homosexual," who can, of course, be parents and espouse reproductive futurism. As Edelman points out, the "conflation of homosexuality with the radical negativity of sinthomosexuality continues to shape our social reality."[17] This conflation is inherent to the sexual binary that emerged in the nineteenth century, and it appears blatantly in the AFA's warning about how homosexuals want to dismantle the carefully constructed heterosexual norm. Projecting the negation of the social order as a very real outcome of allowing homosexuality legitimacy, the AFA writes, "We believe that homosexuality is immoral and leads ultimately to personal and social decay."[18] Edelman quotes the AFA's founder, Donald Wildmon, warning that "'the homosexual movement will result in society's destruction.'"[19] To save society, to save the future, to save the children, the AFA and organizations like it believe they must stop queer negation by oppressing homosexuals.

The logic that conflates homosexuality with this form of negation involves a paradox. Homosexuals must be anti-life, anti-reproduction, and anti-future to make good on the threat of social collapse, but as living beings, they must embrace life just enough to stick around and be a threat worth opposing. Somehow, homosexuals must reproduce while rejecting reproduction. To resolve the paradox, homophobic logic requires two modes of reproduction, one for the heteros and one for the homos. The homosexuals' method of increasing their numbers must be a different, dark, pathological reproduction. This pathological reproduction must produce offspring outside the rules of the heterosexual order. To be sufficiently different from "normal" reproduction, pathological reproduction must create offspring without the combination of woman with man.

Such a feat may currently be beyond real science, but it is not beyond the imagination: in fact, it is a mainstay of nineteenth-century Gothic fiction. The Gothic trope of pathological reproduction evolved over the course of the nineteenth century so that when it appeared, via *Dorian Gray*, in Wilde's trials, it was ready to color Wilde's "crimes." In Wilde's second trial, prosecutor Charles Gill charged the jury "to protect society from such scandals by removing from its heart a sore which cannot fail in time to corrupt and taint it all."[20] The Gothicized conception of Wilde and all homosexuals as propagators of corruption motivated Wilde's enemies to protect society from Wilde's pathological taint, and it continues to make homosexual "pathology" coherent enough to motivate anti-homosexual organizations today.

Mary Shelley's Frankenstein (1818): A Menacing Race without Childhood

Victor Frankenstein's decision to stitch new life together out of corpses presents what might be literature's most famous instance of pathological reproduction. Frankenstein discovers how to create life through a secret scientific process and exults in his power:

> Life and death appeared to me ideal bounds, which I should first break through, and pour a torrent of light onto our dark world. A new species would bless me as its creator and source; many happy and excellent natures would owe their being to me. No father could claim the gratitude of his child so completely as I should deserve their's.[21]

Frankenstein distinguishes "creator," perhaps inseminator, from "source," perhaps the womb; "no father" is as great as Frankenstein because he is two reproductive forces in one. Emphasizing how "completely" he deserves "gratitude," he suggests that his scientific process is like sexual reproduction but better because he need not rely on another person, a woman, for his power to bring new "light" in the world. The *fiat lux* of Frankenstein the Father approaches that of God the Father.

Seeking a reproductive power supposedly better than sex, Frankenstein creates an alternative mode of reproduction that violates the early nineteenth-century order of female and male. Anne K. Mellor explains how Frankenstein's alternative challenges the scientific assumptions of Shelley's time:

> Mary Shelley's novel implicitly invokes [Erasmus] Darwin's theory of gradual evolutionary progress to suggest both the error and the evils of Victor Frankenstein's bad science. The genuine improvement of the species can result only from the conjunction of male and female sexuality. In trying to have a baby without a woman, Victor Frankenstein has failed to give his child the mothering and nurturance it requires, the very nourishment that Darwin explicitly equated with the female sex.[22]

Shelley's Gothic imagination allows Frankenstein's mode of reproduction to succeed, but the success of "bad science" cannot be "genuine improvement." Instead of godly light, Frankenstein can only produce horrific darkness.

The horror of his success strikes Frankenstein when the Creature first draws breath. Frankenstein is so sickened by the Creature's ugliness that, "[u]nable to endure the aspect of the being," he abandons it. Soon after this abandonment, a literal denial of nurturance already figured by his exclusion of the female sex, Frankenstein collapses from exhaustion. In a dream he kisses Elizabeth, his bride-to-be, and she exchanges "the bloom of health" for the "livid ... hue of death"; she then begins to resemble "the corpse of [his] dead mother."[23] The death that consumes Elizabeth spreads like a fast-acting disease from Frankenstein's touch. He is contaminated by his mode of reproduction, and his contamination infects not only the would-be mother of his child by also his own mother and, perhaps by extension, motherhood itself. Frankenstein's mode of reproduction taints the order of female and male; the alternative mode corrupts the original.

Frankenstein's excision of sex from his mode of reproduction is complete enough to create a problem for some readers. Abandoned and lonely, Frankenstein's male Creature demands that Frankenstein create a female for him. Threatened by his Creature's monstrous strength, Frankenstein agrees, but while working on the female, he realizes that "one of the first results of those sympathies for which the daemon thirsted would be children, and a race of devils would be propagated upon the earth, who might make the very existence of the species of man a condition precarious and full of terror."[24] Horrified, Frankenstein destroys the half-finished female creature. Frankenstein's fears and the destruction they prompt seem to involve a ridiculous error, as John Rieder notes:

> I have found that students ... often wonder why Victor did not forestall his fears about proliferating a race of monsters by simply making the female sterile. ... Apparently Victor suffers from a remarkable deficiency of imagination when it comes to understanding or even contemplating the process of sexual reproduction.[25]

Suffering from such a "deficiency of imagination" would indeed be remarkable for someone with enough anatomical knowledge to assemble a living creature from dead parts. Imputing such a deficiency to Shelley, who bore three children prior to *Frankenstein*'s first publication, also seems a bit far-fetched.[26]

A solution to this apparent problem lies in the timing of the female creature's destruction. Immediately after Frankenstein's daydream about the "race of devils," he looks up and sees that his original Creature is spying "to mark [his] progress." Frankenstein already knows what his Creature gains from spying. Earlier in the novel, the Creature describes how, after a short period of life, he seized an opportunity to eavesdrop on an adult Arabian woman's French lessons. Spying on the lessons without direct involvement, he improved "more rapidly than the Arabian." He soon mastered language well enough to read Plutarch, Milton, and Goethe, authors who perplex many human adults for a lifetime.[27] The Creature, super-intelligent from birth, easily learns what he sees and hears.

Rather than suffering a deficiency of imagination when he destroys the female to prevent a "race of devils," then, Frankenstein is imagining the possible results of the Creature observing and learning the asexual mode of reproduction. Seeing that the Creature has had an opportunity to "mark" his asexual reproductive process so far, Frankenstein imagines that, were the Creature to see the process's completion, he might be able to repeat it. Imagining his own great power passing into the hands of his already super-strong and super-intelligent Creature, he recognizes the "madness" of letting asexual reproduction spread. If he were to learn Frankenstein's reproductive process, the Creature could make children "like" Frankenstein's child, children full-grown at the moment of birth. If the Creature represents the standard product of Frankenstein's reproductive process, normal humanity's position would indeed be "precarious" if opposed by an army of superhuman, grown-up children. Allowing Frankenstein's mode of pathological reproduction to spread would place normal humanity in too much danger, so even when his friend Walton inquires about Frankenstein's secret alternative to sex, the scientist remains "impenetrable."[28] Eventually, Frankenstein's pathological mode of reproduction dies with him.

Shelley's vision of pathological reproduction involves the asexual creation of beings powerful enough to wipe out the more delicate human norm. These beings reject normal childhood in favor of assembling new, already grown-up members out of humanity's spare parts — recruiting, as it were, specimens from the incomplete ranks of the normal. Frankenstein's mode of reproduction is pathological, and it threatens the order of female and male with conversion and destruction, but its pathology and the order it threatens are not "homosexual" and "heterosexual." Joseph Kestner and others argue compellingly for a critique of homosocial and homoerotic investments in Shelley's novel, particularly in Frankenstein's relationship with the explorer Walton.[29] However, claiming that Shelley's 1818 novel targets the "homosexuality" that didn't emerge fully until century's end would be inaccurate. Shelley could not have had the TVC and AFA's menacing conception of homosexuality in mind, but she did develop a Gothic trope that would, after almost a century of further literary evolution leading up to Wilde's trials, lend itself well to such nightmares.

Charles Maturin's Melmoth the Wanderer *(1820): Impotent Breeders*

Melmoth the Wanderer's mode of pathological reproduction is a form of influence. The Wanderer describes his unspeakable bargain:

> It has been reported of me, that I obtained from the enemy of souls a range of existence beyond the period allotted to mortality — a power to pass over space without disturbance or delay, and visit remote regions with the swiftness of thought — to encounter tempests without the *hope* of their blasting me, and penetrate into dungeons, whose bolts were as flax and tow at my touch. It has been said that this power was accorded to me, that I might be enabled to tempt wretches in their fearful hour of extremity, with the promise of deliverance and immunity, on condition of their exchanging situations with me.[30]

Melmoth lives longer than normal humans and can travel anywhere with unearthly speed. He uses his superhuman temporal and spatial access to help him "to tempt" people, to influence them strongly enough to adopt his "situation" and become more Wanderers. His tempting influence, then, is a means of propagating the Wanderer line. Judith Wilt observes the resemblance between the relationship Melmoth would have with his victims and a parent-child relationship, calling each victim a "would-be child of his."[31] Through temptation, Melmoth would convert his victims into his children. Like Frankenstein's scientific process, Melmoth's influence is an asexual mode of reproduction, but since Melmoth's influence serves the "enemy of souls"; his pathology is more blatantly evil and opposed to the human order than Frankenstein's bad science.

Frankenstein's mode of reproduction is both asexual and asocial: his insistence on allowing no other person to participate precludes both hetero- and homo-eroticism. Melmoth's influence, on the other hand, requires his victims to be partners in the conversion process, which has an erotic edge. One of Melmoth's would-be children, Stanton, learns that Melmoth once suggested to an Inquisitor that even Jesus Christ, like Melmoth's own "master," might forbid the revelation of Melmoth's horrible secret. Stanton's mind then becomes so "full of his mysterious countryman" that he pursues him for years. When Stanton next sees the Wanderer, the "heart of Stanton palpitate[s] with violence, — a mist overspread[s] his eyes, [and he feels] a nameless and deadly sickness, accompanied with a creeping sensation in every pore." Stanton's rapid heartbeat and watering eyes suggest that the "sickness," or pathology, that Melmoth initiates is quite rousing. Melmoth becomes "the master-passion" and "the master-torment of [Stanton's] life." [32] Marked by such passion and torment, Stanton's years-spanning devotion to Melmoth is at least analogous to a misguided erotic obsession.

Stanton's devotion is not overtly sexual, however. On the surface, what obsesses him is a desire for Melmoth's forbidden knowledge. Eugenia DeLamotte traces a link between "illicit knowledge" and "illicit passion" in *Melmoth* back to Marlowe's Faustus and Milton's Adam and Eve. Whereas Marlowe and Milton tie the association of illicit knowledge and illicit passion to potentially procreative lusts between a man and a woman, Maturin ties it to Melmoth's asexual mode of reproduction. DeLamotte calls Melmoth's temptations "a horrifying parody of normal human intimacy" in part because of the way Melmoth "preys on the desire for knowledge—the insane desire for knowledge about *him*—which his presence inspires in certain people." [33] Desire for knowledge blurs into erotic desire during Melmoth's tempting process of influence. His mode of reproduction involves abnormal erotic intimacy. The seductive lure of his illicit knowledge would make way for reproduction via conversion.

Though Melmoth establishes intimacy with his would-be children, he never succeeds in reproducing. He laments, "*I have traversed the world in the search, and no one, to gain that world, would lose his own soul!*" Melmoth's failure marks his asexual "parody of normal human intimacy" as a mode of reproduction distinctly inferior to its normal, sexual original. Melmoth even attempts sexual reproduction with a female would-be child, Isidora, whom he has already failed to influence. Someone telling Isidora's tale speculates, "It is not impossible that he looked to some future object of his fearful experiment—and a being so perfectly in his power as his own child, might have appeared to him fatally fitted for his purpose."[34] Melmoth wants a biological child because he could more easily persuade his own sexual offspring to become his non-sexual offspring, to be not just another Melmoth but also another Wanderer. He attempts to use the superior power of sexual, normal reproduction to assist with his asexual, pathological reproduction, and he fails: his child dies shortly after birth, making Melmoth's reproductive impotence total.

Even though Melmoth has the superhuman powers granted him by the "enemy of souls," he lacks the normal reproductive powers of humanity and is therefore still inferior. Maturin claims that his novel offers a lesson about what separates the human from the diabolical. The novel's Preface explains that the "hint" of the tale came from one of Maturin's own sermons, which Maturin quotes:

At this moment is there one of us present, however we may have departed from the Lord, disobeyed his will, and disregarded his word — is there one of us who would, at this moment, accept all that man could bestow, or earth afford, to resign the hope of his salvation? — No, there is not one — not such a fool on earth, were the enemy of mankind to traverse it with the offer![35]

Allied with and empowered by "the enemy of mankind," Melmoth traverses the globe, spreading his influence. Melmoth's failure to convert anyone illustrates Maturin's idea that rejection of "the enemy" defines everyone, all of humanity. To be a Wanderer, however, Melmoth himself must have once accepted the enemy's offer; for Maturin's idea to be coherent, Melmoth must be "not one," not human. The name "Wanderer" itself suggests placelessness within the natural human order. By allying himself with humanity's enemy, a Wanderer exits the human race. Like Frankenstein's scientific process, the seductive bargain that creates a Wanderer creates an inhuman being opposed to normal humanity by virtue of its mode of creation.

Melmoth the Wanderer and *Frankenstein* imagine a mode of reproduction that is asexual, sickening, and threatening to the human norm. Frankenstein's Creature and Melmoth both possess superhuman abilities, and both fail to propagate their species. Melmoth's failure is more total than the Creature's: while the Creature gets no mate because Frankenstein denies him the necessary knowledge, Melmoth has the knowledge he needs but fails to reproduce anyway. *Melmoth the Wanderer* deepens the pathology of alternative modes of reproduction by making the pathological reproducer impotent in both normal and abnormal realms. As long as the superior normals defend themselves against the inferior abnormals' evil, seductive influence, they will contain the threat. For containment to succeed, the threat of pathological reproduction must mobilize the forces of normality to reject the tainted policies of the abnormal and thus protect their futures. The moral evil, impotence, and eroticism associated with Melmoth's pathology give it greater commonality with the pathology that Wilde's opponents, the TVC, and the AFA supposedly combat to protect their futures, their children, and civilization itself.

J. Sheridan LeFanu's Carmilla *(1872): Penetrating Sameness*

Carmilla is the story of a female vampire whose evil, impotent, and erotic mode of reproduction draws still closer to the pathological reproduction eventually associated with homosexuality. As a vampire, Carmilla must feed on others for her own survival; "*they* die, and almost invariably, in the grave, develop into vampires." Carmilla's bite, like Frankenstein's secret scientific process and Melmoth's influence, propagates a species without genital contact between female and male. Like Melmoth, Carmilla needs another person to participate in her reproductive process, but unlike Melmoth, she chooses her own sex exclusively. While Carmilla's contact with women does not literally involve their genitals, when Carmilla bites a young woman, Laura, she causes "a sensation as if a hand [were] drawn softly along [Laura's] cheek and neck," "as if warm lips kissed" her "lovingly," all of which causes Laura's heart to "beat faster," leading up to a "convulsion" and, later, "a sense of exhaustion."[36] Laura's response to Carmilla's bite is much more erotic than Stanton's response to Melmoth's influence. Carmilla's reproductive process depends upon an erotic experience between women.

Carmilla's bite offers women the experience and knowledge of sexual pleasure. Tamar Heller links the sharing of sexual knowledge in *Carmilla* to the nineteenth-century concept of "hysterical contagion whereby one hysterical girl infects, and creates, another."[37] Through her exchange of sexual knowledge with Carmilla, Laura catches the "contagion" of "hysterical" sexual deviance, metaphorically becoming a deviant while literally becoming a vampire. Carmilla's act of reproduction functions as a disease that converts a normal human being into a new, abnormal creature through knowledge gained during an erotic same-sex experience. The homosexual "species" that Michel Foucault dates to about 1870 is a pathologized type of being whose interiority is defined by just such knowledge and experience. Lillian Faderman points out several ways in which Le Fanu could have become familiar with this newly emerging concept before the 1872 publication of his novel, but she also grants that Le Fanu "may have thought only to show romantic friendship as a vampire would conduct it — taken to the extreme of bloodsucking."[38] The historical relationship of Le Fanu's fiction with homosexuality is ambiguous. Regardless of this ambiguity, *Carmilla* gives pathological reproduction the dimension of same-sex eroticism later included within the homosexual type that emerged from Wilde's trials.

Le Fanu's woman-biting vampire has phallic teeth that penetrate her victims in order to give pleasure and reproduce. Her attacks meet what Faderman identifies as patriarchy's centuries-old demand for a simulated male in representations of erotic relations between women: "If a man were

3. Pathological Reproduction

not present in fact, one of those who was present must simulate him."[39] In a discussion of the "lesbian phallus," Judith Butler explains that "the phallus signifies the insuperability of heterosexuality and constitutes lesbianism as a vain and/or pathetic effort to mime the real thing."[40] Carmilla's simulation of a male reflects how sexual experiences between women within the patriarchal order must appear as just that, a simulation, an inferior copy. Men eventually rescue Laura, so Carmilla's effort at conversion fails. The vampire's failure to reproduce, like Melmoth's, emblazons her inferiority, and in *Carmilla*, the inferiority of pathological reproduction reflects on same-sex sexual experience.

The men who rescue Laura establish Carmilla's inferiority through violence. The eradication of Carmilla's reproductive threat involves "formal proceedings" that occur "in the Chapel of Karnstein," proceedings that include "two medical men" and two of the fathers of Carmilla's victims.[41] Symbols of religious, medical, and patriarchal authority combine to squash Carmilla's opposition to the normative order they represent. The special method of Carmilla's violent destruction reflects the specificity of her menace. The threat of the evil female vampire who preys on girls — of a figure recognizable today as a phallic lesbian — is that, as Butler claims, "the phallic lesbian [is] potentially castrating."[42] When the patriarchal imagination creates a phallic woman in order to make the idea of sex between women intelligible, it imagines the activity of the phallic woman as a usurpation of its own phallic prerogative. Patriarchal authorities respond to Carmilla's usurpation with her execution:

> The body, therefore, in accordance with ancient practice, was raised, and a sharp stake driven through the heart of the vampire, who uttered a piercing shriek at the moment, in all respects such as might escape from a living person in the last agony. Then the head was struck off, and a torrent of blood flowed from the severed neck. The body and head were next placed on a pile of wood, and reduced to ashes, which were thrown upon the river and borne away, and that territory has never since been plagued by the visits of a vampire.[43]

Heller observes, "Carmilla's execution suggests a feminized version of castration; moreover, the stake driven through the body of the lesbian vampire whose biting had mimicked the act of penetration is a raw assertion of phallic power."[44] Along with her phallus, the patriarchs take Carmilla's life, and as a result, the "plague," or pathology, vanishes from masculine "territory." Whether or not her executioners recognize Carmilla as a lesbian, the details of their response to her mode of reproduction bear a strong resemblance to the violence that often accompanies modern-day homophobia.

The violence in Le Fanu's story that resembles the concept involved in the twentieth-century term "homophobia" contains a paradox: though Carmilla's crime is reproduction involving sameness of sex, when her enemies attack her as a pathologized type, they eliminate not excessive sameness but a type of difference unacceptable to the norm. Edelman elucidates the phenomenon in contemporary terms:

> Homosexuality, though charged with, and convicted of, a future-negating sameness construed as reflecting its pathological inability to deal with the fact of difference, gets put in the position of difference from the heteronormativity that, despite is persistent propaganda for its own propagation through *sexual* difference, refuses homosexuality's difference from the value of difference it claims as its own.[45]

The protection of society from pathological reproduction demanded by Wilde's prosecutors and by the propaganda of the TVC and the AFA requires the confinement — and perhaps the complete elimination — of people who differ sexually from a norm that exalts difference. Casting Carmilla's sexual type as a Gothic horror does not resolve the contradictions involved in her destruction, but the scariness of her pathological, vampiric difference might emotionally justify the violence against her kind.

R.L. Stevenson's Dr. Jekyll and Mr. Hyde (1886): Paradoxical Pathology

In the tradition of *Frankenstein*, the titular doctor in Stevenson's *Strange Case of Dr. Jekyll and Mr. Hyde* employs science as a means of reproducing asexually, using expertise in medicine and chemistry to concoct a potion that releases a new type of being from inside himself. Jekyll, referring to himself in the third person, describes the horror of having Hyde inside of him:

> This was the shocking thing; that the slime of the pit seemed to utter cries and voices; that the amorphous dust gesticulated and sinned; that what was dead, and had no shape, should usurp the offices of life. And this again, that that insurgent horror was knit to him closer than a wife, closer than an eye; lay caged in his flesh, where he heard it mutter and felt it struggle to be born; and at every hour of weakness, and in the confidence of slumber, prevailed against him, and deposed him out of life.[46]

Jekyll carries Hyde like an evil child in the womb, "struggl[ing] to be born." Like Frankenstein before him, Jekyll evades women and the natural sexual order when he gives birth to Hyde.[47] Reproduction in *Frankenstein* results from Frankenstein's aspiration to godhood, from his blasphemous will. Jekyll's reference to "amorphous dust" recalls the story of Creation in the Judeo-Christian tradition, in which God creates His offspring, man, from dust. Jekyll also aspires to godlike creation, and claiming that Hyde is the "wholly evil" product of "moral weakness," Jekyll frames his scientifically-induced asexual reproduction as morally pathological, the result of wicked willfulness.[48]

The role of wicked willfulness is more complex in Jekyll's mode of reproduction than it is in Frankenstein's. Jekyll's transformations begin to occur without his willful ingestion of the potion, and he fears that his "nature might be permanently overthrown [and] the power of voluntary change be forfeited."[49] Jekyll's initial changes resemble Frankenstein's willful decision to reproduce, but Jekyll's later, involuntary changes are closer to Melmoth and Carmilla's reproductive acts. To be a Wanderer is to spread an evil influence: tempting people is a condition of Melmoth's continued existence. Similarly, Carmilla must drink blood, engendering more of her kind, to sustain her vampiric life. For Melmoth and Carmilla, pathological reproduction is a compulsion, not a choice. Jekyll's mode of pathological reproduction seems to occur in two ways, one a scientific choice to create Hyde and another a compulsion resulting from the inclusion of Hyde in his being. Thus, Stevenson's vision of pathological reproduction combines traits from *Frankenstein*, *Melmoth*, and *Carmilla*.

Jekyll's combination of reproductive traits mirrors the medical descriptions of "the homosexual" emerging during Stevenson's time. *Psychopathia Sexualis*, even though it was not yet available in English, had put contradictory ideas about the genesis of homosexuals into circulation by the time of *Jekyll and Hyde*'s publication:

> This perverse sexuality appears spontaneously, without external cause, with the development of sexual life, as an individual manifestation of an abnormal form of the vita sexualis, and then has the force of a *congenital* phenomenon; or it develops upon a sexuality the beginning of which was normal, as a result of very definite injurious influences, and thus appears as an *acquired* anomaly. Upon what this enigmatical phenomenon of acquired homo-sexual instinct depends is still inexplicable, and only a matter for hypothesis.[50]

According to Krafft-Ebing, homosexuality can be a "hereditary" or an "acquired" trait, a compulsion resulting from inner being or, so far as one can choose one's "influences," an injury resulting from choice. Though Jekyll seems to acquire Hyde's bad nature through a willed act of reproduction that later results in compulsory acts, he also indicates that Hyde is the result of something that has always been inside him. Theorizing the "primitive duality of man," Jekyll explains that even before giving birth to Hyde, he had "two natures," one "unjust" and the other "upright." The injustice manifested in Hyde seems, in this formulation, to have been innate all along, but in another formulation, Jekyll describes Hyde as something "worse" than his "original and better self."[51] Jekyll vacillates between characterizations of Hyde's pathology. Taking all characterizations together, the pathology seems to be both innate and acquired, but Jekyll never theorizes a resolution to this apparent contradiction. Such paradoxical possibilities are, to borrow Krafft-Ebing's adjective, enigmatical.

Whether the pathology in Stevenson's *Strange Case* reflects directly on the then-nascent concept of "homosexuality" is as ambiguous as *Carmilla*'s relationship with lesbianism. In a letter to John Paul Bocock written in 1887, Stevenson insists that his study of duality is about hypocrisy, not sexuality. Jekyll, he explains, is not hypocritical about being "fond of women," and Hyde is "no more sexual than another," but "people are so filled full of folly and inverted lust, that they can think of nothing but sexuality."[52] Seeing sexual significance in the novel, according to Stevenson, results from readers' foolish obsessions, not his own representation. His mention of "inverted lusts" might refer to "inversion," a term for same-sex desire sometimes exchangeable for "homosexuality," and thus he might aim to dismiss assignations of homosexual significance in particular. Many literary critics, such as Wayne Koestenbaum and Elaine Showalter, demonstrate that the novel's representation of duality echoes the legal, medical, and cultural discourses on homosexuality loudly enough to deny Stevenson's dismissal.[53] Whatever Stevenson's intentions, his novel adds a dimension to the Gothic trope of pathological reproduction that makes it ripe for association with Krafft-Ebing's paradoxical take on homosexuality. When they debated the significance of pathological reproduction in *Dorian Gray*, Wilde's enemies were able to associate the trope with homosexuality far less enigmatically.

Dorian Gray: The Arts of Reproduction

Like *Melmoth the Wanderer*, *Dorian Gray* is a tale of reproduction through negative influence, but in Wilde's novel, pathological reproduction occurs through the erotic influence of art. Martha Vicinus explains how, in *Dorian Gray*, Basil Hallward "establish[es] art as a tempting alternative to heterosexual reproduction," and Lord Henry Wotton "seduces Dorian ... with a book," using this book and his own words to "reproduc[e] himself through Dorian."[54] Basil does his part to shape Dorian through painting the titular picture, and Henry does his through the sorts of literature and artful conversation that made Wilde himself famous.

Basil explains that when he paints Dorian, he paints Dorian in the image of himself: "'every portrait that is painted with feeling is a portrait of the artist, not the sitter.'" Basil shapes the image, and the image, in turn, shapes Dorian, who in it "recognise[s] himself for the first time." Henry projects himself onto and into Dorian through conversation. Basil complains that Henry "has a very bad influence over all his friends," and Henry explains what influence is:

> To influence a person is to give him one's own soul. He does not think his natural thoughts or burn with his natural passions. His virtues are not real to him. His sins, if there are such things as sins, are borrowed. He becomes an echo of some one else's music, an actor of a part that has not been written for him.

By sharing his libertine views through literature and conversation, Henry fills Dorian with his own "music" and, significantly, his own "passions." Dorian becomes so enamored of Basil's painting that he wishes for the portrait to age while he retains the portrait's beauty. Dorian gets his wish, and he takes up a life of debauchery in the spirit of Henry's libertinism, knowing that the marks of his sins will appear on his portrait and not on his face. Dorian commits, among other sins, the murder of Basil. Eventually, Dorian realizes the horror of his own actions by seeing the ugliness of the "loathsome" portrait, which bears "sign[s] of evil passion" and a bloodstain from the murder that creeps "like a disease."[55] The portrait plainly reveals the pathological results of Henry and Basil's artistic mode of reproduction.

During Wilde's first trial, in which Wilde sued the Marquess of Queensberry for accusing him of "posing as a sodomite," Queensberry's attorney, Edward Carson, tried to justify Queensberry's accusation by proving that *Dorian Gray* "was understood by readers thereof to describe the relations intimacies and passions of certain persons of sodomitical habits tastes and practices." Carson used *Dorian Gray*'s depiction of harmful influences as proof. Noting that once he has embarked on his evil life, Dorian, like Henry, has a profound influence over his friends, Carson read aloud a passage in which Basil asks Dorian why his friendship is "'so fatal to young men,'" men who, after knowing him, seem afflicted with "'shame and sorrow.'" Completing the passage, Carson asked Wilde, "Do you think [the passage] ... would suggest ... they were talking about ... sodomy?" Wilde countered that the passage "describes Dorian Gray as man of very corrupt influence," and he clarified that such influence does not exist "in the world ... except in fiction." Earlier, Wilde had explained that he had left the nature of this fictional corruption deliberately ambiguous. In the manner of Stevenson's letter to Bocock, he dismissed specific sexual assignations of meaning by saying, "he who has found the sin has brought it."[56] Wilde insisted that there is a difference between fiction and reality, that the supernaturally amplified influence in his novel does not specifically belong to a real type of person.

Carson persisted by contrasting his own "common sense" with Wilde's "philosophical point," suggesting that an unrealistic Gothic fiction could unlock the mysteries of real-life homosexuals. Transposing *Dorian Gray*'s Gothic depiction of influence onto real-life "sodomitical" people, Carson segued into a discussion of Wilde's relationship with Queensberry's son, Lord Alfred Douglas, implying equivalence between Douglas's seduction and Dorian's supernaturally facilitated corruptions. Wilde's attorney, foreseeing the consequences of further evidence against Wilde, withdrew the prosecution of Queensberry, submitting "to a verdict of 'not guilty' having reference ... to that part of the particulars which is connected with the publication of *Dorian Gray*." [57] The trial's outcome averred Carson's "common sense" about the equivalence between Gothic fiction and real life. Wilde and his attorney only granted that *Dorian Gray* proved that Wilde "posed" as a homosexual, but Wilde's defeat prompted two trials in which Wilde was prosecuted for homosexual offenses.

During Wilde's second and third trials, the questions once asked about the role of corrupting influence, or pathological reproduction, in *Dorian Gray* became questions asked about the corrupting influence that Wilde had spread in his own life. A week before the second trial began, Gill, the prosecutor who would later direct a jury to protect society from Wilde's corruption, wrote a letter explaining that Douglas should not be prosecuted because, considering "the strong influence that Wilde has obviously exercised ... Douglas, if guilty, may fairly be regarded as one of Wilde's victims."[58] For Gill, the first trial's depiction of Wilde's Gothic influence determined the difference between criminal and victim. To import this depiction into the second trial, Gill read details from Wilde's cross-examination about *Dorian Gray* into evidence. At the second trial's end, the judge, referring to *Dorian Gray*, instructed the jury, "confound no man with the characters he has created."[59] Perhaps the judge's reassertion of a difference between fiction and reality counterbalanced Gill's theory of Gothic influence: the second trial resulted in a hung jury.

The judge in the third trial offered no such counterbalance, and the trial ended with Wilde's conviction for gross indecency. During sentencing, the judge, who had tried murder cases, declared Wilde's "the worse case I have ever tried" and condemned him for being "the center of a circle of extensive corruption of the most hideous kind among young men."[60] The judge labeled Wilde as something more monstrous than a murderer, more "hideous" than the guiltiest of Gothic arch-villains. Wilde's enemies imprisoned him to contain the pathological mode of reproduction practiced by so many Gothic characters before him. Thereafter, the Gothic manner in which *Dorian Gray* supposedly describes "the relations intimacies and practices" of homosexuals became a guidebook for real-life homosexuals' corrupting character.

Max Nordau's seminal late nineteenth-century work *Degeneration* models the logic underlying the use of fiction as a guide for reality. Describing homosexuals within the broader category of the degenerate, Nordau claims, "In perversion of the sexual appetite he has desires which are directly contrary to the purpose of the instinct, *i.e.*, the preservation of the species."[61] This description exemplifies the paradoxical condemnation for both sameness and difference used by Carmilla's executioners. It first condemns the degenerate homosexual as a pervert for having an appetite for sameness, and in doing so, it valorizes difference. Then, it condemns the desires that make the homosexual "contrary" to the preservation of the species; the evil difference of the appetite defines the perverts who possess it as the enemy of humanity.

To rationalize this paradoxical condemnation, Nordau demonstrates how the homosexual enemy operates, explaining how sexually deviant artists, among whom he names Oscar Wilde, reproduce homosexuality through the influence of their work:

> Works of a sexually psychopathic nature excite in abnormal subjects the corresponding perversions (till then slumbering and unconscious, perhaps also undeveloped, although present in the germ), and give them lively feelings of pleasure, which they, usually in good faith, regard as purely aesthetic or intellectual, whereas they are actually sexual.[62]

Making influence the means of homosexuals' pathological reproduction clears up the mystery of Krafft-Ebing's — and Stevenson's — model of a pathology that is both hereditary and acquired. "Abnormal" subjects must first inherit the "germ" of perversion and then awaken it by acquiring an influence with the power to disguise sexual pleasure as something else. Henry Wotton's use of literature and conversation to corrupt Dorian Gray becomes the technique that homosexuals, cast in the mold of Oscar Wilde, employ to reproduce their pathology. The inherited germ is not pathogenic by itself. True pathological reproduction does not occur without an influence, without something that corrupts, converts, seduces, or recruits.

Making influence a necessary addition to an inborn capacity to be led astray—perhaps a gene, perhaps original sin—provides the TVC, the AFA, and others like them a superficial logical coherence as they condemn homosexual sameness for being different. The idea that homosexuals can "recruit" allows the social order to beatify sexual reproduction while excoriating homosexuality as a pathology that, if left unchecked, can spread limitlessly and destroy the fragile norms that ensure the social order its future. Wilde's trials presented a public forum that tested and proved these ideas, making the Gothic trope of pathological reproduction a permanent feature of the "homosexuality" that homophobes attack. Gothic notions of pathological reproduction, from *Frankenstein* to *Dorian Gray*, are, of course, fictional, which means that the counternormative category "homosexual" that emerged with Gothic characteristics might realistically include no one. As long as these fictional notions motivate homophobia, however, their power will remain quite real.

4

Romps in the Closet
The Persistence of Nineteenth Century Notions in Contemporary Pop Culture

Frankenstein's Creature, the vampire Carmilla, and Jekyll/Hyde — icons of nineteenth century Gothic horror — all contributed to the supernatural pathology associated with the concept of homosexuality. The discussions of aberrant sexuality that saturated British culture around 1895 also provided material that Irishman Bram Stoker used to created the century's best-known monster, Count Dracula, whom critics have read as a condensation of all things sexually deviant and even as a direct reflection on Oscar Wilde.[1] Thus the most famous Gothic monsters of all time carry interrelated sexual significations that continue to resonate today.

As they migrated from nineteenth-century novels to twentieth-century cinema, these monsters took their sexual baggage with them. Deviant sexuality suffuses F.W. Murnau's *Nosferatu* (1922), which takes so much inspiration from *Dracula* that Stoker's widow sued the production company, and also James Whale's *Frankenstein* (1931) and *Bride of Frankenstein* (1935), which rework Shelley's brilliant Creature into a brutish, barely-intelligent victim of social prejudice and mob vengeance.[2] Robin Wood, a pioneering critic of the horror film, points out that these films "can be claimed as implicitly (on certain levels) identifying their monsters with repressed homosexuality."[3] Indeed, the repression in Whale's films provides the storyline for the film *Gods and Monsters* (1998), which suggests a parallel between Whale's conception of his films' monster, originally portrayed by Boris Karloff, and his erotic infatuation with his heterosexual male gardener, who at the film's end does an affectionately comic Karloff impression.⁴ By the time *Gods and Monsters* was released, that Whale's own sexuality found expression through his representation of a monster required little explanation. Because they helped to define homosexuality, to greater and lesser degrees, Gothic monsters were and are implicitly homosexual. The legacy of nineteenth-century Gothic is a formula that persists in the cultural imaginary, MONSTER = HOMOSEXUAL, and James Whale stands among countless others who have used this equation to tell stories about themselves.

The Trouble with Reverse Discourse

The formula MONSTER = HOMOSEXUAL is a metaphor that merely visualizes the monstrosity already built into homosexuality as a social construct. Conceived as a pathological category, "homosexual" stigmatizes the people it names; with or without vampire fangs, an image or person labeled "homosexual" is implicitly monstrous. Of course, the meanings associated with any term are negotiable. When people adopt the label "homosexual" for themselves, they have the power to make it signify differently, to make it say something other than *monster*. Foucault explains:

> There is no question that the appearance in nineteenth-century psychiatry, jurisprudence, and literature of a whole series of discourses on the species and subspecies of homosexuality, inversion, pederasty, and "psychic hermaphrodism" made possible a strong advance of social controls into this area of "perversity"; but it also made possible the formation of a "reverse" discourse: homosexuality began to speak in its own behalf, to demand that its legitimacy or "naturality" be acknowledged, often in the same vocabulary, using the same categories by which it was medically disqualified.⁵

Cultural, legal, and scientific discourses of the nineteenth century constructed homosexuality as a pathology in order to identify and control it, but in doing so they created a language of selfhood that enabled people to understand, justify, and defend their desires.

Without terms such as "homosexual" and "gay," there could be no homophile and gay rights movements. The "queer theory" championed by Judith Halberstam, Lee Edelman, and others relies on a more recent instance of reverse discourse: once hurled as an insult meaning "abnormal," the label "queer" now functions as a starting point for attacks on the construction of normality and the insidious operations of heteronormativity. The term "heteronormativity" reflects a set of social norms that valorize opposite-sex relations by vilifying same-sex relations. A person (or subject) in heteronormative culture knows her- or himself not according to what she or he *is* but according to what she or he *isn't*. To be a straight, normal heterosexual is not *to have sex* with someone who has different genitalia; it is *to not have sex* with someone who has similar genitalia. Thus the heterosexual knows her- or himself through what Julia Kristeva describes as abjection, a process through which a person knows who "I" is by contrasting her or himself with the abject, which "has only one quality of the object — that of being opposed to *I*."[6] According to this frightfully circular logic, the homosexual is the heterosexual's opposite, its abject, and the forces of heteronormativity (embodied in their extreme by the Traditional Values Coalition and the American Family Association) ensure that good heterosexual subjects define themselves as anything but homosexual and define the homosexual as anything but I. Those who use "queer" as a position of empowered subjectivity, then, reverse the form of abjectification that constitutes the heterosexual/homosexual binary, marking the heterosexual as "not I" and the queer as the subject defined as "*not* not-I." The queer "not not-I" takes a position that exposes and critiques the threats that heteronormativity poses to the queer social self.

Reverse discourses like queer theory function as interventions in history, redirections of the currents of historical meaning. They can resignify historical terminology, but they cannot erase history. The survival of pejorative meanings in "queer," "homosexual," and "gay" is manifest every time a tittering child on the animated television show *South Park* (or on the real-life playgrounds that the show lampoons) condemns something by saying "That's gay!" Reclaiming the queer, the homosexual, and the monstrous as a viable and valorized category of identity isn't a simple, finite act. Queer theory has been celebrating queerness for decades, but the same queer celebrated in rarefied (and rare) academic circles faces a very real physical threat on Main Street U.S.A. A reverse discourse is a competing discourse, certainly, but its embrace of marginality is by definition distinct from the dominant discourse. When critics and artists try to elevate same-sex sexual relations through retrograde participation in the discourse of monstrosity, then, they risk reinforcing that monstrosity in mainstream culture. Harry M. Benshoff sums up this predicament in his study *Monsters in the Closet*:

> For example, some lesbians find *Basic Instinct*'s killer queer to be an empowering figure, rather than merely a negative stereotype.... Ultimately, however, I would argue that the resultant connotative and cumulative effect of such images on

non-queer spectators remains retrogressive.... And even when the films themselves problematize these figures by linking them to social oppression ... they nonetheless still reaffirm for uncritical audiences the semiotic overlap of homosexual and violent killer.[7]

In other words, while a minority celebrates the powerful queerness embodied by cinematic monsters like the killer lesbians of *Basic Instinct*, the majority sees its fears and discriminations justified.

Monstrous Equations from Dorian Gray to Jeffrey Dahmer

As Benshoff suggests, the primary obstacle confronting those who want to celebrate queer monsters in fiction and film is the monsters' lamentable tendency to kill people. Claiming that these monsters are good unfortunately implies that killing people is good. Oscar Wilde was already grappling with this problem when he wrote *The Picture of Dorian Gray*. If Dorian is, as countless critics have argued, homosexual, he is a homosexual monster, a debaucher of boys and the murderer of his artist-friend Basil. While Carmilla and Jekyll/Hyde's monstrosity appears on their bodies, Dorian's appears on his portrait. After having been kept from the portrait for a long time, Dorian's friend Basil sees it and remarks that it has developed "'the face of a satyr'" and "'the eyes of a devil.'" The portrait becomes the outward manifestation of Dorian's inward monstrosity; Dorian explicitly identifies it as the "conscience" he denies and would "destroy."[8] The portrait therefore represents Dorian to himself and to Basil as the monster he believes his actions have made him. Haunted by his portrait-conscience, Dorian spirals into darkness, seeming to approach what Elaine Showalter calls "the only form of narrative closure thought appropriate to the Gay Gothic": suicide.[9]

However, instead of turning his violence against himself, at the end of Wilde's novel Dorian attacks his portrait. Though the effort kills him, this attack on the portrait differs significantly from a suicide because, instead of trying to destroy the person (himself) whom society has judged a monster, he tries to destroy monstrosity's *image*. As Edward S. Brinkley argues, "the attack on the portrait ... cannot be read as judgment on Dorian or as a suicide per se" but rather as an attack on "the realm in which the moral judgments made against Dorian *obtain*."[10] *Dorian Gray* represents the moral judgments of society in the portrait: if, as the interpretation offered by Wilde's prosecutors suggests, the portrait's pathological corruption represents "homosexuality" as the Victorians understood it, it does *not* represent the homosexual as someone with an intrinsically corrupted soul. The portrait, as an externalization of Dorian's conscience, reflects Dorian's internalization of society's judgment, an internalization of what the twenty-first century would call homophobia. Dorian's attack on the portrait reflects a desire to purge the self-hatred imposed by Victorian culture. The culture proves more powerful, and Dorian dies in the attack.

Fighting against the pathological associations of homosexuality at the very moment of the concept's emergence, Dorian Gray could be interpreted as a homosexual monster/hero, someone whose supernatural pathology carries with it a perverse righteousness. Though it might help to account for why a novel about a putatively homosexual murderer holds a place of reverence in gay culture, this liberationist reading of Wilde's work presents a major problem: though the portrait may very well represent homosexuality, the "loathsome red dew" that appears on the portrait's hand after Dorian kills Basil also represents murder. At first glance, the blood on the portrait's hand may not seem problematic. The portrait's hand isn't Dorian's hand; if the portrait represents the culture's condemnation of Dorian, then the dewy blood is more directly on the culture's hand. Following this logic, the novel blames the culture for shelling out the shame that drives Dorian to murder Basil, for the murder only occurs after a look at the picture that Basil created fills him with "an uncontrollable feeling of hatred." In placing blame for Dorian's actions on the culturally-inflected portrait that inspires him, *Dorian Gray* does not remove all blame from its (anti)hero. Dorian's culpability becomes visible when, after he dies, his body takes on the portrait's appearance.[11] Dorian's assumption in death of his portrait's visage inscribes the culture's crimes into his identity; it figures a retroactive justification of society's judgment. Through his murderous acts, Dorian reveals himself to be what society suspected of him all along. Murder is therefore inextricable from the pattern of queer associations in Dorian's portrait and in Wilde's novel. Unless reverse discourse goes so far as to remove murder from ethical condemnation, the murderous queer monster is reprehensible even if his sexual aberration is, to some, heroic.

The real-life fate of a serial murderer and homosexual — Jeffrey Dahmer — offers a parallel to the fictional fate of Dorian Gray. Though an actual killer rather than a figure from Gothic fiction, Dahmer quickly entered the mythology with which American culture surrounds its madmen, taking the part of a Gothic villain. Just as Wilde's novel suggests that

Dorian murders Basil because he has internalized his culture's homophobia, several analysts of Dahmer's case have suggested that Dahmer's string of homicides was a product of homophobia.[12] However, media coverage of the Dahmer case did not raise a public outcry against homophobia, but as Diana Fuss claims, "in the case of Jeffrey Dahmer, the 'homosexual-murderer-necrophilic-cannibal' equation ... proved particularly fertile ground in the late twentieth century for activating old phobias and breeding new justifications for the recriminalization and repathologization of gay identity."[13] This paradoxical response — strengthening homophobia to combat homophobia's negative effects — indicates the intractability of the MONSTER = HOMOSEXUAL formula as well as its reflexive corollary, HOMOSEXUAL = MONSTER. People who experience same-sex desire can work to reverse the pathologizing tendencies of "queer" and "homosexual" by taking on the labels in acts of resignification, but the dominant culture retains the power to resignify the resignifiers; in the mythologizing of Jeffrey Dahmer, "we see ... a continuation of the colonizing of homosexuality by heterosexual culture, the conflation of heterosexuality with civilization and homosexuality with savagery."[14] The cultural response to Jeffrey Dahmer, the murderer and monster who had the misfortune to inherit the legacy of *Dorian Gray* a century later, demonstrates how reverse discourse ends up reinforcing the pathologies it seeks to undermine.

Judith Halberstam's Skin Shows *and Joss Whedon's* Buffy the Vampire Slayer

Even the most well-meaning of cultural texts can fall victim to the intractability of the MONSTER = HOMOSEXUAL formula. The first book of a foundational queer theorist, Judith Halberstam's *Skin Shows* is very canny about how Gothic texts participate in the articulation of homosexuality, arguing that "monsters are meaning machines," and demonstrating, for example, how medical discourse "produces perversion in exactly the process that Jekyll uses to produce Hyde."[15] Halberstam's work exemplifies literary criticism's potential for denaturalizing homosexuality's negative associations in many ways, but in a reading of the 1986 film *The Texas Chainsaw Massacre 2*, it applies MONSTER = HOMOSEXUAL in order to make a larger point about the horror film and, in the process, reinforces the very association that it would undo.

The heroine of *Texas Chainsaw 2*, Stretch, goes through quite an

4. Romps in the Closet

ordeal. She survives several attacks by multiple maniacs, including a few unwelcome sexual advances from the film's eponymous chainsaw-wielding madman, Leatherface. She witnesses horror after horror: in one scene, she watches a good friend get skinned alive and then has to wear his face in order to avoid being butchered herself. At the end of the film, the only surviving maniac, Chop-Top, chases her through a massive labyrinth until, at the top of a tower-like structure, she discovers the rotten corpse of the maniacs' grandmother. Conveniently, this corpse has a chainsaw between her legs that Stretch is able to pick up and use to defend herself, which she does successfully, dispatching Chop-Top with a whirl of the roaring blade. Leatherface's use of the chainsaw repeatedly identifies it as a phallic symbol — at one point, he rubs an inactive saw between Stretch's legs and becomes sexually excited. When Stretch seizes the mother's chainsaw, she seizes a female phallus and fights the maniacs with a phallic power of her own.[16]

A close-up of Stretch (Caroline Williams), the heroine of *Texas Chainsaw Massacre 2* (1986), reveals her madness, far from a triumph of queerness.

Halberstam accurately represents the film's storyline and its figuration of the chainsaw as a phallic power that women can seize to overcome their male persecutors, but she misrepresents the film's final image. After defeating Chop-Top, Stretch spins around madly, waving the chainsaw over her head in a fashion that exactly duplicates gestures that Leatherface makes throughout the *Texas Chainsaw* series. Halberstam reads this as a positive image of empowerment: "The chain saw has been sutured and grafted onto the female body, rendering it a queer body of violence and power, a monstrous body that has blades, makes noise, and refuses to splatter."[17] The chain saw does become an extension of Stretch's body, creating a phallic woman, but the film consistently associates phallic power with madness: the film's vigilante hero, Lefty (portrayed by Dennis Hopper, who has a tendency to play madmen), wields a chainsaw, behaves as insanely as the killers he hunts, and ultimately fails to accomplish anything. Representations of chainsaw-wielding maniacs throughout the film critique the dangers of violent, uncontrolled masculinity, and the female body that

This long shot of Stretch (Caroline Williams) shows her in a pose almost identical to that taken by the villain Leatherface in *Texas Chainsaw Massacre 2* (1986).

incorporates pathological masculine power shares in the pathology. Stretch is indeed empowered by seizing the phallus, but her empowerment is emphatically negative.

Stretch's traumatic ordeal drives her insane, causing her to identify with her attackers. She becomes a monstrous phallic woman, but the phallic woman in *Texas Chainsaw* is not necessarily a phallic lesbian. Stretch's monstrous body does not combine monstrosity with a "queer," or non-normative, sexuality. No scene in the film suggests she is attracted to women, and there are no verbal or visual cues that indicate she might identify with lesbianism or any other non-normative sexual category. If "queer" identity is a category for those who refuse normative categories, affirming "not not-I" as an (anti)identity, Stretch never offers such a refusal or accepts such an (anti)identification. The only thing that might mark her as queer is the fact that, like Carmilla, she wields the phallus: Halberstam, not the text, attaches the queer label to her phallic transformation. While many representations from the nineteenth century forward associate deranged phallic women with lesbians and queers, this film, on its own, does nothing to duplicate or reinforce such associations. Halberstam claims that one of the purposes of her book is to imagine "a posthuman monstrosity that is partial, compromised, messy, and queer."[18] By forcing such a reading on *Texas Chainsaw 2*, Halberstam seems to want to reclaim "monstrosity" and relate it to queerness in a kind of valorizing reverse discourse. Because the film only associates pathology with its images of monstrosity, the monstrosity that Halberstam would reclaim is far from valorous. Halberstam's reading of *Texas Chainsaw 2* merely repeats the negative, homophobic association between non-normative sexuality and monstrosity.

Halberstam's treatment of *Texas Chainsaw 2* shows how attempts to resignify "monster" along with "queer" within the context of Gothic horror are significantly more vexed than attempts to resignify "queer" alone. Resignification of "queer" has succeeded in some quarters because it valorizes the abnormality that the word denotes, reversing the normal/abnormal hierarchy. It changes meanings by shifting the value of abnormal from bad to good. Accomplishing similar shifts, recent films such as those in the *Shrek* series, which is about a lovable and misunderstood ogre, make "good guys" out of creatures who look like monsters but do not behave monstrously.[19] However, *Shrek* isn't a horror movie. The resignification of an abject figure — such as an ogre or a queer — typically succeeds by removing that figure from abjection, from the status of vilified other to valorized self. When monstrosity leaves abjection and ceases to horrify, it ceases to be Gothic. As Halberstam points out, the Gothic monster "can represent any *horrible* trait," and a "monster functions as monster ... when it is able to condense as many *fear-producing* traits as possible into one body" (emphasis added).[20] Queer abnormality is not necessarily horrific, but Gothic monstrosity is. Valorizing Gothic monsters means valorizing homicidal maniacs, creatures, human and otherwise, who literally destroy life. If Dorian Gray found the secret to immortality and then did nothing but make friends, Wilde's novel would have no place in this study. If Stretch from *Texas Chainsaw 2* took the phallic chainsaw and went on a picnic, Halberstam's reading of her as a queer-positive figure would be unproblematic. But she doesn't — instead, Stretch kills someone and spins around like a lunatic, and thus her story's ending is true to its genre, and her monstrosity remains pathological.

The hugely popular Gothic television show *Buffy the Vampire Slayer*, which aired in the U.S. from 1997 to 2003, offers an example of an artifact from contemporary popular culture that, like Halberstam's academic treatment of *Texas Chainsaw 2*, tries and fails to resignify Gothic monstrosity. In the series' fourth season, the episode "New Moon Rising" involves parallel storylines that serve as a commentary on diverse sexualities. Willow, one of the show's main characters, is involved in a sexual relationship with another woman for the first time in her life, and she has not yet identified herself to her friends as a lesbian. At the beginning of the episode, Willow's ex-boyfriend Oz, who abandoned her abruptly and mysteriously earlier in the season, comes back to town. Oz is a werewolf, but he is not a villain. Buffy, the show's vampire-slaying lead character and Willow's best friend, has gotten a new boyfriend, Riley, since Oz left, and Riley does not know about Oz's hidden, monstrous identity. A member of a monster-hunting military organization called the Initiative, Riley is displeased by what he learns about Willow's past. He shares his displeasure with Buffy:

> RILEY: I didn't know Willow as the kind of girl ... into dangerous guys ... she seemed smarter than that.
> BUFFY: Oz is not dangerous.... Something happened to him; it wasn't his fault. God, I never knew you were such a bigot.
> RILEY: ... It's a little weird to date someone who tries to eat you once a month.
> BUFFY: Love isn't logical, Riley. It's not like you can be Mr. Joe Sensible about it all the time. God knows I haven't been.[21]

Though Buffy doesn't explain what she means about her own lack of sensibleness in matters of love until the end of the episode, the long-time viewer knows that she is referring to her own non-normative sexual history: she had an extended, sexual relationship with a male vampire named Angel. Riley's reference to Willow as the "kind of girl" who likes "weird" relationships, combined with the way Buffy defends Oz by claiming his condition is not his "fault," echoes the sort of conversation two straight people might have when trying to make sense of the experience of finding out one of their best friends is gay. The fact that Willow does indeed come out to Buffy later in the episode, which pushes the usually articulate Buffy into a condition of shocked babbling, turns these echoes into deafening screams. Willow's relationship with a werewolf, Buffy's relationship with a vampire, and Willow's relationship with another woman all parallel and inform characters' understandings of themselves and one another.

The show's message is ultimately about how people shouldn't judge people just because they are unconventional: it encourages toleration and acceptance of difference. At the end of the episode, Riley explains to Buffy that he has learned his lesson:

> RILEY: I was wrong about Oz. I was being a bigot.
> BUFFY: ... You found out that Willow was in a sort of unconventional relationship, and it gave you the wiggins. It happens.

4. Romps in the Closet

> RILEY: Still, I was in a totally black and white space, people versus monsters, and it ain't like that. Especially when it comes to love.
> BUFFY: I have to tell you some stuff ... about my past ... and it's not all stuff you're gonna like.

Riley has seen that Oz is a good person, so he knows that his prejudice was unfounded. He rejects the "black and white" binary opposition "people versus monsters." Buffy has also learned to understand her boyfriend's difficulty with revelations about unconventional relationships because she had the same sort of difficulty when Willow came out to her. After hearing Willow come out about her unconventionality, Buffy is now ready to face such difficulty and tell the truth about herself.

If anything could resignify the negativity of associating homosexuality with monstrosity, this show's handling of the werewolf/vampire/lesbian parallels might, but the negativity inherent in the horrors of lycanthropy and vampirism ultimately thwarts resignification. As Buffy's description of Oz's lycanthropy indicates, being a werewolf means Oz has contracted a disease; it was "something that happened to him." Similarly, Angel's vampirism was something that happened to him, an invasion of his body by a demon. The conditions that the show parallels with lesbianism are pathological conditions — conditions that bring no culpability but are nonetheless a horrible "fault." Several episodes of the series focus on the horrors of what could happen if Oz or Angel ever loses control of his monstrous nature: if the werewolf's or the vampire's desires for the flesh and blood of his fellow man take over, he will murder people.

In addition to being a lesbian, Willow is a witch. The association of lesbians with monstrous witches is older and more prevalent than even the association of lesbians with phallic vampires. Though this association might seem to make Willow's witchcraft another indicator of her

Buffy the Vampire Slayer's lesbian character, Willow (Alyson Hannigan), shows her grief as she weeps over her slain lover in the episode "Villains," from the show's sixth season.

monstrous lesbianism in itself, in "New Moon Rising" it doesn't in any overt way. Up until this point, the series has gone to great lengths to show that, despite the occasional bad witch, witches and witchcraft are parts of valid religious traditions and are usually forces of good. This positive meaning ascribed to lesbian witchiness fades by the show's sixth season. Near the end of the season, Willow's girlfriend, Tara, is shot and killed. In the

In this shot from "Villains," from *Buffy the Vampire Slayer*'s sixth season, Willow (Alyson Hannigan) shows her magic-fueled rage as she seeks to avenge her lover's murder.

episode "Villians," Willow goes into a rage, turns her hair and eyes black, and starts hunting her girlfriend's murderer, Warren. Warren is a stereotypical nerd who has become a misogynistic killer; even after Willow has mystically lashed his arms to two trees, he continues to spout gynophobic slurs, calling the first girl he killed a "bitch" and making fun of Willow's grief. Willow takes a bullet and uses magic to make it slowly penetrate Warren's skin. Then she flays him and burns him to cinders.[22]

Willow's rage-driven spree of mystical violence continues until, in the season finale, she tries to destroy the entire world, and Buffy and her friends must oppose her or perish. Her male friend, Xander, a simple carpenter, talks her down by saying he loves her.[23] Thus a man calms lesbian rage and lulls the monstrous lesbian back into the proper social order. *Buffy* falls into the same trap that many well-meaning representations of lesbian witches fall into, as Paulina Palmer observes:

> [Such representations] illustrate, in this respect, the difficulties that confront the writer who attempts parodically to rework the grotesque images which patriarchal culture projects upon women. Rather than redefining the boundaries of the abject, she may end up reinforcing them and perpetuating, unchanged and unchallenged, existing prejudices.[24]

Repetition of gyno- and homophobic images perpetuates the negativity of the associations the repetition would resignify. That *Buffy* succumbs to an overtly homophobic representation of lesbian monstrosity reflects the

Buffy the Vampire Slayer's Willow (Alyson Hannigan) reflects the lesbian monstrosity that emerges when she uses witchcraft to flay her lover's murderer, Warren (Adam Busch), in the episode "Villains," from the show's sixth season.

negativity inherent in monstrosity, a negativity that the show never managed to evade fully in the first place.

Back to the Closet: The Films of David DeCoteau

Facing the intractability of the MONSTER = HOMOSEXUAL formula and the failures of even the most well-meaning texts from Gothic criticism and Gothic fiction, is resignification of the queer monster even possible? Halberstam's reading of *Texas Chainsaw 2* is problematic because it sees queerness and positivity in the fate of a character who is neither queerly identified nor sane. *Buffy*'s representation of tolerable queer monsters reinforces homosexuality's negative associations because it persists in representing lesbianism as pathological and subject to world-destroying lapses in judgment. Both of these failures stem from the requirement for monsters in Gothic horror to behave monstrously. Faced with such a requirement, can the queer monster be recuperated?

Most attempts at recuperation fail, but the direct-to-video horror movies of gay filmmaker David DeCoteau present a surprising form of success. That success is difficult to see, however. Though DeCoteau directed the same-sex romance *Leather Jacket Love Story* (1998) and is frank about his sexuality in interviews, his horror films usually do not deal openly with women who have sex with women or men who have sex with men. DeCoteau, who once described coming out of the closet as "the best thing I've ever done in my life," is coy about his horror films' eroticism, grouping them not as gay horror but as "horror movies for girls."[25] Assuming that girls derive the same voyeuristic pleasure from horror films as boys, this claim makes a kind of sense. Since film's earliest years, horror movies have featured scantily clad young women in distress, revealing their bodies as they fight to protect themselves from assaults that have either direct or implied sexual motivation. The young men in DeCoteau's films do exactly the same thing, spending much of their screen time in boxer briefs running from a variety of menaces, from the supernatural forces of *Voodoo Academy* (2000) and *The Brotherhood* (2001) to the mutants named in the title *Leeches!* (2003). If most horror films target male audiences by showing scantily clad women, then DeCoteau's films must target female audiences by showing scantily clad men.[26] Right?

This question gets divided answers from DeCoteau's viewers. The user-written reviews of *The Brotherhood* on Amazon.com provide a useful sample. One reviewer, Alec Scudder, announces that "David DeCoteau is the queen of gay horror," explaining that the "movie is an excuse for delivering underwear homoerotic scenes of some of the most hot [sic] young males that the director could find." Reviewer Lynne A. Wallace isn't so sure. Wallace explains that she didn't like the films and so passed them along to her niece, and at the end of her review, she reflects on all four films in the *Brotherhood* series: "This series is supposed to contain some sort of gay connotation? *Where?* None of the guys moved on each other, only some half-witted groping of a few idiot women."[27] Wallace is correct. If *The Brotherhood* and DeCoteau's other horror films contain "gay connotation," it's hidden — closeted. The closeted-ness of DeCoteau's films allows both of the Amazon reviewers to find support for their assessments: *The Brotherhood* both is and isn't a gay film.

Queer Institutions: Homosexual Connotations from *Blackwood* to The Brotherhood

Wallace's choice of "connotation" to describe what she doesn't see in DeCoteau's movies is apt. Discussing Alfred Hitchcock's *Rope* (1948), another film that has divided viewers on the question of homosexuality, D. A. Miller notes that connotation has "a certain semiotic insufficiency" that gives it "an abiding deniability." For Miller, connotation becomes "the dominant signifying practice of homophobia," and in *Rope* it helps to "construct a homosexuality held definitionally in suspense on no less a question than that of its own existence."²⁸ In other words, connotation associates meanings with words and images in ways that are always questionable, and it allows homophobic viewers to dismiss claims about a film's homoeroticism with "You're seeing something that isn't there," the same deniability involved in the worried parent's refrain, "You're not gay — you just haven't met the right [member of the opposite sex] yet!" In this heterosexist way of thinking, the burden of proof always falls on the person who claims homosexuality's existence, and without solid evidence — such as images of one guy making a definitively sexual move on another — the claim is doomed to perpetual uncertainty.

This uncertainty, though founded in the homophobic assumption that homosexuality shouldn't be detectable because it simply shouldn't *be*, has had some historical benefits. As Miller notes, *Rope* wouldn't have made it past Hollywood's Production Code in 1948 if it had dealt openly with homosexuality, so connotation — maintaining plausible deniability — served as a passing strategy. Simply put, *Rope* was allowed to exist because it allows viewers to question its homosexuality's existence. Mark David Guenette links the passing strategy that Miller sees in *Rope* with none other than *Dorian Gray*, noting that "Wilde succeeded in sealing the homosexual content of the books by using the general unwillingness to discuss homosexuality to his advantage (there is no other way he could ever have gotten away with *The Picture of Dorian Gray* as long as he did)." Guenette calls this reliance on connotation a "homophobic escape hatch."²⁹

The need for an escape hatch in the late nineteenth and early twentieth century is easily understood, and even though DeCoteau's milieu is gay-friendlier than Wilde's and Hitchcock's, one motivation for denying homosexuality has survived the centuries: economics. DeCoteau's movies make more money in the Horror section of the video store than they would in the Gay and Lesbian section. Films not cordoned off (quarantined?) as productions for minorities tend to reach larger audiences and thus receive bigger profits. The effects of the escape hatch in DeCoteau's films don't stop with the economic, however. The films use the escape hatch differently, in a way Wilde wouldn't have dared to dream, and this difference creates a break in the Gothic tradition that allows for the resignification of the queer monster.

A comparison between *The Brotherhood* and the short story "Secret Worship," which Algernon Blackwood published in the collection *John Silence* in 1908, illustrates this break. In Blackwood's story, a man named Harris returns to the isolated religious school he attended as a youth. The religious school "left an imprint of its peculiar influence" when he was an "impressionable youth of fifteen." The school gave Harris the "discipline" that his "soul and body needed," and when, thirty years later, he travels back to the school, "his mind travel[s] back somewhat lovingly," and "he [feels like] a boy again." The words "imprint" and "impressionable," which evoke John Locke's conception of the human mind, liken Harris to a work of clay molded by "the devout Brotherhood" that disciplined him. An all-male religious society has given Harris his core physical and spiritual identity, and the parallel travels of his body and mind result in a regression to that core. He meets one of the brothers at the school, who remarks, "'Your memories possess you.'" Harris joins the schoolmasters in an evening of music and drink, not realizing how literal his possession is until too late. The schoolmasters confuse Harris when they thank him for giving himself so "freely" and "unconditionally," and though he speaks fluent German, he does not understand why they call him an "*Opfer*," or sacrifice. The meaning finally strikes him when the schoolmasters, who are really demonic ghosts, begin to summon the demon that will claim Harris's soul. Harris cannot run; "his mind" and "the very muscles of his body" are "out of control."[30] Harris's mind and body are not his own; they belong to the schoolmasters who have molded them.

Harris's supernatural possession provides an analogue for the power of education to forge identity, and his regression to the vulnerable state of adolescence in which he was "imprinted" reflects the centrality of childhood development in the theory of sexual identification circulating in Blackwood's day. In *Three Essays on the Theory of Sexuality*, published in 1905, Freud states, "In the case of many inverts, even absolute ones, it is possible to show that very early in their lives a sexual impression occurred which left a permanent after-effect in the shape of a tendency to homosexuality."

"Every pathological disorder of sexual life," Freud argues, "is rightly to be regarded as an inhibition in development." He notes that heredity and education work together to create "mental dams against sexual excesses — shame, disgust and morality," and warns that before the erection of these dams, "under the influence of seduction children can become polymorphously perverse." Without proper oedipalization, young boys can "go astray" in their choices of sexual objects. An all-male education lacks the ingredients for oedipal identification, so "education of boys by male persons ... seems to encourage homosexuality."[31] In Freudian terms, Harris regresses to a state of pre-oedipal polymorphous perversity and becomes a victim of his schoolmasters' seduction. He is a vulnerable adult because his schoolmasters inhibited his development in childhood, sowing the seeds for pathological reproduction.

Harris's "sacrifice" would complete his process of wayward sexual identification. From the beginning, Harris realizes that the feelings his memories "stir in his heart" are "queer." As he observes the schoolmasters in action, he feels there is "something queer about it all." Though the word "queer" doesn't necessarily mean "homosexual" in Blackwood's usage, it does emphasize the abnormality of both Harris's feelings and the feelings of the men around him. This abnormality takes on the aura of sexual inversion when Harris notices that the hands of one schoolmaster are "like the hands of a woman," and it impinges on the homoerotic when the schoolmasters' "excess of ... admiration" makes Harris "a little uncomfortable." Harris's discomfort increases when he hears the schoolmasters, who address each other as "Bruder," call "him 'Bruder' too, classing him as one of themselves." When the demon comes to claim Harris as a sacrifice, forces rise "all about him, transforming the normal into the horrible." The sacrificial transformation from normal to queer occurs violently: forceful hands change his clothes, fasten his arms to his waist, and push him to his knees. While this figurative rape, which Harris feels is "the death of the soul," continues, Harris hears "impassioned chanting" saying "'We worship! We adore! We offer!'"[32] Adoration and offering — love, sex, and sacrifice — merge as Harris loses his "soul," and along with it his "normal" adult male identity.

A man named John Silence, Blackwood's hero in several stories, arrives in the nick of time and stops the ritual. Silence explains that Harris had fallen under the spell of devil-worshippers, and he says, "'had they accomplished their object you, in turn, at the death of your body, would have passed into their power and helped to swell their dreadful purposes.'" The ritual rape-as-sacrifice would have allied Harris with what Silence calls "'perverted powers,'" which the schoolmasters practiced "under cover of the very shadow of saintliness and holy living."[33] The "purposes" that Harris would help the brothers to "swell" could have a sexual subtext, but even without such a level of deliberately naughty encoding, the sacrifice is an attempt at same-sex recruitment: if the ritual had been completed, Harris would have become a demonic ghost in saintly clothing. The idea that an all-male holy order could nurture great evil, particularly great sexual evil, has roots going back to eighteenth-century Gothic fictions. As chapter two discusses, the titular character of Matthew Lewis's *The Monk* hides his evil passions behind the cloak of religious devotion, passions that include an illicit affair with a girl who dresses like a boy.[34] Blackwood's story combines a traditional critique of all-male religious societies' hypocrisy with a generalized warning about male educators' lasting influence. Noting how Harris's upbringing made him susceptible to the devil-worshippers' seduction, Silence cautions, "'And if thought and emotion can persist in this way ... how vitally important it must be to control their very birth in the heart, and guard against them with the keenest restraint.'"[35] "Secret Worship" ends with this admonition that at least parallels a common form of homophobic didacticism, commanding readers to monitor schools and other sites of influence in order to prevent future formations of non-normative identity.

"Secret Worship" and Freud both suggest that ensuring normative development requires a policing of the homosocial, particularly in education. Explaining how heterosexist cultures protect homosociality from homosexuality, Eve Sedgwick's *Between Men* describes a "radically discontinuous relation of male homosocial and homosexual bonds" that is "culturally contingent." The police-work of socially mandated homophobia ensures this discontinuity; in John Silence's words, homophobia "guards against" the "birth" of feelings that could confuse the normal with the queer. Sedgwick notes that a "tradition of homophobic thematics was a force in the development of the Gothic." "Secret Worship" and *The Brotherhood* both participate in this tradition, but while Blackwood's story manages its homophobic theme through the moralizing of John Silence, DeCoteau's film uses a different mechanism, a graphic representation of the triangular "routing of homosocial desire through women" that Sedgwick describes as a way to keep the homosocial from blurring into the homosexual.[36] In relations between men, women act as figurative buffers between the social and the sexual, and DeCoteau's film makes this trian-

In *The Brotherhood* (2001), Devon (Bradley Stryker, left) prepares to sacrifice Chris (Sam Page, a.k.a. Nathan Watkins, center) in a manner that recalls the ritual in Algernon Blackwood's "Secret Worship (others shown unidentified)."

gular buffering painfully — and hilariously — literal, incorporating them into a storyline that is very similar to Blackwood's.

The film begins with a group of fraternity brothers hunting down and killing a pledge who is guilty of an unarticulated (unspeakable?) betrayal. After the credits, the film's protagonist, Chris, watches a news report about the crime as his new roommate, Dan, arrives for their first meeting. As Chris and Dan start to get to know one another as well as the campus, the fraternity brothers from the opening scene, led by buff blond Devon, identify Chris as the proper recipient of their attention, attention that, the film eventually reveals, would ultimately make Chris a sacrifice in a demonic ritual. Despite Chris's general dislike of the Greek system, the fraternity zealously recruits him, introducing him to the privileges of social status, expensive clothing, and fast cars that they can offer. They then introduce him to their secret: they're pseudo-vampire blood-drinkers who practice dark magic to sustain their immortality. As Chris transforms into one of these literal blood brothers, Dan, along with new female friend Megan, investigates the fraternity's history. He discovers the plot and rushes to Chris's rescue, interrupting the sacrificial ritual during which the frat brothers surround and grope Chris in a manner almost identical to the ritual in "Secret Worship." Megan reveals herself as a "shill" who helps Devon to lure in male victims, and she turns against Dan. Just when the balance of power seems to have shifted in the Brotherhood's favor, Dan hits Devon with an axe, Megan and the frat brothers all suffer mystical deaths, and Chris and Dan leave together as happy, smug survivors.

The Brotherhood and "Secret Worship" involve schools that hold the

In *The Brotherhood* (2001), Devon (Bradley Stryker) approaches Chris (Sam Page, a.k.a. Nathan Watkins) from behind, introducing him to the woman who is offering them her blood. Even though they're technically preying on a woman, their positions and body language suggest a homoerotic encounter.

potential to corrupt young men's souls, focus on all-male "brotherhoods," and deal with recruiting/corruption processes that mirror Freud's spin on nineteenth-century conceptions of pathological reproduction. Instead of John Silence's moralizing about fighting against the corruption of youth, *The Brotherhood* has Megan and several other female characters who at least superficially mark the story as one about homosociality instead of homosexuality. Megan provides a heteroerotic object of interest for Dan, a slight and awkward boy whose rescuer-rescued relationship with Chris might otherwise seem to have overt homoerotic motivation, and the women who offer the fraternity brothers their blood provide heteroerotic objects for Devon and Chris, whose recruiter-recruited relationship also might otherwise seem homoerotic.

The triangulation of Devon and Chris's desire for one another through a blood-offering woman becomes graphically obvious in the scene during which Devon introduces Chris to his blood-drinking ways. As a woman offering them her blood stretches on the bed in front of them, Devon stands behind Chris, setting a hand on Chris's shoulder as he goads him forward. Chris and Devon join the woman in the bed, and each man sucks on one of the woman's wrists. They form a neat visual triangle, the woman's body providing visual discontinuity between the almost-naked men. As the blood-drinking continues, the woman seems to vanish into the pillows and sheets. Part of her is almost always visible, but the parts become less and less, creating an image that suggests Devon writhing on top of Chris. They're still in their underwear, of course, but their movements seem to

4. Romps in the Closet

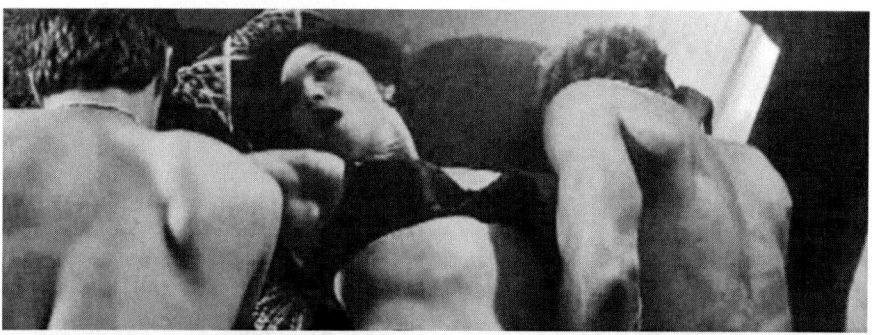

Top: In *The Brotherhood* (2001), from left, Chris (Sam Page, a.k.a. Nathan Watkins), Sandy (Chloe Cross) and Devon (Bradley Stryker) form a triangle as the men consume the woman's blood. The triangle is a perfect visual representation of the break in the continuum from male homosociality to male homosexuality required by heteronormativity. *Above:* The visual triangle formed by *The Brotherhood*'s Devon (Bradley Stryker, top), Chris (Sam Page, a.k.a. Nathan Watkins), and Sandy (Chloe Cross) almost dissolves when the woman mostly disappears from the camera's view, leaving an image that suggests one man writhing on top of another, realizing the homoerotic possibility that begins with Devon standing behind Chris at the bedside. Note that Sandy never becomes completely invisible: her knee remains as a (laughable) barrier between the homosocial and the homoerotic.

realize the homoerotic possibility that begins with Devon standing behind Chris at the bedside. As Devon completes this final act of recruiting and initiation, we see the two young men's bodies in a configuration tantamount to anal sex. After the scene's climax, Chris rolls over onto his back, blood dripping from his lips. Using a finger, Devon samples the blood directly from Chris's lips, and Chris says he feels "alive." The scene that follows shows Chris with the fabulous clothes and superior attitude that are the Brotherhood's hallmarks.

In *The Brotherhood*, as in "Secret Worship," homosocial institutions abound with homoerotic possibilities. *The Brotherhood*'s substitution of women for moralizing to contain the institutions' homoerotic potential creates competing visual imagery. On the one hand, a woman is always present to keep male bodies from making erotic connections, but on the other, that presence becomes so visually insignificant that the male bodies, at least symbolically, seem to connect. The connotation of Devon's body looming on top of Chris's is, of course, deniable, because the visualization of anal sex never moves beyond seeming. Nevertheless, the male bodies are in moments so close to one another that the scene could offer visual pleasures like those associated with gay soft porn. In fact, the deniability of the scene's homoeroticism, despite the obviousness of semi-naked men in bed together, gives the eroticism an illicit edge. If a viewer sees the eroticism as both present and hidden, then that viewer is in on a secret. This sneakiness could provide a thrill, at once nostalgic (remember when homoeroticism had to be sneaky?) and subversive (just think of those idiots who don't *get* this!), that compounds the visual pleasure of eroticism. The visual dimension of the medium, then—film as opposed to print—gives DeCoteau's closeted connotations something that Blackwood's lack: a chance for viewers to revel in the very eroticism that heteronormative triangulation of male desire would deny.

The Queer Camera and Visual Belonging

This visual difference, in this single example from *The Brotherhood*, is unlikely to overcome the heteronormative and homophobic impulses that require discontinuity between the homosocial and the homosexual. After all, the images from *The Brotherhood*, if they're about two guys making a move on one another, are also about two guys drinking blood, so if the configuration of bodies encodes homosexuality, it also associates homosexuality with monstrosity. What DeCoteau's films offer that many other representations of queer monstrosity lack is repetition: images of semi-naked men in potentially homoerotic configurations saturate *The Brotherhood*, *Voodoo Academy*, and *Leeches*, as well as a few others (*Speed Demon* (2003) is a standout). But even this saturation of imagery wouldn't necessarily resist heteronormativity; after all, some vampire films, such as *Vampyros Lesbos* (1971), abound with nude women in eroticized same-sex configurations, and these films don't play as moments of queer liberation because they seem to exploit lesbian stereotypes for the pleasure of straight male audiences. DeCoteau's films stand apart from others because they couple saturation of homoerotic imagery with reflections on the cinematic gaze. The eye on these putatively straight guys is constructed as queer.

In one of the *The Brotherhood*'s early scenes, Chris is out for a run, and when he pauses to stretch, the camera slowly pans over his shirtless arms and torso, touring his muscles and skin. The camera cuts between slow-motion shots of Chris's body and slow-motion shots of the evil frat brothers coming toward him. At first the frat boys are too far away for the camera's perspective on Chris to be their own, but they eventually get into range and pause beside a tree to watch Chris finish his stretches. They're all wearing sunglasses, but eyeline matches between their faces and Chris's body makes the object of their gaze certain. "He's beautiful," Devon says, "perfect. I've been watching this one since the semester started." When one of his friends asks whether Devon wants to keep searching, Devon says, "I want this one." What Devon wants Chris for is unclear at this point in the film. Immediate context might suggest that he wants him to join the fraternity; the film's ending reveals that Devon wants to take Chris's body as his own. Though the narrative provides different options for interpreting Devon's wanting, the immediate visual relationship between Devon's gaze and Chris's objectified body allows and encourages an erotic interpretation of Devon's desire. In this scene and several others, point of view cinematography makes the camera's gaze both male and determined by desire for another male.[37]

Voodoo Academy more thoroughly explores and troubles the identities motivating the camera's perspective, triangulating gazes in a manner parallel to the triangulation of erotic blood-drinking in *The Brotherhood*. Like "Secret Worship" and *The Brotherhood*, *Voodoo Academy* centers on a predominantly homosocial academic institution; the all-male Bible college of *Voodoo Academy*, like the Brotherhoods of the other two tales, seeks to seduce, entrap, and sacrifice young men. Unlike the other two tales, *Voodoo Acad-*

In *Voodoo Academy* (2000), shirtless Mike (Ben Indra) goes into a masturbatory frenzy inside the Reverend Carmichael's confessional. His affection for his crucifix provides a homoeroticized object for the camera's gaze.

emy places a woman at the head of the evil plot. The only significant female character in the film, Mrs. Bouvier, conspires with male Reverend Carmichael, who leads the school's six young male students in "alternative Bible study." Mrs. Bouvier's evil plan is to transfer the boys' heads to the heads of voodoo dolls in a ritual that will somehow raise an army of zombies to help her take over the world. She therefore lures the boys, one by one, into a secret lair where she performs the head-transferring magic. In many horror films, violence escalates through the course of the narrative as characters fall victim to a monstrous killer one by one. In *Voodoo Academy*, boys do fall victim to a monstrous killer, but instead of increasing amounts of violence, the camera provides increasing amounts of skin, as the boys who fall under Mrs. Bouvier's spell stop coming to class in their uniforms and wear torn jackets and skimpy undershirts instead. Though the camera does show one particularly comical voodoo-doll transformation, it seems far more interested in seeing what's going on beneath the boys' clothes than in what's going on in Mrs. Bouvier's secret lair.

Following the same skin-revealing narrative trajectory, the film also gradually reveals what goes on in Reverend Carmichael's special confessional booth, which uses electronics to combine science and religion. About midway through the film, Reverend Carmichael leads a student, Mike, into his confessional booth, and instead of cutting away as it has during earlier confessional scenes, the camera follows the boy into the booth. After they get situated on either side of the booth's divider, Reverend Carmichael tells the boy that the booth's energy is "changing" him, and he says, "Confess your lust ... it's perfectly natural. Do you touch yourself? What do you think about when you touch yourself? What excites you? What makes you want to touch yourself? ... Open your shirt.... Show me how you touch yourself." Mike rips off his shirt and

A series of eye-line match cuts in *Voodoo Academy* (2000) identifies Reverend Carmichael (Chad Burris) with the camera's gaze as the camera captures Mike, Carmichael's pupil, going into a masturbatory frenzy. When Mike rubs his crucifix within his lips, Carmichael kisses his own crucifix, sealing a homoerotic connection.

begins to rub his body. At one point Mike suggestively slides a crucifix on a rosary along his lips, and the scene cuts to Carmichael, watching through the window that separates his side of the confessional from the boy's, kissing his own crucifix reverently. The scene cuts back and forth between the boy and the spying Reverend until a dissolve replaces the Reverend's lips with Mrs. Bouvier's, suggesting that she has been the true audience for the erotic display. Mike asks about with whom he's speaking, and Mrs. Bouvier calls herself "the purveyor of your dreams, the tongue inside your mouth." She says, "You want me more than anything in the world," and the boy repeats, "Anything in the world." She says she has shaped him, molded him, watched him every night. At the end of the exchange, Mrs. Bouvier asks, "Who owns you?" "You," the boy says, "you are my queen." Mrs. Bouvier smiles and says, "Tonight I shall have you." This last-minute switch from homoerotic masturbation and voyeurism to a promise of heteroerotic consummation posits the film's ultimate telos as heterosexual. It also posits the camera's gaze, up to this point identified with Reverend Carmichael as he watches Mike's body-rubbing, as female.

Gaze-switching happens again in a series of scenes scattered through the film that provide the film's highest points of homoerotic interest. In the first of these scenes (titled "Noctural Gyrations" on the DVD), the young male protagonist, Chris (not a typo — DeCoteau reuses hero names), awakens to see the other boys in his dorm room writhing in the grip of the erotic nightmares caused by Mrs. Bouvier's dark magic. As Chris watches this masturbatory frenzy, over-the-shoulder shots and other point-of-view cinematography equate the camera's gaze with his, but the end of the scene reveals that the real audience for the scene is Mrs. Bouvier, who watches the boys in her power through a spyhole drilled in a crucifix. The second scene involving erotic nightmares ("Nocturnal Gyrations Part Two") occurs as Chris discovers the vantage Mrs. Bouvier has used to spy through the crucifix. Chris pulls away from the peephole, exclaims "That sick bitch has been watching us!" and resumes spying. On the level of plot, the misogyny in "sick bitch" might be motivated by Mrs. Bouvier's murderous scheme, but Chris's exclamation associates her sickness with her watching of "us." That Chris pronounces his judgment on Mrs. Bouvier as he partakes of some watching of his own heightens the significance of Chris's use of "us": it's okay for one of the boys to watch the boys, but a woman, an outsider, is sick to intrude on the homosocial scene.

If Mrs. Bouvier and Chris stand for possible viewers for the film — girls who see the film as one of DeCoteau's "horror movies for girls" or

Leeches! (2003) opens with voyeurism from an unidentified perspective, giving the viewer ample time to examine the athletic body of Jason (Josh Henderson).

boys who see the film as a skin flick for gay boys — then Chris's exclamation about Mrs. Bouvier's sickness contradicts the film's homophobic triangulation of gazes. In the director's commentary on the DVD, DeCoteau points out that one erotic exchange between Mrs. Bouvier and a boy is "a little heterosexual moment ... one of the few in this movie." Heterosexuality is the minority in this film; its attempts to guard against the sexuality in scenes of erotic homosociality are overwhelmed by the sheer number of those

A mutant leech with a bulbous head in *Leeches!* (2003) violates the mouth of an unidentified young man, creating an image that evokes homosexuality.

scenes, and the attempt to establish a heterosexual perspective as the authoritative eye stands out as "sick." *Voodoo Academy*'s self-conscious reflections on voyeurism undermine the film's use of a homophobic mechanism, the triangulation of scopic desire through a woman, by calling attention to it as an intrusion. Since Mrs. Bouvier is at the head of *Voodoo Academy*'s evil plot, the male eye that desires other males may not have the most power in the film's narrative, but it structures the film's visuals with the greatest frequency and with the hero's approval. The queer gaze is the one that *belongs* in this film, and that belonging offsets the obligatory and hollow operations of homophobia within the Gothic narrative.

Repositioning the Escape Hatch

Though it lacks *Voodoo Academy*'s degree of self-consciousness about the cinematic gaze, the camera in *Leeches!* might be the queerest of them all. After cartoonish credits reminiscent of 1950s B-movie horror, *Leeches!* opens on an Olympic-style swimming pool. One of the film's main characters, Jason, clad in only a Speedo, moves in slow motion toward the pool (see page 106). Quick cuts show Jason's body from multiple angles and at distances ranging from extreme close to medium long, filling the frame with his torso, sides, back, and feet. The camera picks apart Jason's body for almost a full minute before he finally dives into the pool. The narrative soon reveals that the scene has actually been an anxiety dream Jason has about his performance as a swimmer, but this revelation does not account for the camera's perspective — unless Jason dreams about his own body as an object to be analyzed from a distance. Since the plot of *Leeches!* centers on a college swim team's use of steroids, steroids that infect and mutate the leeches in a lake near the college, one could argue that the camera's focus on Jason's form relates to narcissistic anxiety about his physical fitness. However, the argument for an anomalous level of psychological sophistication in this sequence requires reading the eventual development of the steroid plot backward. Lacking an immediate context that could support such a reading, the sequence plays as pure voyeuristic objectification of the young man's body, and the identity of the objectifier is up for grabs.

The camera's objectifying eye becomes even queerer when the leeches start to attack Jason's friends on the swim team. The leeches' first on-screen victim is taking a shower, and the camera provides multiple perspectives on his body just as it does with Jason in the opening sequence. After exploring the boy's body, the camera tracks over the shower-room floor and shows a giant leech climbing out of the drain. As the leech — long, thick, and with a slightly bulbous head that makes it look more than a little like a penis — crawls toward its prey, the camera cuts between it and shots of the boy's back. Conveniently for the leech, the boy slips and falls on his back, hitting his head. The camera then moves to a floor-level shot of the splayed body, taking the leech's perspective. As the camera tracks closer and closer, the leech's destination appears not to be the boy's back (now covered), but his mouth. When it arrives, it uses its head to pry open the boy's lips and crawls inside of him (see page 106). The scene cuts to a different location, a girls' dorm room where several of the swimmers' girlfriends are discussing the boys. After this brief interlude, the scene cuts back to the leech's victim writhing in slow-motion, clutching his stomach. He vomits first a viscous fluid, then the leech. He falls dead, and the scene cuts to two of his teammates, one of whom asks the other, "Where's the girls?" These cuts form a pattern that juxtaposes images that might have homosexual significance with invocations of heterosexuality.

The pattern continues with the second leech attack, which begins when a disposable male swimmer strips down to his underwear for a nap, lying conveniently above the sheets on his bed. The film's suspense music signals a danger of which the boy is unaware as the camera pans slowly along his body; when the camera reaches his calves, a giant leech enters the frame and crawls across the distance the camera has just traveled. Quick cuts show multiple leeches taking similar paths until finally all the leeches attack his face at once. Even more graphic than the shower scene, this death sequence presents images of creatures inching along a prone young man's body so slowly that they almost seem incapable of the speed they finally exhibit when they suddenly converge on his mouth. Like the camera, the leeches seem to enjoy the spectacle of flesh, choosing to take the body in gradually before rushing to oral climax. After the attack, the scene cuts to one of the other male swimmers dragging his reluctant girlfriend to a social event.

The cartoonish opening credits, the exclamation point in the title, and the giant leeches themselves suggest that this film has a sense of humor, and that sense of humor is nowhere more apparent than in these death sequences that linger on penis-shaped giant leeches, still smaller than their athletic male prey, feeling up young men before they violate their mouths. If the leeches' predations, aligned with the camera's gaze, suggest homoeroticism, then the cuts to boys either talking about or being with girls may seem like gestures of containment, reminders of the characters' heterosexuality that might allow the film to pass as straight, too. However, although discussions and images of girls may remind viewers that the male characters are heterosexually identified, they do nothing to offset the homoerotic horror, and humor, of the leeches. Standing beside shots that blatantly objectify and eroticize the male body, these editorial gestures toward erotic containment are ineffective and end up looking just as absurd as the leeches themselves. Absurdity becomes contagious: it spreads from the homoerotic scenes that feature bizarrely lascivious leeches to the mechanisms of homophobia and heteronormativity themselves, the weakness of which lies open to the same ridicule and derision as the monstrous queerness they would contain.

Absurd, failed heteronormative containment also suffuses *Leeches!*'s dialogue, with the question "What's the supposed to mean?" overtly calling attention to the problems of sexual connotation at key moments. One example occurs immediately after the dream sequence that opens the film. Following the pattern of juxtaposing the potentially homoerotic with a reminder of the characters' (and the film's) heterosexuality, Jason has a conversation in bed with his girlfriend, Casey, in which she associates Jason's steroid use with his nightmares:

> CASEY: Those things are messing with your mind. God knows what they're doing to your body.
> JASON: Hey, you didn't seem to have any problems with my body a few hours ago, now did you?
> CASEY: Yeah, well, I don't think I can take this much longer. I just may start spending my nights back in my room again.
> JASON: You know what, I don't think Steve-O and Sabrina would appreciate the company, to tell you the truth, actually, so....
> CASEY: You've got to lay off the steroids, I mean it! This wasn't happening before you started using.
> JASON: You make it sound like it's crack, and it's not just me, the whole team's taking them.
> CASEY: I really doubt that, Jason. As far as I know, it's just Steve-O. But I guess as far as you're concerned, he is the whole team.
> JASON: What's that supposed to mean?

After Jason asks this question, the scene cuts to Jason and Steve-O, shirtless, walking close to one another, and discussing Casey's objection to their use of steroids. Steve-O says he doesn't understand Casey's objection and asks, "It hasn't affected your performance, has it?" In response, Casey asks if Steve-O has had any weird dreams, and Steve-O describes a heterosexual fantasy about his mom's tennis partner. Steve-O and Jason's intensely close relationship is triangulated through their girlfriends, Casey and Sabrina, and Steve-O's guy-talk reference to his heterosexual dream content reinforces this triangulation. Nevertheless, Jason's conversation with Casey marks his relationship with Steve-O as open to interpretation, and that openness defies total containment. As Casey questions the homosocial relationship's meaning, and as Jason questions her questioning, the film pairs its homophobic theme with perpetual doubt about whether homophobia can truly make the homosocial and the homosexual discontinuous.

In a later conversation with Casey, Steve-O frames his homosocial relationship with Jason as competing with Casey's heterosexual one. Jason tells Steve-O that he shares Casey's concern about steroids, and Steve-O confronts Casey:

> STEVE-O: There are certain things between me and Jason that are just none of your business, okay?
> CASEY: Well if it's affecting his health, it *is* my business.
> STEVE-O: Jason is as healthy as a damned horse.
> CASEY: Really. Shows how well you know him.
> STEVE-O: I've known him since freshman year. You guys have been going out, what, five months?
> CASEY: So what is that supposed to mean? You got dibs on him or something?

Steve-O establishes the priority of his homosocial relationship by claiming that the "certain things" that characterize his relationship with Jason are beyond the purview of the opposite sex's attention. Just like Mrs. Bouvier's spying in *Voodoo Academy*, Casey's intrusion into the homosocial scene is marked as inappropriate. When Steve-O tries to reinforce the priority of his relationship with Jason by claiming that its longer history affords him greater knowledge of his friend's physical health, Casey becomes suspicious of his meaning, repeating the question that Jason asked when Casey implied that his relationship with Steve-O might be inappropriate. If Steve-O has "dibs" on Casey's boyfriend, his possession of another male might cross the normative boundaries of the homosocial, and thus Casey proves to be a dubious agent for triangulating men's desire for other men.

Using ineffective juxtapositions of the potentially homosexual with the putatively heterosexual and dialogue that casts doubt on the triangulations of male desire, *Leeches!* simultaneously calls attention to and undermines its homophobic mechanisms. The success of connotation as an escape hatch depends on homosexual meanings' potential to remain invisible, and pointing out where the meanings might be diminishes their ability to hide. To the queer gaze that DeCoteau's camera constructs as belonging, then, escape hatches stand out in bold relief, and, like the penis-shaped leeches themselves, they look absurd. This absurdity might be most poignant in the double entendres that appear throughout DeCoteau's films. The double entendre is Wilde's escape hatch *par excellence*, but DeCoteau's lines lack Wilde's subtlety, as when *The Brotherhood*'s Devon says to Chris during the final ritual, "Let me enter you." Deniability persists in these absurd lines, but they don't bear scrutiny, and when such a clumsy escape hatch becomes visible, it becomes risible. The clumsy, ineffective homophobia that seems to mandate such transparent duplicity becomes a site of laughter and pleasure. Reduced to a humorous frame for homoerotic imagery, in De Coteau's films repetition of the homophobic mechanisms developed in the nineteenth century becomes a gay romp.

Performativity, Camp, and the Powers of the Closet

DeCoteau's horror films employ homophobic mechanisms in ways that make the mechanisms seem absurd and ineffective, turning them into visible objects for critique. The films' homophobia is insincere and inauthentic, a parody: dressing up homoerotic images of young men in homophobic conventions from nineteenth-century Gothic, these films perform homophobia as drag. Considering how drag, specifically gay male crossdressing, reflects on gender identity, Judith Butler explains drag's political potential:

> The performance of drag plays upon the distinction between the anatomy of the performer and the gender that is being performed.... *In imitating gender, drag implicitly reveals the imitative structure of gender itself—as well as its contingency....* In the place of the law of heterosexual coherence, we see sex and gender denaturalized by means of a performance which avows their distinctness and dramatizes the cultural mechanism of their fabricated unity.[38]

According to Butler, gender is always produced through performance— someone produces male or female identity by acting in manners culturally prescribed for (implicitly heterosexual) manliness and womanliness. An anatomically male drag performer, acting in manners culturally prescribed for womanliness, is only doing what anatomical females do to be womanly, but the anatomical difference makes the performance more transparent as a performance. Revealed as mere performance, gender loses "natural" status, and so do gender's implications for sexuality, i.e., the notion that real men love women and vice versa. Much of heteronormativity's power stems from the status of "normal" heterosexuality as natural and therefore just, right, and the way things ought to be. Denaturalizing gender, which implicitly denaturalizes heterosexuality, deals a serious blow to heteronormativity, disrupting and weakening it by exposing its claim to naturalness as fake. DeCoteau's films operate similarly, exposing homophobic mechanisms as absurd and ineffective in their efforts to enforce a supposedly natural discontinuity between the homosocial and the homosexual.

If DeCoteau's films open homophobia to critique through parody — and if the monstrosity they associate with homosexuality is as absurd and insincere as their homophobic triangulations of men's desire for men through women — then they might seem to accomplish denaturalization through a perspective that has characterized Gothic since its beginning: camp. Often taken as a manifesto for camp, Susan Sontag's "Notes on Camp" approaches camp as both a sensibility and a form of aestheticism that emphasizes artifice; it "sees everything in quotation marks."[39] Camp's figurative scare quotes suggest artifice and insincerity behind the term captured within the inverted commas. As a sensibility, camp involves imposing scare quotes on the world; as an aesthetic, camp involves artifacts that draw attention to their own artifice through strategies that have a scare-quote effect. Sontag rightly identifies Gothic novels as foundational influences on the formation of the camp aesthetic. The Gothic is almost always hyper-conventional, and it often conveys self-awareness of its hyper-conventionality in a manner that makes the use of conventions seem somewhat, if not entirely, insincere. If DeCoteau's films make fun of their own artifice, drawing attention to the Gothic's homophobic conventions, then they may merely be participating in the Gothic's long tradition of subverting social norms.[40]

Leeches!'s absurd phallic mutants, *The Brotherhood*'s fashionable pseudo-vampires, and *Voodoo Academy*'s doll-making Mrs. Bouvier are certainly campy, and signs that the films don't take themselves seriously might seem to qualify them as what Sontag calls deliberate, as opposed to naïve, camp. The endings of *Voodoo Academy* and *The Brotherhood* are telling: *Voodoo Academy*'s Chris leaves the Bible school saying, "I was gonna go to business school anyway," and when Dan succeeds in rescuing the other Chris at the end of *The Brotherhood*, Chris assures his pal, "I told you I'd never join a goddamned fraternity." These dismissive final lines trivialize the horrors the characters have experienced, putting the films' conventional representations of witchcraft and monstrosity in figurative scare quotes. However, this trivialization does more than make the films' Gothic elements campy because it points toward the films' priorities. If the horrors in the films are trivial, what, if anything, do the films offer to be enjoyed sincerely? The answer is all those boys running around in boxer briefs, offering themselves up for the enjoyment of the queer camera's eye. Significantly, Sontag includes on her list of things camp "stag movies seen without lust." Porn can only be camp if it's seen as a source of humor rather than titillation, and DeCoteau's camera encourages and fulfills sincere voyeuristic desire. The subversive potential in these films depends on their being both camp and not camp, insincere in their horror and homophobia but genuinely enjoyable for their eroticism.

DeCoteau's films succeed in resignifying queer monstrosity by denaturalizing Gothic homophobia while turning its representations into sites of homoerotic pleasure. The denaturalization works because the films perform homophobia as if they mean it, just as drag performers act like the opposite sex as if they were it. Just as a viewer can mistake a man in drag for a woman, a viewer can mistake DeCoteau's films for heterosexually-oriented, homophobic Gothic, but once the drag is revealed, the viewer who has made the mistake becomes the laughable dupe. The monstrosity in DeCoteau's films loses its abhorrence because the queerly desiring eye is the one that is not sick, not monstrous, but belonging, correct in its perception, and welcome in a diegetic world of trivial, laughable monsters and serious, beautiful skin. Ironically, the films defeat homophobia by retreating inside heteronormativity's most powerful institution, the closet. But as the films turn queer monsters into sexy jokes — delectable in their appearance and ridiculous in their murders — the closet becomes a fabulous place to be, and the reality of MONSTER = HOMOSEXUAL finally starts to recede.

PART THREE
Gothic Ghosts

5

Ghost Stories and Ghostly Belief

Conventional Horrors That Make Good Truths

Belief in a thing's reality usually depends on perception of the thing as meeting some criteria for "real" status. The most common criteria for reality are empirical: someone can know an object to be real because it satisfies empirical tests such as seeing, hearing, and touching. Even sexualities, which are purely discursive constructions, tend to get their status as real from empirical support, and thus a viewer of *The Brotherhood* might argue the film isn't *really* gay because she doesn't see guys making moves on one another. Belief in the supernatural is different; it accords supernatural entities a special type of reality because they only sometimes, if ever, require conventional empirical evidence to gain their status as real.

The realities accorded to the supernatural primarily stem from texts about the supernatural. Most Protestant Christians do not need to see God to know He is real; the Bible describes Him as real, and belief in the Bible's truth grants Him "real" status. Similarly, many believers in ghosts rely on textual accounts to determine the reality of ghosts. Coleridge and other critics must fight to distinguish "true" religion from "absurd" superstition in part because both forms of belief stem from perceptions of texts' value as truth.[1] Whether or not ghosts have an actual, "objective" existence, their reality is a product of discourse, and so those who would govern people's beliefs must govern *which* texts, which discourses, people use as the bases of their supernatural realities. The eighteenth-century critics who, like Coleridge, feared that Gothic fiction would upset normative codes for gender and sexual desire also feared that it would encourage heretical belief in the supernatural. This chapter and the next argue that Gothic fictions have, in a sense, justified these fears, too, by providing material that can make supernatural entities beyond Christian canons qualify as real. This chapter focuses on ways that this reality can be purely textual or discursive; the next chapter explores ways that Gothic fictions can even help the supernatural to gain empirical support.

Claiming that fictional discourse shapes the discourse of real ghosts does nothing to limit ontological claims for the paranormal. Indeed, many parapsychologists and others who study paranormal phenomena acknowledge that fictional ghost stories exert formative pressure on "true" ghost stories. H.J. Irwin, author of the 1999 textbook *An Introduction to Parapsychology*, explains, "fictional ghost stories (and folklore too) promote a particular stereotype of an apparitional experience, and it is feasible that witnesses' accounts of their experience unwittingly are distorted to conform to these popular expectations."[2] Since *The Castle of Otranto* set out to combine the ancient and modern forms of romance, Gothic fictions have sought a degree of mimetic authenticity, a way to make their fictional ghosts seem real by making their attributes conform to popular expectations. True ghost stories also seek to make their ghosts seem real, and to do so, they often adopt the same strategy. Seeking the same effects, the fictional and the true borrow from and shape one another, and the repetition of ghostly attributes in either form of representation reinforces the attributes' status as either realistic or real.

A Brief History of Modern Ghosts

In *The Rise of Supernatural Fiction*, E.J. Clery cites a true ghost story that serves as a kind of precedent for the first Gothic novel: the story of the "Cock Lane Ghost" that haunted London in 1762. "The well-documented opinions of two members of the crowd who visited the ghost, Samuel Johnson and Horace Walpole," she argues, "offer points of departure for the investigation of two techniques for ghost-seeing that posit two distinct objects: a 'real' supernatural and a 'spectacular' supernatural." She explains that Johnson sought to experience the ghostly rapping noises that haunted Cock Lane because he wanted to overcome the "impasse in the debate over the reality of spirits"; Walpole, on the other hand, went for the spectacle of the affair, accepting the "real" ghost (soon revealed as a hoax) as a kind of fiction fit for his entertainment in a way that would lead him to compose and publish his own entertaining ghost fiction, *Otranto*, in 1764.[3] Johnson's and Walpole's encounters on Cock Lane represent two approaches to the ghostly, the truth-seeking and the thrill-seeking, that would flourish and intermingle throughout the nineteenth century. Seeking the truth about ghosts by hunting for real ones became very popular, as did Walpole's sensational ghost novel and the Gothic tradition it inaugurated. If contemporary television shows proliferating on the Syfy cable network — *Ghost Hunters*, *Ghost Hunters Academy*, and *Ghost Hunters International* — as well as the phenomenally successful low-budget film *Paranormal Activity* (2009) are any indication, that popularity is stronger than ever.[4]

Popular interest in hunting for real ghosts got a significant boost in 1848, when more ghostly rapping sounds summoned a whirlwind of activity that surpassed the hubbub on Cock Lane. John Fox and family, residents of New York state, heard "rappings, bangs, and scrapings"; suspecting an intelligent agent behind the sounds, Mrs. Fox "decided to use the 'ghost's' percussive responses to questions as a means of communications," and soon the publicity the events received allowed "the idea of communicating with deceased persons [to capture] the imagination of the American public." The Spiritualist movement was born, and scores of spirit mediums with reputed aptitudes in spirit-communication as well as regular people began attempting contact with the dead through séances and other means. Spiritualism became a kind of religion, which Irwin describes as a "compromise" between "agnostic science" and "a Christianity under siege from Darwin's theory of evolution."[5] The movement spread across the Atlantic, becoming an international phenomenon and making ghosts perceived as real part of the everyday lives of thousands.

While Spiritualism spread, ghosts also entered the everyday worlds of fiction. Robert F. Geary describes how the Victorian ghost fiction, "shorn of its pseudo-medieval trappings ... found what the Gothic novel never provided — a coherent context for the supernatural in a credible contemporary setting."[6] The nineteenth-century ghost story and the twenty-first century ghost story that continues its domestic traditions are the Gothic in a new phase, a phase in which the mimetic ingredients in Walpole's original formula increase dramatically. In the supernatural horror story, terror becomes more terrible by abandoning the extravagance of ancient romance and invading the modern routine. The heightened realism of these fictions relies on increasing popular knowledge about "real" ghosts.

Several nineteenth-century Gothic writers participated in Spiritualist activities and in the controversies that surrounded them, getting their knowledge of the real supernatural — or at least the sort of supernatural that people believed could be real — first-hand. A seldom-read author today but a major force in his time, Edward Bulwer Lytton was infamous for his interest in occult activities. His 1859 fictional ghost story "The Haunted and the Haunters" solidified some of the conventions that now define the "classic" haunted tale. According to C. Nelson Stewart, this story "was based in part on his impressions of a haunted house in Berkeley Square," and Lytton's novel *Zanoni* was "likely ... based ... upon what we should now call 'astral experiences' beginning in early youth."[7] The poets Elizabeth and Robert Browning, whose works occasionally reflect a Gothic influence, participated in a séance with the celebrated medium Daniel Home.[8] Charles Dickens expresses humorous skepticism in his short-story satire on Spiritualism entitled "Well–Authenticated Rappings," but even he claimed "'not in the least [to] pretend that such things cannot be.'" As if to settle Dickens's doubts, Arthur Conan Doyle, "a dedicated proponent of spiritualism," conferred "with the spirit of Charles Dickens at a séance."[9] When not writing about the supreme skeptic Sherlock Holmes, Doyle penned stories such as "Playing with Fire," a fictional account of the sort of séance that he supposedly experienced. Among the literary elite, both skeptics and believers blurred the line between fiction and reality by seeking in their lives the sorts of sensations they recorded in their realistic fictions.

As paranormal truth-seeking changed through the course of the nineteenth century, so did ghost fiction. At the end of the nineteenth century, paranormal truth-seeking moved away from the quasi-religious realm of Spiritualism and toward inclusion in the realm of science. "Cambridge intellectuals" who "felt the implications of parapsychological phenomena were so great that science could not afford to ignore [them] or to reject them out of hand" founded the Society for Psychical Research in 1882, the date that most parapsychologists cite as the inception of the scientific discipline devoted to such phenomena, parapsychology. Irwin defines his science as the "study of experiences which, if they are as they seem to be, are in principle outside the realm of human capabilities as presently conceived by conventional scientists."[10] As Irwin indicates, most parapsychologists see nothing un- or super-natural about paranormal phenomena — conventional science just has a narrow view of nature.

Long before 1882, dissatisfaction with the narrowness of conventional science started to appear in fictions of the so-called supernatural, further shifting the emphasis of the ghost story from the fantastic to the mimetic.

Geary argues that scientific explanations in the ghost stories of Le Fanu reflect "the desire for an enlarged sense of the real" that "animated alike the horror tale ... and the work of the Society for Psychical Research."[11] Jack Sullivan notes the way Le Fanu's "synthesis of psychology and supernaturalism" survives in the works of later supernatural (or perhaps super-scientific) fiction writers such as Arthur Machen and Algernon Blackwood.[12] In *Zanoni*, Lytton places "the fanaticism of unbelief" in the scathing light usually reserved by materialists for fanatical believers.[13] The materialism of conventional science and intellectuals' fanatical unbelief were oppressive, so fiction dealing with the paranormal offered a liberating and attractive alternative.[14] While fringe scientists and other truth-seekers began researching the reality of phenomena conventionally regarded as unreal, writers of ghost fiction crafted their work not as representations of unreality but as representations of reality reconceived. Their form of Gothic writing does not necessarily oppose realism but instead functions within it, expanding the boundaries of realistic representation to include elements called supernatural only by those limited by the narrowness of mainstream science.

Authentication Strategies and the Interplay of Conventions

In a sense the fiction and the science of the paranormal are both unconventional, but they are not without conventions. Fictional and true ghost stories follow general rules and use commonplace characteristics that encourage their readers to assign them the status of either fiction or truth. "Terrorist Novel Writing" is one of many anonymous eighteenth-century attacks on the Gothic that include satirical "recipes" for producing a Gothic novel, indicating ways Gothic works tend to be hyper-conventional, extremely repetitive in their uses of plot devices and thematic motifs.[15] Ghost stories from the nineteenth century onwards offer few deviations from the eighteenth-century norm: though the list of conventional ingredients changes over time, a ghost story's generic markers consistently create a well-defined horizon of expectations that allows readers to anticipate the horrors they will find on each succeeding page.[16] Familiarity establishes a kind of verisimilitude; ghost stories create shocks and suspense by validating some popular expectations and violating others. A ghost fiction's conventionality allows readers to recognize and believe in the parameters of its fictional world just enough to deliver thrills when the rules of that world are broken.

The ghost story presented as true also relies on conventionality for its effects. Jay Anson's 1977 book *The Amityville Horror: A True Story*, which sits on the border between fiction and true reporting, begins with an introduction that supports its claim that "the phenomena reported in this book do happen" with evidence that "the case is not atypical." The book's epilogue lists some of the story's spookiest features and states assuredly that they "are all familiar elements to readers of the voluminous literature about poltergeists or 'noisy ghosts,' whose behavior has been documented by professional investigators."[17] While real ghost hunter Hans Holzer might be right in his estimation of *Amityville* as "embellished," the basic claim that *Amityville*'s plot points recur in scores of documented poltergeist investigations contains no exaggeration.[18] In *Poltergeist! A Study in Destructive Haunting*, Colin Wilson comments on how hundreds of years of "poltergeist observation" have produced a list of fairly reliable "rules" for the poltergeist's behavior.[19] Ghosts' rule-abiding and repetitive behaviors earn them a place in the natural world that is governed by fundamental scientific principles. The repeatability of experimental phenomena is such a principle, and though truly repeatable experiments that demonstrate ghosts' existence have eluded most (if not all) parapsychologists, repetition among true ghost stories nevertheless authenticates them as objects of scientific inquiry. If a report of a real haunting lacks elements already observed in other real cases, its truth-value diminishes. For a poltergeist to earn "real" status, it needs to follow the rules.

Fictional and true ghost stories both take hyper-conventional forms in order to produce verisimilar or actual authenticity. To foster sensation and belief, the fictional and the true mime and repudiate one another; authenticity often comes not from mechanisms within a particular story but from that story's relationship to other stories. Oscillations between miming and repudiating occur not only from story to story but also within a single story: a story might deploy multiple and sometimes inconsistent strategies to achieve the effect of authenticity. A fiction might mime true accounts one moment and then repudiate them the next, or a true account might showcase both its departures from and its adherence to fictional stereotypes. The symbiotic relationship between fictional and true ghost stories creates a state of uncertainty in which no story falls comfortably into one category or the other. This uncertainty renders the perception of discursive ghosts as either real or fictional objects of knowledge unstable, and this instability increases the burden of proof for the sciences that deal with supernatural phenomena. Placed at the limit of "true" science, parapsychology must defend the authentic reality of the objects it studies, but it can do so only through the very fiction-inflected language that marginalizes it.

Seeking to evade marginalization, true ghost stories often attempt to secure their contents' status as "real" by distancing themselves as much as possible from their fictional counterparts. After warning about the problems that fictional ghost stories cause by influencing witnesses' accounts of apparitions, Irwin poses a solution: "One way of minimizing this problem is to give greater credence to consistencies that are not a feature of the popular stereotype."[20] According to this approach, the most credible consistencies, or conventions, among true stories are the consistencies *inconsistent* with "the popular stereotype" that comes from fiction. This strategy portrays the "true" as that which is absent in fiction. In its most reduced form this approach is definitional: fiction is that which is untrue, and nonfiction is not that, so the un-untrue is authentic. The double negative employed by this strategy posits the real ghost as an inverse construction of the fictional ghost: fiction constitutes the real through opposition.

Aware that double absence does not equal ghostly presence, those who rely on inverse construction for authenticity rarely place fiction in the position of an original of which the true is only a negative copy. Irwin cautions against going to the "extreme" of denying all credibility to true stories that recall fictions, explaining that "some aspects of the fictional stereotype may well be drawn from authentic experiences."[21] Irwin's reservation makes fictions' conventions available to the true reporter while establishing true accounts as fictions' origins. He makes inverse construction compatible with other strategies while affirming its claim to superior authenticity. Tom Ogden's *The Idiot's Guide to Ghosts and Hauntings* exemplifies how inverse construction works as an authentication strategy without repudiating fiction entirely. Ogden identifies how "most people ... see a haunted house" according to Gothic clichés such as "towering gables" and the "huge staircases," and then he offers a correction: "The majority of houses that are reported as haunted, however, do not fit any of these stereotypes."[22] Ogden would establish the truth of his accounts with this claim about how the "majority" of true stories differ from fiction, and he invokes this qualifying difference without disqualifying the minority. In fact, Gothic clichés appear in most of Ogden's true accounts. Marked as a minority, these accounts share in the underrepresented majority's authenticity because of their stated exceptionality.

Holzer adopts a similar strategy in *Ghosts: True Encounters with the World Beyond*. He states, "Many of the false notions people have about ghosts come from fiction," and then he corrects, "Only in fictional ghost stories do ghosts threaten or cause harm." Despite this maxim, one of Holzer's true accounts describes a woman who slept in a room with a history of mysterious deaths and awoke to find a ghost poised to suffocate her.[23] If this case implies that the ghost might have harmed its percipient if she had not escaped, it invalidates Holzer's absolute generalization. The majority of Holzer's stories do uphold his claim about harmless ghosts, so if his generalization fails, it does so because he uses the absolute "only" instead of Ogden's more careful qualifier "majority." The generalization's failure may be less significant than its effect: the overstatement with which Holzer would banish the "false notions" of "most people" foregrounds the extreme difference between the true reporter's knowledge and the popular stereotype. By making strong claims that contradict popular wisdom, true reporters generate an aura of elite, authoritative knowingness, and they use their authority to divide the truth from fiction.

Another common form of inverse construction appears in claims that real ghosts, unlike their fictional counterparts, tend to be boring. Raymond Bayless's study *The Enigma of the Poltergeist* cites an "appropriate" comment about poltergeist phenomena made by the Reverend Joseph Glanvil in his 1666 *Philosophical Considerations concerning the existence of Sorcerers and Sorcery*: "'I confess the passages recited are not so dreadful, tragical and amazing, as there are some in a story of this kind, yet they are nevertheless probable or true, for their being not so prodigious and astonishing.'"[24] This comment suggests that less sensational true accounts have proportionally greater claims to authenticity. Wilson states the same idea more boldly when discussing the reliability of an anonymous poltergeist report: "How, then, can we assume it is true? Because it is so completely pointless."[25] Fictional ghost narratives usually have beginnings, middles, and ends that endow their apparitions with accessible motivations and goals; stories without such points rarely succeed in producing sensational effects. Un-sensational pointlessness, by contrast, becomes a hallmark of truth.

Reliance on the un-sensational to magnify a true account's aura of authenticity appears within the very language that parapsychologists use. like members of any scholarly discipline, scientific or otherwise, parapsychologists use a specialized vocabulary, a jargon that marks its users as members of an exclusive group. Turning to the subject of ghosts, Irwin establishes his idiom: "The survival hypothesis concerns the notion of

5. Ghost Stories and Ghostly Belief 125

postmortem survival, that is, that a disembodied consciousness or some such discarnate element of human personality might survive bodily death at least for a time."[26] It's not a ghost theory; it's a "survival hypothesis." It's not a ghost or spirit; it's a "disembodied consciousness" or a "discarnate element." This language's usefulness within the discipline exceeds the merely sesquipedalian, but the pointed absence of popular, sensational names like "ghosts" for the discipline's objects of inquiry suggests that one of the jargon's primary purposes is to convey legitimacy through its rejection of the sensational, unscientific subjects of fiction. Parapsychologists employ the language of sensational fiction from time to time, but their preference for anti-fictional jargon establishes both their professionalism and their commitment to truth.

The survival hypothesis, or the existence of ghosts, is only one possible explanation parapsychology offers for the paranormal phenomena that fictional ghost stories tend to depict. Bayless still uses the word "ghost" when discussing the enigmas his title names, but he condescends to the popular notion of ghosts by claiming, "Probably none but the most naïve Spiritualist believes today that the poltergeist is necessarily an actual human spirit."[27] In his influential study *The Poltergeist*, William G. Roll attributes most poltergeist phenomena to "RSPK," recurrent spontaneous psychokinesis. "I do not know of any evidence for the existence of the poltergeist as an incorporeal entity other than the disturbances themselves," he states, "and these can be explained more simply as PK effects from a flesh-and-blood entity who is at their center."[28] Behaving like a good scientist, Roll uses a version of Occam's Razor in his quest for simple explanations, and like many materialists who use the Razor to discredit all claims about the existence of an intangible world, he calls a tangible "flesh-and-blood" person a more likely explanation for strange phenomena than an intangible, "incorporeal" ghost. Parapsychology uses scientific jargon and reasoning to distance the scientific pursuit of paranormal nature from the pursuit of fictional thrills. If the paranormal is natural, it is in a limited sense normal, unusual but nevertheless part of science's everyday world.

Many true accounts carefully describe the locations of their phenomena, detailing their normalcy. In a move similar to Ogden's dismissal of fictional clichés from the "majority" of real-life hauntings, Le Fanu's non-fiction "Authentic Narrative of a Haunted House" describes its haunted location as "comfortably furnished," with "a completely modern character [and] a very cheerful air."[29] Like the titular setting of Jane Austen's *Northanger Abbey*, Le Fanu's real haunted house defies the expectations aroused by the dilapidated locales of eighteenth-century Gothic. The "modern character" of Le Fanu's true account is, however, the same modern character that appears in many of his fictional works and in the ghost fictions of other Victorian writers. H. P. Lovecraft surveys the Gothic tradition up to the early twentieth century in his essay "Supernatural Horror in Literature" and concludes, "Serious weird stories are either made realistically intense by close consistency and perfect fidelity to Nature except in the one supernatural direction which the author allows himself, or else cast altogether in the realm of phantasy." He cites early twentieth-century master of the ghost story M.R. James as "gifted with an almost diabolic power of calling horror by gentle steps from the midst of prosaic daily life."[30] Modern ghost stories that introduce horror within the quotidian focus on the unusualness that normalizing jargon would obscure, making the everydayness of haunting one of its most sensational features. They appropriate anti-fictional aspects of true accounts and transform them into some of the commonest and most effective conventions of fiction.

Fictional ghost stories further invade the territory of truth by miming true accounts' claims to actuality, claims such as the boast on *The Amityville Horror*'s dustjacket about the book's "one vital difference" from "*The Exorcist, The Omen,* or *Rosemary's Baby,*" enormously popular works of fiction: "the author reports, '... all the events in this book are *true.*'"[31] As Dorothy Scarborough observes in *The Supernatural in Modern Fiction*, a foundational study of the form first published in 1917, "Certain volumes of ghost stories have appeared, claiming to be not fiction but fact, accounts of actual apparitions seen and snap-shotted." Scarborough cites Daniel Defoe's "Apparition of Mrs. Veal" as an early example of a fictional work passing for true but allows that "recent evidence leads one to believe that it is a reportorial account of a ghost story current at the time, which missed being reported to the Society for Psychical Research merely because the organization did not exist then."[32] Given Defoe's and other eighteenth-century writers' tendency to pass off their fictions as facts, Scarborough's doubts about how to categorize "Mrs. Veal" indicate the way such truth-claims allow ghost fictions to increase their verisimilitude by obscuring the boundary between truth and fabrication. When *Amityville* claims to be true—unlike *Rosemary's Baby* and others—it distances itself from fiction. When stories otherwise identifiable as fictions make the same sort of claim, they close that distance.

Rhoda Broughton's significantly entitled ghost fiction "The Truth, the Whole Truth, and Nothing but the Truth" concludes with the sentence,

"This is a true story."[33] The repetitiveness of the title and of the concluding line overplays the insistence on veracity to the point of irony, exposing the eagerness for authenticity that renders both fictions and true reports suspect. Mary Louisa Molesworth's "The Story of the Rippling Train" goes a step further, opening with a group of people discussing ghost stories, one of whom complains, "'One hears nothing else nowadays ... they're all 'authentic,' really vouched for, only you never see the person who saw or heard or felt the ghost.'" Someone soon arrives and gives the complainer what she wants, a first-person account of a ghost. The complainer's scare quotes around "'authentic'" underscore the crisis of credibility inherent in all ghost stories' truth-claims. Acknowledging this crisis at the outset sets up the subsequent first-person account as an exception with superior credibility. The complainer within the story might see this first-hand account as authentic, but Molesworth nullifies the account's exceptional status for the story's reader by giving it a fictional third-person frame. In another authenticating move within this frame, the first-person narrator explains that the story lacks "'ghost-like circumstances.'"[34] Contrasting its tale with popular stereotypes, "The Story of the Rippling Train" hijacks true accounts' strategy of inverse construction in both form and content. By miming inverse construction to increase verisimilar authenticity, the fiction inverts the inversion and closes the distance that would establish actual authenticity for true tales.

Ghost fictions' parasitic technique of gaining verisimilitude at the expense of true accounts extends to miming true accounts' attacks on fiction. A man who encourages the narrator of Lytton's "Haunted and the Haunters" to investigate a haunted house advises, "'It is better that you should judge for yourself, than enter the house with an imagination influenced by previous narratives.'"[35] Though the man refers to the true accounts of other people who have fled the house in terror, his warning about how "narratives" might "influence" the protagonist resonates with warnings such as Irwin's and Holzer's about the biases and "false notions" derived from the stereotypes popularized by fiction. The fiction evokes the vulnerability of perception to expectation, producing an aura of authoritative knowingness that competes with that of its non-fictional counterparts.

Lytton amplifies this authority by antagonizing other kinds of ghost stories throughout the tale. The narrator rails against "popular superstition" and "American spirit-seers," condemning both folklore and Spiritualism. He claims that the force he has encountered in the haunted house could not be "against nature" but is instead "only a rare power in nature," aligning himself with the thinking that would later define the Society of Psychical Research and parapsychology. The narrator's interlocutor aims more directly at the stereotypes that come from fiction when he grants, "'I accept any crotchet ... rather than embrace at once the notion of ghosts and hobgoblins we imbibed in our nurseries.'"[36] This statement echoes Addison and Locke's concerns about how "foolish maids" might "inculcate" certain "ideas of goblins and sprites" in "the mind of a child."[37] Similarly, in Le Fanu's "The Haunted Baronet," a character berates his own fear of supernatural goings-on at a nearby lake by saying, "The nursery is to blame for it—old stories and warnings," and in "Captain Murderer and the Devil's Bargain," Dickens refers comically and semi-autobiographically to the "impossible places and people ... none the less alarmingly real ... introduced ... by my nurse."[38] Though their approaches to their own content range from the sincere to the ironic, these stories make references to superstitions and nursery tales that set up a class of ghost stories beneath themselves. The stories of Lytton, Le Fanu, and Dickens claim authority and superiority by characterizing others' fictions as wayward and ludicrous. They place their fabrications on the high level with others' truths, damaging the truth/fiction hierarchy.

Though fiction's miming of true accounts' inverse construction strategy does weaken that strategy's potential for effecting authenticity, it does not deprive the strategy of all efficacy. Irwin's claim that "some aspects of the fictional stereotype may well be drawn from authentic experiences" turns true accounts into origins and fictions into mere derivations. According to this reasoning, true accounts should not be judged inauthentic simply because they look like the fictions derived from them. Without a clear timeline to establish the direction of derivation, this logic fails the test of history, and self-consciously scientific studies of the paranormal such as Irwin's and Roll's therefore tend to use it sparingly and with the tentativeness suggested by Irwin's "some" and "may well be." Many approaches to relating true encounters with the spirit realm do not, however, adhere to the rigorous standards of parapsychological reporting. True accounts sometimes purposefully employ fiction's stereotypes, directly or indirectly suggesting that they report the actual phenomena that inspire verisimilar fictions. Fiction can drain authenticity from true tales, but true tales can reclaim that authenticity in a form more potent for having been fictionalized.

Though Bayless condescends at times to those "naïve" people who believe that poltergeists are human spirits, his tendency to refer to the poltergeist as a "ghostly visitant" instead of using parapsychology's drier polysyllables pushes him beyond the boundaries of scientific rigor and toward the popular sensibility he labels naïve. The dustjacket of Bayless's 1967 work frames the study with overt sensationalism, punctuating almost every sentence with an exclamation point and using all capitals. The front flap proclaims Bayless's systematic overview of his evidence, "POLTERGEIST ATTACK MAY TAKE MANY DIFFERENT FORMS!" The back flap characterizes the book as a survival manual, calling "a strange chapter on EXORCISM AND POLTERGEISTS ... the most useful chapter you've *ever read*, for it contains many of the rituals which have succeeded in dispelling poltergeists down through the centuries!" A publisher's marketing does not always reflect an author's content: Bayless does not produce the degree of sensation that the book flaps suggest, but he does pile up sensational adjectives, describing the "actions of the poltergeist" as "grotesque" and a particular "poltergeist's intentions" as "completely malign and murderous," perpetuating what Holzer calls the false fictional notion of the harmful ghost.[39] Wilson moves even further from the dry rigor of parapsychology. Roll's title, *The Poltergeist*, somberly proclaims the study's object, but Wilson's title, *Poltergeist!*, abandons that somberness, suggesting a difference in tone comparable to the difference between Dickens's *Oliver Twist* and the popular musical *Oliver!*

The somberness and rigor of parapsychology's approach to its topic reflects the burden of proof it carries as a science: it must appeal to the primarily skeptical academic community, so it must eschew the expressions of excitement common among believers. Most audiences, however, are not as demanding as academics. Irwin notes, "According to Gallup Poll data (Gallup & Newport, 1991), the majority of the American population believes in the authenticity of one or more paranormal processes."[40] Trent Brandon's *The Ghost Hunter's Bible* provides more exciting data without the rigor of a citation: "Over 80% of people polled believe in the existence of ghosts."[41] To win the status of "reality" from the vast numbers who already believe in the paranormal, true accounts need not offer a foundation for belief but rather an expansion of the believed, new data that readers can either accept or reject as authentic based on their preexisting faith in the possibility and relative probability of a true ghost story's authenticity. Sensationalized true accounts deal more directly with matters of faith in their search for authenticity, so they can shift their focus from the intellectually compelling to the emotionally compelling. Fictional ghost stories that scare believers often do so because they are verisimilar enough to attain credibility. True ghost stories can achieve authenticity by striving for the same emotional credibility, which they gain by becoming more like fiction in both form and content.

True ghost stories must negotiate an apparent contradiction: similarities between fictional stereotypes and the portrayal of actual events can both decrease and increase the effect of authenticity. True stories' struggle to go beyond the suspension of disbelief and into the realm of belief hinges on the dispositions of readers, and perhaps by consequence, a range of true stories exists to appeal to a variety of readers. At one end of the continuum, parapsychological studies tend toward an inverse relation with fiction in order to appeal to skeptical academics, and at the other end, sensationalized true accounts tend toward a direct relation with fiction that aims at believers' hearts more than their minds. Moving toward the sensational end of the continuum, Bayless is a step away from pure parapsychology, and Wilson is another step further.

Holzer's true accounts come even closer to the sensational end. He crafts his stories with many of the standard techniques of horror fiction, introducing characters, building suspense, and withholding information until climactic moments, as in this example:

> The light followed her to her room *as if it had a mind* of its own!
> When she entered her room the light left, but the room felt icy. She was disturbed by this, but nevertheless went to bed and soon had forgotten all about it as sleep came to her. *Suddenly, in the middle of the night*, she woke and sat up in bed.
> *Something* had awakened her. At the foot of her bed she saw a man ... she stared at the apparition [emphasis added].[42]

A parapsychologist's scientific case report would omit the anthropomorphizing of the light in the first sentence because it suggests a human spirit through metaphor instead of evidence. The exclamation point and the choppy one-sentence paragraph build excitement and tension, tension relieved momentarily — while the character finds forgetful sleep and the reader catches a breath — and then reintroduced "suddenly" at the scariest, most vulnerable yet nonspecific time of night. The next paragraph teases with the idea of "something" in its first sentence. Its second sentence delays the revelation of the something with a prepositional phrase before calling it first a "man" and then, most horribly, an "apparition."

Holzer announces his proximity to fiction when, setting the scene for a séance he attended, he describes the striking of a clock at a dramatic moment as happening "like a well-rehearsed television thriller."[43] Similarly, when recounting the true case of "The Smurl Poltergeist," Trent Brandon states, "The horrible events that took place in the Smurl home could have come straight out of a horror movie."[44] With this overt comparison of the stipulated reality to fiction, Brandon summons a host of stock images to give color to his tale, images that his audience, likely to consist of sensation-seekers who enjoy fictional ghost stories as well as true, will find familiar. The familiarity of fictional conventions lends substance to true stories when those conventions recur as truth: Brandon needs to do less work to describe the events realistically because his readers already know what they look like. For the right kind of reader, overt approximation of fiction authenticates the real.

Beth Scott and Michael Norman's *Haunted Heartland: True Ghost Stories of the American Midwest* straddles the border between true reporting and fictionalized narration. Its stories often bear not only the marks of fictional style common in Holzer's work but also dialogue, action-driven narration that spans multiple pages, and dramatic curtain lines to conclude stories such as, "And that's the last that has been heard from George [the ghost]. Or is it?" In small print at the end of their introduction, the authors admit, "Although all the material in this book is based on 'true' incidents, the authors have, in some cases, expanded upon the original circumstances to create scenes which may not have actually taken place." The uncertainty they express about scenes that "may not have actually taken place" does not cohere with their admission that they created them. If this uncertainty is at all credible, its credibility stems from the idea that, since the scenes are "based on 'true' incidents," the stories' relation to truth is secure enough that the fictional interpolations very well *could* have happened. The people in the accounts might not have said the exact words in the fabricated dialogue, but the precise details of the events are immaterial to the core truth of the ghostly manifestation it embellishes. The authors state that they don't know whether or not their stories are actually true: "What matters most, we believe, is that these stories have been *told* by the people involved as if they were true." What matters most is that someone at some point testified to the reality of "George, the Mischievous Ghost."[45] A truth-claim not even verified by the authors sets each story before the judgment of a reader who probably already believes in ghosts, and the compelling narration must do the rest of the work of authentication.

Anson's *Amityville Horror*, as Holzer points out, is also "embellished." To establish the book's adherence to truth, Anson includes blueprints of the haunted house, photos of George and Kathleen Lutz, whose testimonies form the book's basis, and a drawing one of the Lutz children made of a ghostly manifestation. The book carefully alludes to television newscasts and other media reports that corroborate some of the story's most violent details, and it narrates the Lutzes' experiences sequentially, noting the precise dates and time of each occurrence, often down to the hour. The documentary detail creates a strong aura of authenticity, but there is too much detail for the book to be wholly accurate. Like the stories in *Haunted Heartland*, this book includes word-for-word accounts of unrecorded dialogue and moment-to-moment formulations of characters' thoughts, feelings, and impressions. Exclamation points, choppy paragraphs, and climactic revelations mark the entirety of the narration. The superfluity of stylized details makes a novel-length book out of a story Holzer manages to recount in three photo-enriched pages.[46] The extent of *Amityville*'s embellishments and the degree of its stylization would probably justify the book's inclusion in a survey of supernatural fiction. *Amityville* and other fictionalized true accounts, like fictional ghost stories that employ true accounts' anti-fictional conventions, close the distance between truth and fiction. The disposition of a true account's reader will determine whether the closing of that distance will increase or decrease its authenticity. As reviews quoted on the back of *Amityville*'s dustjacket describing it as "the scariest true story I have read in years" and "far more unsettling than fictional works" indicate, the superfluity of fabricated details has not stopped readers from receiving Anson's book as a description of an actual haunting made all the more thrilling and authentic by fictionalization.

Alongside fictionalized true accounts, straddling the same blurred line but leaning toward the opposite side, are fictions merely based on or "inspired by" real events. A standout example of the based-on-truth type of ghost fiction is Frank DeFelitta's novel *The Entity*, a contemporary of *Amityville* published in 1979. The back of the Warner Books paperback edition claims it is "based on a real-life case," and the author's "Acknowledgments" page thanks "Barry Taff, Kerry Gaynor, and Doris D., whose lives inspired part of it."[47] These claims of a true basis and real inspiration are the book's only true-story trappings. Otherwise it behaves like a novel, using fictional character names, internal monologues, and other narrative elements reserved for fiction. As Troy Taylor explains in *The Ghost Hunter's Guidebook*, "The real-life 'Entity' case (on which both a fictionalized book and film were based) began in August 1974 when a woman called 'Doris B.' [sic] overheard parapsychologists Barry Taff and Kerry Gaynor talking about haunted houses in a Westwood Village, California bookstore."[48] Taylor's brief account focuses almost exclusively on the reported experiences of the parapsychologists, while DeFelitta's long novel focuses on the perspective of Doris (renamed Carlotta), a woman who believes a ghost follows her, speaks to her, rapes her repeatedly, and attacks other members of her family.

The Entity does not claim to be anything more than a novel sprung from a seed of truth, but it does strive for a high degree of verisimilitude in the way it depicts its ghostly phenomena. It includes many of the conventional elements found in true accounts of hauntings, which the fictional versions of Taff and Gaynor (renamed as Kraft and Mehan) recognize as "rather basic elements of poltergeist activity." In many twentieth-century true accounts, the involvement of parapsychologists with the reported phenomena is itself a distinguishing trait, and *The Entity* makes parapsychology and parapsychologists not only a factor in its plot but also its secondary subject. The novel's title refers to parapsychologists' preferred name for the phenomenon attacking Carlotta, and at one point Kraft speculates, "'It could be RSPK.'"[49] Proving that even parapsychology and parapsychological jargon can offer thrills, instead of being dry and stuffy, terms such as "entity" and "RSPK" become mysterious and chilling.

DeFelitta divides his story into four sections, one named after Carlotta, one after her psychiatrist, one after Kraft and Mehan, and one after the Entity itself. The section names indicate not just the major players in the tale but also the factors that might be involved in any case of its type: the percipient of the phenomenon, the institution of psychiatry that explains it as unreal, the institution of parapsychology that explains it as a different order of reality, and the phenomenon itself. Much of the book focuses on the struggle between the explanations of psychiatry and parapsychology, which keeps Carlotta wondering whether she is mentally ill or the victim of a spectral rapist. Carlotta becomes the battleground of the two disciplines as, outraged by the intrusion of a marginal science, her psychiatrist tries to have the parapsychologists, whose "existence as a division within the Department of Psychology was tenuous," banished from their university.[50] The struggle over the legitimacy of parapsychology doubles Carlotta's struggle with the reality of her experiences, and both struggles involve the ontological issues that make distinguishing true ghost stories from fictions so problematic.

The central position of parapsychology's struggles as a discipline in *The Entity* serves to heighten the novel's verisimilitude. Parapsychology is the most prominent non-literary discipline that deals with ghosts as if they were real, and its appearance in fiction imports all of the discipline's anti-fictional, authenticating attributes into fiction, sensationalizing everything from its jargon to its electronic devices that measure unusual atmospheric activity. This importation, however, does not necessarily have a purely parasitic effect on parapsychology's claims of authenticity for its narratives of the paranormal. Though *The Entity* keeps the question of Carlotta's sanity and the Entity's objective reality somewhat open, the number of witnesses who share Carlotta's experiences increases throughout the narrative. When a university dean and a highly skeptical psychiatrist both witness the Entity's final, explosive manifestation, the former asks for an explanation, and the latter, "without conviction," answers, "'A mass illusion.'"[51] The psychiatrist's lack of conviction about his explanation casts psychiatry's explanatory power as feeble when compared to that of parapsychology. Though the parapsychologists fail to record the evidence that will prove the validity of their discipline to the world once and for all, the novel suggests that they, the underdogs, are the real winners of the academic struggle. Framing parapsychologists as heroic for believing and helping the victimized Carlotta, the novel generates sympathy for the discipline, sympathy that a reader might carry from her or his experience of DeFelitta's fiction to experiences of parapsychological truths.

One of the best-known ghost fictions of the last thirty years, Tobe Hooper's 1982 film *Poltergeist* also uses the involvement of parapsychologists to increase its verisimilitude. The film opens with sounds and images that, in the tradition of ghost fictions that mime the inverse construction strategy, emphasize the everyday-ness of its American setting. The first sounds are the notes of the United States' national anthem, and the first images follow the family dog from room to room of the unremarkable suburban household of the Freeling family. Suburban American life in many ways becomes the film's subject: the oblivious construction of cookie-cutter homes on ground that was once a cemetery becomes the film's most compelling justification for the ghostly manifestations that terrorize the Freelings and kidnap their daughter Carol Anne. Shortly after these terrors invade the Freelings' typical suburban home, parapsychologists receive an invitation. They set up cameras that record apparitions and instruments that measure "psychotronic energy," and the lead parapsychologist, Dr. Lesh, helpfully explains the difference between the "classic haunting" and the "poltergeist intrusion." Though real-life parapsychologists would probably wince at many of their filmic counterparts' inaccuracies, they might be pleased by the heroic role their discipline plays in giving comfort and support to the iconic American family and, by enlisting the help of the medium Tangina Barrons, in rescuing Carol Anne. The kindly Dr. Lesh describes herself as a "professional psychologist" with a "ghostly hobby" because "parapsychology isn't something you get a Master's in"; she establishes the discipline's derogated status within the academy, and her heroism frames that derogation as unjust.[52] The verisimilitude of the film, bolstered by the involvement of parapsychologists, is such that the authors of *Haunted Heartland* explain that "a haunting as in the film 'Poltergeist' can actually happen," and "events like those described in the movie *did* occur ... during the early 1970s."[53] The movie reinforces the reality of the 1970s haunting that preceded it, and it also reinforces the authority of parapsychologists and mediums to the extent that Zelda Rubinstein, the actress who portrays Tangina Barrons, was asked to write an endorsing introduction to *The Idiot's Guide to Ghosts and Hauntings.* Instead of parasitic, the relationship between fictional and true accounts can be mutually beneficial, symbiotic in the best sense of the word.

Conversion Narratives

Whether they help or hinder one another in the quest for authenticity, most fictional and true ghost stories seek to stimulate their readers' belief in the paranormal to gain the status of either "realistic" or "real." With motives ranging from the hedonistic to the religious, both types of tales employ their authentication strategies in order to make readers accept — for at least the duration of the narrative — the possibility of real ghosts. Clery remarks on how, "in the 1660s, attested apparition narratives [were] offered as an antidote for the spread of atheism," exemplifying one way that the "need to demonstrate the existence of the invisible necessitated a resort to the tools of language and testimony."[54] Scientific atheism can use tools such as Occam's Razor to invalidate not only ghost stories but also stories about other "supernatural" beings such as the Christian God; testimony about ghosts becomes a tool that atheism's opponents can use to shore up a general belief in the supernatural. Underlining the perceived power of such testimony, Geary discusses spiritual leader John Wesley's struggles with unbelievers and quotes Wesley's claim "'that if but one account of the intercourse of men with separate spirits be admitted, their whole castle in the air (Deism, Atheism, Materialism) falls to the ground.'"[55] If a reader believes just one true account of a ghost — or perhaps even the basis of just one ghost fiction — that one instance of belief overpowers every other instance of unbelief. Just one story can convert an unbeliever into a believer.

Comparing the authenticity of a ghost story to that of a newspaper reporter's account of a crime that, like a ghost's appearance, cannot be reproduced in a laboratory, Troy Taylor explains that, while the existence of ghosts may not be provable "scientifically," testimony makes it provable "historically."[56] For this reason, the ghost hunter — or the parapsychologist — must grant witness testimony the utmost importance, and works ranging on the unsensational-to-sensational continuum from Irwin's *Introduction to Parapsychology* to Brandon's *Ghost Hunter's Bible* all tend to devote pages to guidelines for interviewing witnesses in their discussions of evidential proof. Victor Sage's study *Horror Fiction in the Protestant Tradition* notes how "testimony tends to assimilate itself to 'fact' and 'evidence'" in reactions to true tales of the supernatural recorded in the eighteenth century.[57] Witnesses and witnessing play a central role in the generation of belief that results in conversion, and, as seventeenth-century spiritual autobiographies and the act known among twenty-first-century Protestants as "witnessing" attest, stories *about* conversion often appear to be the most capable of *performing* conversion. Thus conversion, through an operation similar to pathological reproduction, can spread either sanctioned or heretical belief. Seizing this potential, many ghost stories, true and fictional, take the form of conversion narratives.

Conversion narratives make the defeat of skepticism by belief their subject as well as their enterprise: their stories as well as their ideal readers start in skepticism and move toward belief. Irwin states that in parapsychology "in no way is there any presumption ... of the existence of 'the paranormal.'"[58] Parapsychologists gather and interpret evidence, proving rather than presuming; as Dr. Cooley, *The Entity*'s most authoritative parapsychologist, explains, "'You do much better ... if you start in the traditional world and move outward.'"[59] By this reasoning, any good parapsychologist's account of a ghost (or a disembodied consciousness) is, in a sense, a conversion narrative that moves from skepticism to belief. The disbelief common in "the traditional world" also provides a starting point for many fictional accounts of ghosts. Geary argues, "For the modern horror story to arise ... the dominant view of reality must be one where what we call the supernatural is not a normal part of what is assumed to be real, but something denied, rejected as superstitious, and thus made

5. Ghost Stories and Ghostly Belief

alien, strange, eerie."[60] Ghost fictions achieve their strongest affects by staging a conflict between two explanations of the real. The coexistence of two contradictory explanatory frameworks in one story creates tension, suspense, horror, and the thrills that can result from all these emotions when fiction arouses them.

While many fictional ghost stories move toward the defeat of one explanatory framework by the other, some avoid a decisive movement toward belief or disbelief and maintain the tension of contradictory explanations for the apparently paranormal throughout their narratives. Henry James's 1897 *The Turn of the Screw* is perhaps the best-known example of this type of story: the governess's first person narrative about specters who plot against the innocence of her two young charges gives the reader insufficient information to decide with certainty whether the ghostly experiences have any reality beyond the governess's own disturbed mind. James's story builds on a tradition of ghost fictions that exploit the ambiguities of first-person testimony.[61] The narrator of Charlotte Riddell's 1882 "The Open Door" frames her tale with the disclaimer, "There are persons who ... say ... the whole affair was a delusion ... I am going to tell what happened to me exactly as it happened, and readers can credit or scoff."[62] Similarly, in her 1873 novel *Monsieur Maurice*, Amelia B. Edwards raises this tension almost dismissively when her narrator remarks, "I cannot prove those events ... I can only relate them in their order, knowing them to be true, and leaving each reader to judge of them according to his convictions."[63] These stories frame the credibility of first-person testimony about ghosts as a question that readers must answer according to their predispositions; their insistence on multiple explanations allows them to illustrate the contingency of conversion on the delicate relationship between the credibility of testimony and the credulity of its judges.

"The Open Door" introduces ambiguity by foregrounding the contingent reliability of testimony, but it strongly encourages its readers to regard the narrator as credible. The story follows its first sentence, "Some people do not believe in ghosts," with "For that matter, some people do not believe in anything," which frames those who do not believe in ghosts as prone to extravagance in their doubts, the fanatical unbelief lampooned by Lytton. The narrator represents the starting and end points of his conversion at once: "I ought to premise there was a time when I did not believe in ghosts either ... If you had asked me one summer's morning years ago ... if I held such appearances to be probable or possible, you would have received an emphatic 'No' for answer."[64] He first identifies his past self as one of the extravagant unbelievers he has already subtly critiqued, a figure for the potentially skeptical reader, and he then identifies his present self as one who knows better from his experiences, a figure for the wise reader who will undergo the same sort of conversion after hearing his testimony. Admitting the problems of first-person testimony at the same time that it gestures toward the testimony's potential for conversion, "The Open Door" invites its readers to cross through ambiguity and into belief by accepting the wisdom gained by another's experience.

Le Fanu's short story "The Familiar" reveals the conversion of its central character, Barton, more slowly, in correspondence with the measured revelations of the haunting phenomena that bring about the conversion. The narrator introduces Barton as a man who "was himself, from the deliberate conviction of years, an utter disbeliever in what are usually termed preternatural agencies." After an escalating series of experiences with haunting noises, apparitions, and threats, Barton seeks a doctor and, hearing his experiences dismissed as figments of diseased imagination, explains:

> "I am not a credulous — far from a superstitious man. I have been, perhaps, too much the reverse — too sceptical, too slow of belief; but unless I were one whom no amount of evidence could convince, unless I were to contemn the repeated, the *perpetual* evidence of my own senses, I am now — now at last convinced to believe — I have no escape from the conviction — the overwhelming certainty — that I am haunted."[65]

The repetitiveness of Barton's outbursts about his conviction and his emphasis on "*perpetual* evidence" demonstrate the extremity of his original skepticism; the only stronger skepticism would come from "one whom no amount of evidence could convince," one who is more stubborn than wise. Barton winds up dead, which legitimizes his concern that he was "too slow of belief." Had he believed faster, like the sinner wise enough to convert before damnation, he might have been saved.

Le Fanu presents "The Familiar" not as Barton's testimony but as the testimony of "the Rev. Thomas Herbert," who writes, "I was a young man at the time, and intimately acquainted with some of the actors in this strange tale; the impression which its incidents made on me, therefore, were deep and lasting."[66] While the reader cannot know with certainty if the young man has become a Reverend because his acquaintances' story converted him, his reference to an "impression" that was "deep and lasting" hints strongly at a conversion. By basing the testimony on second-hand information, Le Fanu produces a warning to the skeptic in the fate of Barton and a model for the convert in the character of Herbert. The story

5. Ghost Stories and Ghostly Belief   139

seems to have had the same effect on Herbert as the experiences had on Barton: step by step, the haunting events converted Barton, and learning about them converted Herbert. Herbert was not foolish enough to need the empirical convincing that killed Barton: Herbert's testimony suggests that the wise reader will follow his example and believe, at least for the duration of the tale, in a reality for ghosts derived solely on their textual representation.

A model convert in both fictional and true conversion narratives is the man or woman who is not only a skeptic but also a member of the authoritative professional class. Authority can qualify a witness for expert testimony, as highly educated parapsychologists like Roll and Irwin — or their fictional counterparts, Drs. Lesh and Cooley — might insist. Dick Donovan, a.k.a. J.E.P. Muddock, begins his fiction "The Corpse Light" with a narrator who announces his conversion: "I no longer scoff when somebody reminds me that there is more in heaven and earth than is dreamt of in our philosophy." The reference to *Hamlet*'s ghost-related epiphany underscores the narrator's own movement from scoffer, or skeptic, to believer. In the very next sentence, the narrator casually mentions his "medical practice," suggesting that his original skepticism was that of a scientist, a doctor.[67] This introduction gestures toward the converting power of the experiences it will relate by establishing the extremity of the conversion that has occurred. The narrator was and is a scientist, and since a man of his erudite and ingrained materialism has converted, so should the reader. Medical authority combines with *Hamlet*'s literary authority to add force to the story's exemplification of a dramatic fictional conversion.

Conversion stories favored by true reporters tend to be no less extreme. At the outset of his study, Wilson provides copious details of the real-life conversion of "Professor Cesare Lombroso," whom he describes accurately as "one of the most celebrated scientists" of the nineteenth century after he published his best-known work, *Criminal Man*, in 1876. Once "a thoroughgoing materialist," Lombroso's "scepticism received a severe setback" when he encountered a girl who justified her claim to paranormal abilities with demonstrations that passed all the scientist's tests. "Slowly, and with painful reluctance," Wilson writes of Lombroso's later life, "the sceptical scientist was converted to the view that the world was a far more complex place than his theories allowed."[68] Setting forth theories of humanity's degeneration that had a strong influence on the work of Max Nordau, *Criminal Man* was widely discredited in the century following its publication. Wilson's snide attack on the simplicity of the scientist's "theories" transfers the weight of *Criminal Man*'s discredit to his scientific materialism in general. In Wilson's characterization, Lombroso's experiences with the paranormal moved him from the erroneous path of the skeptic to the right and righteous path of the believer.

Taking pride of place as the first account in Wilson's study, the conversion of Lombroso, a celebrity scientist, serves as a model for the many other conversions that Wilson describes and, by extension, for any readers also encumbered by simplistic and erroneous theories. Whenever possible, Wilson notes his converts' positions of authority. Describing " a typical poltergeist story" in which a lawyer and his family visit friends' poltergeist-infested home, Wilson gives some of the story's participants actual names but calls the lawyer only "the lawyer," working the word "lawyer" into almost every sentence so that the educated man's status cannot escape the reader's attention. The lawyer starts out "completely sceptical about the 'ghost'" but ends up cowering in bed with his wife and daughter after hearing noises that the home's owners could not hear.[69] Holzer provides similar models, describing in one case "an advertising man" who "had scoffed at the idea of a ghost" but who, after fencing with a ghostly intruder, found himself "no longer a scoffer."[70] Holzer augments his aura of authoritative knowledge with stories about educated people who give up their own false notions and come around to his point of view. By modeling the conversions of educated doctors, lawyers, and advertising men, true reporters can usurp the authority of skeptical science and make it their own.

Fictional and true conversion narratives both feature converts who begin not only as skeptics buts as "scoffers," people who disbelieve to the point of ridiculing claims of ghosts' existence. Arthur Myers begins his collection of true ghost stories *The Ghostly Register* with a description of his own conversion: "When I began writing this book, I wasn't at all sure I believed in ghosts," but after "six months ... spent researching ... I believed in ghosts as much as I believe in anything."[71] His testimony provides the kind of introductory model that Wilson gets from Lombroso's story; by using his own foolish disbelief as an example, he allows sympathy for incredulous readers who nevertheless should, after reviewing the research his book lays out, follow his example and wise up.

Such sympathy has limits, however. Telling the story of two young women who lived in a haunted house, Myers describes how suitors "ridiculed the women" about their ghostly belief "until they experienced it for themselves." "Then a sudden conversion occurred," Myers states, and the "usual quips then ceased."[72] In such examples the scoffers who go as far as to ridicule believers look ridiculous when proven wrong; the ridiculers, whose quips ultimately point out nothing but their own ignorance, stand worthy of ridicule. Holzer revels in the reversal of ridicule, turning his own experience and education against scoffers whenever possible. He relates an encounter with "a well-known TV personality ... [who] proudly proclaimed himself a skeptic":

> "The term skeptic," I lectured him patiently, "is derived from the Greek word *skepsis*, which was the name of a small town in Asia Minor in antiquity. It was known for its lack of knowledge, and people from skepsis were called skeptics.
> The TV personality didn't like it at all, but the next time we met on camera, he was a lot more human and his humanity finally showed."[73]

Holzer depicts himself as having been as "patient" with this famous scoffer as one would be with an ignorant child, and he shows some glee in recounting how his etymologically inaccurate lecture about the foolishness of all skeptics, while perhaps not making a conversion, apparently endowed the man with greater "humanity." Conversion narratives about scoffers are also cautionary tales: though they might not all end up dead like Barton in "The Familiar," some of them might very well end up looking like asses, perhaps even on television.

While bolstering the authority of the believer who recounts the tale, conversion narratives that illustrate the "falls" of educated skeptics have a leveling effect. They suggest that if a great scientist or doctor could fall into the error of unbelief, then anybody could — the regular person and the great, equal in error, can both rise above the mistake of incredulity. The ultimate conversion is the conversion of the everyman, the person whose change in outlook could be anyone's change. Holzer states that conversion is not a change in "belief" but the dawn of a higher "awareness," and he maintains that "everyone, except the skeptic" will find that "the evidence of this is overwhelming." Holzer argues that everyone but the ignorant, fanatical unbeliever will come around to this awareness. Conversion narratives make belief available and compelling to all, insisting in one way or another, as Holzer does, "The people who come across ghostly manifestations are people like you."[74]

Causal Beliefs

Conversion narratives encourage conversions, and sometimes these conversions produce more conversion narratives. Narrative shapes belief, and belief proliferates through narrative. Since Gothic fictions shape the language and strategies that encourage belief, without these fictions, the beliefs might not be (or be recorded) in the shapes that they are. Belief in the discursive reality of ghosts has effects that extend beyond the merely discursive: in many cases, belief that a ghost can be perceived provides a necessary condition for its sensory perception. As the next chapter demonstrates, through their encouragement of belief, Gothic fictions shape what empirical phenomena people perceive as ghostly and how they perceive them. The idea that ghost stories might not only make people believe in ghosts but also see them motivates some of the critics who decry the Gothic's threat to stimulate heretical belief. Radcliffe's metafictional critique of the dangers of imagination in *Udolpho* dramatizes this fearful result: as one character, Ludovico, reads a ghost story, he begins to interpret sensory phenomena as ghosts of the type he has read about, and his misinterpretation almost costs him his life.[75] Radcliffe reflects on the dangerousness of the relation between belief and perception, and in doing so she reflects on the dangerousness attributed to the Gothic.

Ghost stories that produce erroneous beliefs provide the basis for other pseudo-ghost stories in Radcliffe's metafictional tradition. Michael Arlen gives his 1925 short story "The Gentleman from America" a common set-up: three men make a bet that one of them won't stay the night in a supposedly haunted room. The titular gentleman, Puce, stays the night and makes the mistake of reading a ghost story, "The Phantom Footsteps," which he believes his main opponent in the bet, Quillier, has left for him. In "The Phantom Footsteps," twin sisters, Geraldine and Julia, hear a noise downstairs, and Julia goes to investigate. Geraldine cowers while she hears the slow footsteps of Julia's reanimated corpse coming back upstairs. The girls' father returns home to find Geraldine insane from the ghostly encounter. The father learns that a homicidal maniac, recently escaped from an asylum, half-decapitated Julia, and Julia's ghost came back to warn Geraldine. Geraldine, now a lunatic, takes the maniac's vacant place in the asylum. Puce finishes reading, sleeps, and wakes to strange sounds. He immediately associates his predicament with the story, and when he sees a headless phantom, his first thought is that "Julia's head had only been half-severed." After a fruitless fight with the phantom, Puce passes out, and eleven years later he learns that Quillier had dressed up as the phantom to trick him into losing the bet. Puce tries to strangle Quillier, whom warders rescue when they arrive to return Puce to his place in an asylum. Puce is now an escaped lunatic who believes he had "'a sister ... called Julia who was murdered.'"[76]

5. Ghost Stories and Ghostly Belief 143

Arlen's fiction-within-fiction leads to a misinterpretation that results in horror. Puce, who at first insists he doesn't "believe in that no-head bunk," stands for the model convert who goes from total skepticism to all-consuming belief.[77] Arlen's tale derives terror from the idea that a ghost fiction can increase a reader's belief until the reader's senses become deranged, trapping him (or her) in a world made from fiction. Though this story shares many elements with *Udolpho*, it might be a celebration rather than a critique of the ghost story's power: if a ghost story can make its readers believe that a ghost story might have that kind of power, ghost stories become much more terrifying and much more thrilling. For the thrill-seeker, Arlen's story pays off by increasing the payoff of other stories.

That belief might change sensory reality provides chills for readers of ghost fiction and hope for seekers of ghost truth. According to Wilson, at least one group of parapsychologists has tested the power of belief to produce empirical phenomena:

> In the early 1970s, members of the Toronto Society for Psychical Research, under the direction of A.R.G. Owen, decided to try to manufacture a ghost. For this purpose, they invented the case history of a man called Philip, a contemporary of Oliver Cromwell, who had an affair with a beautiful gypsy girl. When Philip's wife found out, she had the girl accused of witchcraft and burned at the stake; Philip committed suicide.
>
> Having elaborated this story and created a suitable background — an ancient manor house — they set about trying to conjure up the spirit of Philip. For several months, there were no results. Then one evening, as they were relaxing and singing songs, there was a rap on the table. They used the usual code (one rap for yes, two for no), to question the 'spirit,' which claimed to be Philip, and repeated the story they had invented for him. At later séances, Philip made the table dance all around the room, and even made it levitate in front of TV cameras.

Using well-tried, sensational material, these scientists supposedly used a fiction to create objective sensory data. Wilson suggests that the ghost "*may* have been a manifestation of their collective unconscious minds," or it might just have been a different spirit that took on Philip's identity to amuse itself.[78] Either way, if this particular ghost story is "true," the belief encouraged by ghost fictions can open the door for the phenomena that the fictions help to qualify as real. This experiment suggests that the payoff of fiction-inspired belief could be the belief's substantiation. If the Gothic creates belief, and belief creates empirical reality, then the Gothic is more dangerous than eighteenth-century critics ever imagined.

6

Ghost Epistemology
Five or Six Ways to Haunt the Senses

Interpretation gives meaning to empirical data, and although sense-objects might exist independently from language, language facilitates the interpretive, perceptual process that makes empirical data meaningful.[1] As a result, sense-perception is vulnerable to the prejudices of experiences, expectations, and beliefs. By shaping beliefs, Gothic fictions won't necessarily shape the objective world beyond discourse (assuming such a thing has ontological validity), but within discourse they can shape the sensory perception that makes that world accessible. The discursive reality that Gothic fictions shape for ghosts also shapes the sensory reality that their percipients attribute to them.

Fictional ghost stories that achieve verisimilar authenticity, and true ghost stories that achieve actual authenticity, have the capacity to shape their readers' interpretations of sensory data. The sharing of conventions between fictional and true accounts — the fact that a reader might find ghostly phenomena described in the same ways on the pages of either — means that a difference in truth-labels may not equate to a difference in truth-value. Kate Ellis argues, "The Gothic in fiction ... is a set of conventions to represent what is not supposed to exist."[2] Both fictional and true ghost stories can tell readers what to expect if what is not supposed to exist actually does; the verisimilar and the actual can be equally informative. Images of ghosts in discourse — auditory, visual, olfactory, and tactile — tell people what to look for when they believe they are in a haunted place, and they explain how to know if an experience is really a ghost. Together, ghost stories classified as fictional and true lay out an epistemology grounded in empiricism. William Roll demonstrates the centrality of observational data in parapsychological research when, in his "Questionnaire for Poltergeist and Haunting Investigations," he emphasizes "unexplained sounds, sights, smells, and touches."[3] Troy Taylor defines true haunting as "the repeated manifestation of strange and inexplicable sensory phenomena at a certain location," marking unusual sensory experience as the essence of a ghostly encounter.[4] When, in "A Christmas Carol," Marley's ghost asks Scrooge, "'What evidence would you have of my reality beyond that of your own senses?'" he points toward the status of sensory experience as the ultimate verifier of a phenomenon's reality.[5] According to both fictional and true accounts, even though empirical data might not be the primary way to attain knowledge about the supernatural, the best knowledge about real ghosts comes from the senses.

Marley's ghost, seeing Scrooge's hesitation, follows up, "'Why do you doubt your senses?'" and Scrooge replies:

> Because ... a little thing affects them. A slight disorder of the stomach makes them cheats. You may be an indigested bit of beef, a blot of mustard, a crumb of cheese, a fragment of an underdone potato. There's more of gravy than the grave about you, whatever you are![6]

With typical comic flair, Dickens represents the senses' limitations. While the senses might provide strong evidence of a thing's reality, dyspeptic and other disorders can derange them. When the narrator of Poe's "The Tell-Tale Heart" assures, "what you mistake for madness is but over-acuteness of the senses," he unwittingly suggests that madness and "over-acuteness" are, at least in this case, the same thing.[7] The narrator of Amelia B. Edwards's "Was it an Illusion?" foregrounds the unreliability of witness testimony by wondering, "Could I, in truth, no longer rely upon the testimony of my senses?" Like Poe's mad murderer, this narrator hinges the tension of two coexisting explanatory frameworks for ghostly phenomena on the senses' shortcomings.[8] Discussing the nature of real ghosts, Brandon warns potential ghost hunters, "They play tricks on the human senses," suggesting that physical and mental disorders are not the only reasons why sensory data merit scrutiny.[9] For many reasons, the senses share narrative testimony's capacity for deception. The same variables that inform the perception of narrative truth can inform the perception of empirical validity. Sensory and narrative authenticity both depend upon the standards of those who judge them.

A survey of the data drawn from reports about people's sensory experiences of ghosts reveals trends, norms that ghost researchers can use to measure the reliability of further data. Irwin explains "Phenomenological Characteristics of Apparitional Experiences":

> Apparitional experiences tend to be restricted to one or two sensory modalities. Green and McCreery (1975) report that of their cases 61 percent were in one modality only, with a further 25 percent limited to two senses. Most apparitional experiences are visual, 84 percent according to Green and McCreery ... a third have an auditory component, with 14 percent being a wholly auditory experience.[10]

The enlistment of norms to establish generalized characteristics of actual experiences suggests that conformity or deviation has consequences for judgments of an experience's "real" merit. A ghost researcher can more readily rely on a report of an experience that reflects the tendency for experiences of its type to occur in only "one or two sensory modalities" than on a report of an experience that deviates by claiming four or five types of sensory data. As Irwin's norms would predict, phenomena that affect a limited number of senses do appear in many verisimilar and actual ghost stories.

Not just any inexplicable sensation qualifies as a real ghost experience. Real or realistic ghost-sensing happens in particular ways, working in particular modalities according to particular rules. Sensory absences and sensory presences both factor into the authentic ghost experience, and distinctive absences and presences will factor into any reliable representation of ghosts, be it factual or fictional. Reflecting their own status as both present and absent, or lingering while departed, ghosts usually register to only part of the sensorium, combining the presence of one type of sense-data with the absence of another in a way that advertises their ghostliness. Each sense has significance in the manner it either provides or fails to provide data. Familiarity with enough ghost stories will allow thrill-seeking readers and truth-seeking researchers to anticipate how they will hear, see, smell, and feel ghosts in ways they will know to be real.

Hearing

Haunting sounds lie at the roots of both Gothic fiction and the modern habit of ghost-seeking. Knocking unaccompanied by other sensory stimuli was the principle manifestation of both the ghost on Cock Lane, which provided the cultural context ripe for *The Castle of Otranto*, and the ghost that haunted the Fox family, which fomented interest in ghosts into

Spiritualism. Knocking noises have been a mainstay of ghost stories ever since. In both of these cases, the knocks were purposeful. Using what would become the system that Colin Wilson calls "the usual code (one rap for yes, two for no)," both of these alleged ghosts managed to communicate sordid tales of unsolved murders.[11] In his true "Authentic Narrative of a Haunted House," Le Fanu, after noting the phenomenon's "resemblance to what we hear described of 'Spiritualism,'" describes a "knocking" with "this peculiarity, that it was always rhythmical, and, I think, invariably, the emphasis upon the last stroke."[12] Lytton includes "three slow, loud, distinct knocks" in "The Haunted and the Haunters," and both his story and Le Fanu's suggest (the latter somewhat facetiously) that the knocks pertain to a long-concealed crime.[13] The "Well-Authenticated Rappings" that Dickens satirizes in his story of that name tend to be sounds with substance; in Dickens's case that substance is again dyspepsia, but more often the substance relates to the reason for an actual haunting. Even the pointless phenomena heralded in true accounts that use the inverse construction strategy tend to be patterned: Wilson's "completely pointless" poltergeist case involved "tapping ... almost every night, and always at about ten o'clock."[14] Story after story depicts ghost knocks as regular and patterned, providing recognizable norms that the ghost-seeker can use to separate actual ghosts from merely suspicious sound.

Another common ghost sound is the "Phantom Footsteps" named by the framed story within Arlen's "The Gentleman from America." Wilson's pointless poltergeist followed its tapping noises with footsteps "loud and clear, like a man in leather shoes with solid heels, tramping loudly over the wooden floor."[15] "Unnaturally loud and distinct" footsteps pursue Barton in Le Fanu's ghost fiction "The Familiar," harbingers of the ghostly pursuit that culminates in Barton's death.[16] While not all ghost footsteps are part of a ghostly game of cat-and-mouse, like ghost knocks, they tend to communicate something that can range from the ghost's potential description ("a man in leather shoes") to the ghost's intention (murder). Too loud, too clear, or otherwise "unnaturally" specific, these noises communicate.

Some ghosts employ voices in their communications. Worrying about "incipient decay of the brain," the haunted man in M.R. James's "The Stalls of Barchester Cathedral" admits, "I hear voices," at least one that speaks "distinctly and with a peculiar emphasis."[17] Most ghosts that speak do so strangely; Wilson describes one as "incapable of polite conversation" and that on tape "sounds so breathless that he can only get out one word at a time."[18] Irwin devotes a section of his textbook to "the electronic voice phenomenon (EVP)," which is "voicelike sounds ... found on a magnetic tape when they had not been present on the occasion of the original recording ... generally ... faint, isolated, very brief and banal phrases or sentences."[19] EVP is the subject of the appropriately named 2005 film *White Noise* and shows up in the fictional television show *Supernatural*, the recent film *Paranormal Activity*, and the allegedly nonfictional *Ghost Hunters* shows. The titular phenomenon of Thomas Street Millington's ghost fiction "No Living Voice" involves a "groaning ... too dreadful, too intense, for human utterance."[20] Other ghost voices are better developed. In Lynne Sharon Schwartz's ghost fiction "Sound is Second Sight," a man's dead wife returns to him as a disembodied voice, which "talk[s] with him and [keeps] him company," but its appearance is subject to a dog's howling.[21] Whatever these voices communicate, some peculiarity distinguishes them from the mortal kind. Messages from beyond tend to sound unmistakably different from the messages of the living. Their difference authenticates them.

More often in fictional but occasionally in true tales, ghosts' aural communications perform the function of testimony, providing accounts of murders and other deeds that the witness's posthumous condition tends to grant the force of inarguable truth. Hamlet might question the revelations of the apparition that claims to be his father's ghost, but the suggestion that someone has opened the gates between worlds to let the ghost deliver his testimony makes the being's aura of authority greater than the merely paternal. Aural testimony by ghosts takes the form of knocks, as with the Fox family, the form of speech (usually less eloquent than *Hamlet*'s and sometimes downright impolite), and occasionally the form of music. Myers speculates that the singing in a true case he titles "A Musical Spirit" might have been motivated simply by a desire "to make its presence known."[22] Musical testimony about the reality of life after death is, in itself, a powerful thing; it gains even more power in M.R. James's short fiction "Martin's Close," in which reports of a murder victim's post-mortem singing help to convict her murderer. The "singular character of the evidence" in James's story might weaken its claim to legal authenticity, but it nevertheless underscores the meaningful potential of ghostly noise.[23] Stories such as Algernon Blackwood's "A Case of Eavesdropping" and Ambrose Bierce's "The Secret of Macarger's Gulch" depict ghosts who recreate in detail all the sounds that accompanied their murders, vividly telling and retelling their tragic tales.[24] *Haunted Heartland* provides a true account of ghosts producing "the sound of men fighting and a body falling to the floor," which some speculate is a "reenactment" of a murder whose victim's "name has been long forgotten."[25] In all of these cases, ghost sounds have a revelatory purpose, a testimonial concern with truth that reinforces their ghostly validity.

Sound's absence can be just as or even more useful than its presence in determining whether strange phenomena indicate the involvement of a real ghost. The narrator of Elizabeth Gaskell's "The Old Nurse's Story" remarks:

> It fairly made me tremble ... all the more, when I remembered me that, even in the stillness of the dead-cold weather, I had heard no sound of little battering hands upon the window-glass, although the Phantom Child had seemed to put forth all its force; and, although I had seen it wail and cry, no faintest touch of sound had fallen upon my ears.[26]

The noiselessness of the visual image makes the narrator "tremble" because its unexpectedness confirms the child as a Phantom. An eerie absence of sound accompanying a visual image alerts witnesses to a phenomenon's ghostly status quite frequently in ghost stories both true and fictional. The tell-tale absence of sound need not be a total silence. Bayless describes a policeman's "observation of considerable interest" that the stones that appeared in a mysterious rock-fall "made much less sound when they struck than normally expected," an observation that helps Bayless to justify the phenomenon's inclusion in his study of poltergeists.[27] Sounds that defy normal expectations by being present when they shouldn't be or absent when they should both qualify as evidence for ghosts, and thus they merit both study and chills.

Reversing the convention of footsteps with no visible walker like those in Le Fanu's "The Familiar," visible ghosts take noiseless steps so often that an anonymous 1887 poem called "Ghosts" generalizes in the voice of its titular subjects, "noiseless is our tread."[28] Sullivan cites a passage from Le Fanu's "Mr. Justice Harbottle" and comments, "The striking thing about this passage is that Le Fanu manages to make these figures both ghostly and physical ... not glide or float about like old-fashioned ghosts, but walk 'as living men do,' causing physical vibrations without making actual sounds."[29] In keeping with ghostly norms, one type of sensory data obeys physical laws, but one type of sensory data does not. Natural laws are both present and absent, and this present absence indicates the entity defined as present absence, the ghost.[30] Ghost noises and silences follow rules that announce their ghostly identities through their otherworldly logic of contradiction without cancellation.

Sight

Commenting on why Samuel Johnson was so anxious to see the Cock Lane ghost, Clery equates "the truth of seeing" with "the truth of empirical philosophy" and explains, "Sight was privileged above the other physical faculties in Locke's theory of mind to an extent that it became a metaphor for knowledge."[31] In one of Wilson's true conversion narratives, a woman encounters a visual apparition and goes from insisting that childish pranks must be behind certain strange phenomena to saying, "'You've got the devil in this house.'"[32] Sight, a metaphor for knowledge itself, creates and confirms belief more than other sensory mode. It resists misinterpretation: the narrator of Arthur Conan Doyle's "Playing with Fire" sees a ghostly vapor at a séance and knows it isn't a "delusion" because "all could see it."[33] Ogden states that even though photography "was less than a decade old when the Fox sisters first heard rappings ... it was only a matter of time before mediums began to use this new sensation as a tool to prove the existence of ghosts and spirits."[34] Pursuers of ghostly truth seek visual images, particularly those that recordings or multiple witnesses can confirm, as the ultimate proof of the real. Sight more than any other sense has the power to grant a phenomenon reality.

Sight's privileged relation to truth extends to a privileged relation to identity, and visual identification of someone as passed but present is identification of a ghost. Though Doyle and others frame sight as more reliable than other senses, it is not invulnerable. To combat the suggestion of delusion, many ghost stories describe visual apparitions with excessive detail "to make identification absolute."[35] A footprint's lack of the titular "Middle Toe of the Right Foot" in Ambrose Bierce's story confirms the footprint's maker to be the identically disfigured and deceased Gertrude, and in Dinah Maria Mulock's "M. Anastasius," a man knows he encounters "'no living man'" but his wife's dead uncle when he sees "'exactly the same face ... [with] the same mark — a scar, cross-shape, over one temple.'"[36] Ellen Wood (a.k.a. Mrs. Henry Wood) tips the scales toward reality in her fiction "Reality or Delusion?" with the climactic revelation that the story's ghost-seer has described the apparition to the narrator as wearing a "seal-skin cap tied over the ears and the thick grey coat buttoned up round him," and she could not have known when describing them that the man had already "died in these things."[37] Similarly, a true account in *Haunted Heartland* provides the description of a woman's burial outfit, which, unbeknownst to those who saw her, was the same they had "seen the ghost wearing ... fifty years after her death."[38] Impossibly known and impossibly precise visual data confirm that unexplained visual phenomena are ghosts.

There is no single visible attribute that identifies all ghosts as such, but there are recurring characteristics by which their percipients can know them. Taylor names a few of the most prominent in his description of real ghosts:

> Some reports say that they are white, mist-like forms that only resemble a person. They are sometimes transparent and you are able to see through them. In other cases, the ghosts are reported as appearing very life-like. In fact, witnesses sometimes mistake ghosts for living persons, at least until they vanish into the wall or disappear through a solid door![39]

Taylor's "until" represents ghosts' inevitable turn toward visual deviance. Ghosts can look exactly like non-ghosts *until* they do something that demonstrates their membership in a different order of being. Holzer quotes a woman's description of her mother's experience, "'Oh no, it looked just like someone of flesh and blood — until that last moment when she dissolved before Mother's eyes.'"[40] Mistiness, transparency, and dissolution characterize a great number of ghosts' visual manifestations; initial data might suggest normalcy *until* the ghost displays characteristics that are impossible for the living. The real ghost announces itself in Louisa Baldwin's "The Real and the Counterfeit" with impossible movements, "slowly gliding over the floor which its feet did not touch"; John Harwood's "Underground Ghost" suggests its unliving status with an image of motion's absence, standing "motionless as a statue."[41] Like the auditory, visual images of ghosts defy the laws of biology and physics, as Le Fanu notes in his "Authentic Narrative" when he recounts a shadow that "seemed to have no sort of relation to the position of the light ... in manifest defiance of the laws of optics."[42] As a rule, ghosts' images break the rules.

The ghost in Algernon Blackwood's short fiction "The Listener" supplies sensory data in an impossible sequence, building up images until the final visual revelation. It begins with isolated creaks and knocking noises, and then it adds a "cold and moist" touch, causing the narrator to conclude, "Two senses had been affected ... I could not believe that I had been deceived." The ghost then supplies a "fetid odour," brief glimpses of "a man's legs," and finally, near the story's end, a vision of its full, nauseating form.[43] After this climax, the permutations of sensory absences and presences end, and so does the action. Closing with some facts gathered later, the narrator confirms what the reader might have already guessed from the visual description, that the ghost had been a leper in life. Visual revelations provide climaxes for many ghost fictions; these climax apparitions turn the temporality of true accounts' "until" into a formal structure. The climactic moment of Charlotte Riddell's (a.k.a. Mrs. J.H. Riddell's) *The Uninhabited House* occurs when the narrator and his companion see "that which no man can behold unappalled," the apparition of a murdered man who, when he takes noiseless steps toward his murderer, the narrator's companion, frightens the murderer so much that he soon confesses and dies.[44] The ghost's visual manifestation brings forth a truth that can no longer be concealed, a revelation about a death that causes a death. The overwhelming, climactic power of the visual apparition reflects the power of sight to signify the truth and to provide the ultimate — and sometimes fatal — distinction between the living and the dead.

Smell

The "fetid odour" that precedes the climactic visual apparition in "The Listener" is one of many haunting scents in the history of ghost fiction. Scarborough argues that smells "seem less subjective than sights or sounds, and are not so conventionalized in ghostly fiction, hence ... they are unusually effective."[45] Ghost smells — particularly of the fetid and sulfurous varieties — are, in fact, highly conventionalized, and they are almost as common as visions in both fictional and true accounts. Unlike seeing, however, smelling is not necessarily believing. The sense of smell has a low rank in the traditional empirical order, so odors seem like unlikely and unconventional ways to demonstrate a ghost's reality. By claiming unconventionality in the same way that hauntings of modern, un-spooky homes claim unconventionality, smells seem antithetical to fiction and therefore more true. A playwright's insistence in Wilkie Collins's *The Haunted Hotel* that a "'terrible smell from an invisible ghost is a perfectly new idea'" lacks accuracy, but the suggestion of novelty gives the "strange doubly-blended odour" that eventually accompanies a ghost's visual appearance the effectiveness of inverse construction.[46] Like "apparition," "hallucination" usually implies the visual. Olfactory hallucinations do, of course, appear in the annals of behavioral science, but the relative obscurity of the nose's capacity for deceit combined with its data's unconventional appearance allows it to communicate a strong suggestion of objective existence.

Part of smell's strength comes from the way an odor such as the one in *The Haunted Hotel* tends to "spread its fetid exhalations."[47] Olfactory apparitions fill up a place, taking over, overwhelming their percipients more easily than their usually more localized visual counterparts. Wilson reports how a seventeenth-century poltergeist responded angrily to misguided attempts to pray by "leaving behind a disgusting sulphurous smell — presumably to imply it came from Hell."[48] An unavoidable stink can be a ghost's most potent weapon. Listing the unmistakable signs of haunting in a particular room in the West Virginia State Penitentiary, Brandon remarks, "The putrid stench of sulfur can fill the room making visitors gag and vomit."[49] The entire body responds to strong odors, offering testimony about smell's objective accuracy that exceeds the organ of sense. Odors invade the body; they are a ghost's way in. Through sickness the body sends one of its most undeniable messages that something *wrong* has come inside. Though almost always wrong or unnatural-seeming, ghost smells don't have to be intrinsically nasty. Any excessive smell can sicken, as the narrator of Ralph Adams Cram's fiction "No. 252 Rue M. Le Prince" illustrates when he describes the "odor of musk" attached to ghostly goo as "nauseating."[50] Ghosts emit perfume almost as often as sulfur. Wilson describes one case in which a "flower-like perfume ... indicated that the ghost was around."[51] Even a pleasant scent can offer distinct, insistent, and overwhelming evidence of a real encounter with a ghost.

Smells overwhelm by filling rooms and bodies, and while they indicate that a ghost is non-specifically "around," they can also communicate very specific information. An investigator in Nigel Kneale's short fiction "The Patter of Tiny Feet" interprets a "'kind of talc, gripe-watery, general baby smell'" as "'a poltergeisted maternal impulse,'" culling a meaning from the odor that helps him to develop a more general theory of the haunting.[52] The meanings of odors might stem from their general associations, as of baby smells with maternity, or they might stem from more personal associations. When in the presence of the supernatural, the narrator of E.F. Benson's "Bagnell Terrace" observes, "I was conscious that there was a stale, but aromatic, smell in the room that reminded me of the curious odour that hangs about an Egyptian temple." Drawing conclusions from the associations of his own memory, the narrator speculates that the disturbance might have been "the essence or spirit of one of those mysterious Egyptian cults."[53] Smells conjure the sorts of rooms one remembers them filling, and in doing so they provide the raw material for interpretation.

The greatest source of interpretive instruction offered by ghost smells might, however, lie in the absences of other types of sensory data that might help to explain them as something other than ghostly in origin. In his foreword to *The Mammoth Book of Haunted House Stories*, Peter Haining shares one of his experiences with actual ghosts. He describes an "unmistakable smell" of smoke that "seemed to have no identifiable source," and this absence helped him to conclude that the phenomenon "had no other explanation than yet another instance of the supernatural at work." The fact that the phenomenon was "smelled rather than ever being seen" deprived it of natural interpretability.[54] The absence of the other senses results in an absence of explanation, and the absence of explanation suggests the supernatural. Implying similar reasoning, a psychologist in Blackwood's fictional "The Wendigo" systematically explains away the strange impressions of sight and hearing as misperceptions, but he admits reluctantly, "'The only thing I find it uncommonly difficult to explain is — that — damned odour.'"[55] A smell must have some explanation, and if that explanation does not appear in complementary sense-data, then it might lie in the realm of ghosts.

Touch

Ghosts' intangibility is one of their most significant sensory absences. The visual characteristics of mistiness, transparency, and dissolution indicate ghostliness in part by implying a lack of touchable substance. After breaking phantasmal encounters into basic categories, Holzer notes, "The only thing these four categories of phenomena have indeed in common is their density: they *seem* three-dimensional and quite solid most of the time (though not always), but try to touch one, and your hand will go right through."[56] A visual apparition invites an attempt at touching, an attempt that most ghosts doom to failure. Irwin concisely describes the consequences of ghosts' want of solidity:

> Most attempts to touch an apparitional figure are unsuccessful but people who did so generally report their hand to have gone through the apparition. The figure may seem to pick up an object or to open a door when physically these have not been moved at all. Apparitions usually leave no physical traces such as footprints.[57]

Ghosts usually can't touch or be touched in the ways expected of human physicality, so a visual apparition that has this particular lack is much more likely to qualify as a ghost in the eyes of ghost hunters and parapsychologists. Ghosts do, however, have the ability to affect the tactile sense. Though not a specific property of a visual apparition's form, Irwin suggests that "close to the apparition a sensation of coldness may be felt," and Wilson states, "One of the commonest features of hauntings is a sudden feeling of coldness in the room."[58] Denied the living's methods of touch, ghosts access the tactile through alternate means.

Causing sensations of cold allows haunters to touch the haunted in a way more definitive than a slap or a punch. In Shirley Jackson's *The Haunting of Hill House*, the house's intended victim, Eleanor, describes her encounter with a "vicious cold," "'I felt it as *deliberate*, as though something wanted to give me an unpleasant shock.'"[59] Ghostly cold communicates the ghost's personality and intentions, which in the case of Hill House, though not in all cases, are profoundly evil. Cold allows the phenomenon's percipient to know the ghost, and, in the case of Jean Rhys's fiction "I Used to Live Here Once," it also helps a ghost to know itself. When the arms of Rhys's ghost reach "out instinctively with the longing to touch" a child, the child says, "'Hasn't it gone cold all of a sudden,'" and that is "the first time" the ghost knows that she has died.[60] A ghost's cold touch signifies the cold of death and can convey the horror of its condition as well as the horrors it threatens for those it haunts.

A ghost's ability to access the tactile sometimes goes beyond mere drops in temperature. With a slimy texture familiar to many from Ivan Reitman's *Ghostbusters* (1984), the ghostly goo known as ectoplasm, the appearance of which during séances Irwin explains as "a substance allegedly issued from the body of the medium," provides a way for ghosts to leave a lasting physical impression.[61] One of the most horrific moments in the film *The Haunting in Connecticut* (2009), which purports to be based on a true story, depicts a black cloud of ectoplasm emerge from a child medium's mouth. The ectoplasm signals the spirits' invasion, which is ghastlier because the invasion is a physical violation, a malicious touching of the child's body.[62]

Ghosts' power to touch can allow them to manipulate objects as well as people. Many accounts both true and fictional describe invisible ghosts, often poltergeists, who cause objects to move visibly, as if by themselves. According to Irwin, "One of the most common features of poltergeist activity is the movement of objects."⁶³ The inverse of the intangible visual apparition, the invisible poltergeist has manipulative powers that become tactile when they focus on a living body. *Haunted Heartland* describes a haunted restaurant where a waitress who "scoffed at ghost tales ... quickly became a believer in the supernatural" after "her ponytail shot straight up in the air ... remained upright a moment, dropped limply and again was yanked up ... when no one else was around."⁶⁴ Since no one was around to provide a non-paranormal explanation, these phenomena suggest a poltergeist with the ability to grab, lift, pull, and otherwise create tactile sensations. The waitress's conversion reflects on the convincing power of a tactile sensation most easily explained by a ghost's involvement.

H.P. Lovecraft associates M.R. James's disturbing realism with the fact that his typical ghost is "usually *touched* before it is *seen*."⁶⁵ Though the combination of these two sensory modalities is rare, as Charles Willing Beale writes in his novel *The Ghost of Guir House*, "when the sense of sight is corroborated ... what *better* evidence have we of the existence of those things we are all agreed to call real?"⁶⁶ A ghost's touch corroborates the reality of its visual image, and it also makes a strong impression on its own. Noting cold, heat, and other tactile sensations that ghosts might cause, Scarborough comments, "Seeing a supernatural visitant is terrible, hearing him is direful, smelling him is loathsome, but having him touch you is the climax of horror."⁶⁷ Though seeing a ghost more often has the force of a narrative climax, Scarborough's point about the insuperable horror of experiencing the touch of the dead points to the way touch, like smell, carries the strength of objectivity. It also carries more than any other sense the suggestion of a being with the capacity to do physical harm. Pinching is supposed to help a person know whether what she or he sees is real or a dream; pain indicates the possibility that an experience could have lasting consequences. Ontological uncertainty evaporates when the flesh senses danger. Potentially the most horrifying of the senses, touch can be the most compelling arbiter of reality.

The Sixth Sense

Psychic powers have intimate associations with ghostly realities. Mediums such as *Poltergeist*'s Tangina Barrons use their special link to the world beyond to bring forth evidence of ghosts in many ghost stories.

Holzer takes mediums with him on almost every one of his real-life ghost-hunting expeditions, causing most paranormal investigators not to "consider him a serious researcher."[68] Clairvoyance, psychokinesis, and other mental abilities apparently not possessed by the majority of human beings fill more pages of current parapsychological studies than ghosts do; RSPK and other theories often appear to replace the survival hypothesis. Irwin defines extrasensory perception, ESP, as "direct apprehension of information by the mind ... *not* via the usual sensory channels."[69] The world of psychics is elite, but according to this broad definition, just about anyone could have an ESP experience, and according to many ghost stories, one need not "see dead people" like the special little boy in M. Night Shyamalan's *The Sixth Sense* (1999) to have an extra sense of the dead.[70] Story after story assures regular people that they can perceive ghosts while data from all of the usual sensory channels are notably absent.

No distinct, universally-recognized name exists for the most common way of perceiving a ghost without using the five conventional senses. In one case Holzer refers to regular people having "the intangible feeling of a presence" and "the uncanny feeling that they were not alone."[71] Holzer's use of the definite article in these descriptions of "the feeling" gestures towards its apparent universality. Common wisdom associates a particular strangeness with feelings of being not alone or of being watched that are not corroborated by the usual senses. This feeling is *that* feeling, describable only by ambiguous, negative adjectives such as "intangible" and "uncanny." After the description of the Egyptian odor, the narrator of Benson's "Bagnell Terrace" states, "I knew, by what sixth sense I cannot tell, that I was not alone in the room and that the presence there was no human presence."[72] The number six in "sixth sense," as it appears here to describe the strange sense of a presence that Holzer calls by other names, distinguishes the sense from the other five by suggesting that those five have contributed nothing to it. The nomination of the sixth automatically implies the absence of the other five; it is the sixth because it is not the other five just as ESP is extra because it is "not via the usual sensory channels." Benson's narrator has a negatively defined sixth sense that tells him not only of a presence but that the presence is not human, suggesting that the mind has an extrasensory mode of perception specifically designed for ghosts, present absences, walking negations. Vaguely formulated in these accounts, "the feeling" equates with ghostly presence. The feeling is a ghost's special way of making itself known.

Taste

Ghosts have other ways of making themselves known that go beyond the usual senses. They can appear in dreams. Le Fanu's "The Haunted Baronet" and Bierce's "The Death of Halpin Frayser," two examples from fiction out of many, both depict ghosts exerting their influence on the world while people sleep.[73] Myers offers a true account of a woman who asked a relative why she was having dreams about their dead cousin and heard in reply that "this was the dead woman's way of communicating from the other side," an explanation that this woman's experiences and many other accounts both true and fictional support.[74] Ghosts can also make themselves known by disturbing a non-human animal, as Scarborough explains: "Animals are supposed to be peculiarly sensitive to ghostly impressions, more so than men, and the appearance of a specter is often first announced by the extreme horror of some house-hold pet, or other animal."[75] The dog in *Poltergeist* occasionally acts as an early warning system for ghostly manifestations, as do many other animals in many other ghost narratives. If each of these modes of perception counted as senses, there would be a seventh sense, an eighth, and possibly more. But what about the *fifth* sense — what about taste?

In her 1917 study Scarborough comments, "The taste as a medium of impression has not yet been exploited by fiction writers though doubtless it will be worked out soon." She offers some amusing suggestions for what ghost fictions about taste might include, including a rather grisly idea "that gastronomic ghosts might haunt cannibals," but she can cite no concrete examples of how ghosts appear to the taste.[76] There are enough ghost stories in and out of print to fill a lifetime of volumes, and one or more of them may have covered the spectral flavor, but in 2010, that flavor has not yet become conventional. The conventions of fictional and real ghost stories establish rules for ghost epistemology, and as a conglomerate they can act as a guide, making suggestions by which people can choose or not choose to shape their expectations for the world and their definitions of the real. Since acceptance or rejection of this guidance ultimately becomes a matter of personal judgment, the reality of ghosts depends on another kind of taste, the ineffable basis of human distinctions. Predisposed toward the Gothic, some readers are also predisposed toward belief. Both truth-seekers and thrill-seekers, these readers can go through fictional and non-fictional norms for ghosts like they can go through their libraries, carefully selecting the foundations of their realities.

Part Four
Gothic Violence

7

Fictions That Kill
Columbine, Virginia Tech, and Stephen King's Only Out-of-Print Novel

On April 20, 1999, Eric Harris and Dylan Klebold murdered thirteen people at Columbine High School in Littleton, Colorado. The teenage shooters also killed themselves. At the end of 2009, the event continues to haunt American culture. Around the ten-year anniversary, a new group of publications offered new perspectives on the tragedy, and this chapter will pay particular attention to three of them: Dave Cullen's *Columbine* reframes the circumstances surrounding the shootings, Jeff Kass's *Columbine: A True Crime Story* provides a narrative account with excruciating detail, and Peter Langman's *Why Kids Kill: Inside the Minds of School Shooters* puts Harris and Klebold in context with similar criminals in order to arrive at a broader understanding of the motivations and tendencies behind such crimes.

No account of the Columbine story would be complete without some mention of the Gothic subculture initially associated with the killers and, as a result, repeatedly attacked by an array of politicians and pundits. As Carol Siegel observes in *Goth's Dark Empire*, "The press erroneously, and very insistently, attributed the tragedy to the Goth subculture," and "as a result of the moral panic that followed, anyone with the slightest interest in youth cultures ... has probably heard of Goths by now."[1] Even though Cullen and others have successfully dispelled the myth that Harris and Klebold were part of their school's Goth subculture, for some, Columbine seems to have fulfilled the prophecies of eighteenth-century critics who warned that Gothic influences could corrupt the young and cause violent disturbances of social order. Columbine is, in this sense, a Gothic event.

Because they have influenced the construction of "homosexuality" and "real" ghosts, Gothic fictions have, in a sense, caused homosexuality and ghosts to be in the ways that they are. Homosexuality would not be a thing associated with pathological reproduction in the way that it is if Gothic fictions had not contributed significant dimensions of those associations. If, however, Gothic fictions contributed to the event called Columbine, to the deaths of fifteen people, claims about causality become far more serious. The power to shape a social construction is formidable, but it lacks the directness and urgency of the power to kill. This chapter explores debates about media violence, charting a shift from a tendency to blame specific sources—especially violent entertainment—for large-scale tragedies to rhetoric emphasizing complex causality. This emphasis on complexity, which crystallized around the tragic shootings that took 32 lives at Virginia Tech in 2007, appears most clearly in accounts of tragedies that use the conventions of narrative fiction—especially, but not exclusively, Gothic conventions—to represent and interpret events. The writers who adopt this narrativizing tendency don't simply suggest that the Gothic causes violent realities: they suggest that the Gothic is reality, and reality is Gothic.

Columbine and Debates about Media Violence

Did the Gothic cause Columbine? Many people asked this question in the days following the massacre, and the question's urgency propelled Columbine into the center of contemporary debates about the effects of media violence. The April 22, 1999, edition of London's *Independent* newspaper features an article by David Aaronovitch with the headline "All-American Gothic; Columbine High: A Suburban Horror Story." An article from the same day by Bill Hutchinson, K.C. Baker, and Virginia Breen in New York's *Daily News* claims that Harris and Klebold "embraced a warped version of doom-and-gloom Gothic culture." An article in the April 27 issue of *The Ottawa Citizen* refers to how Columbine's shooters acted out "the crude imaginings of a 'gothic fantasy'"; the author, Graeme Hunter, frames the event in these terms to justify his belief that schools need to teach better literary and moral values. In 1995, U.S. Senator Bob Dole, then Bill Clinton's rival for the presidency, warned that "popular culture shapes [children's] view of the 'real world'" and that violent popular culture "threatens to undermine our character as a nation."[2] Dave Grossman and Gloria DeGaetano begin their 1999 book *Stop Teaching Our Kids to Kill: A Call to Action Against TV, Movie and Video Game Violence* by quoting a statement that President Bill Clinton made less than two months after Columbine: "Kids steeped in the culture of violence do become desensitized to it and more capable of committing it themselves."[3] After Columbine, rival American leaders agreed that violent, Gothic fictions corrupt children and shape the horrors of their crimes. The Gothic causes these crimes to be in the ways that they are, and thus, some critics reason, it deserves censure.

Blaming the Gothic for threatening America's stability in the twenty-first century relies on the same mode of thinking that blamed the Gothic for social upheavals in the eighteenth century: the Gothic supposedly has the power to exert a negative influence on impressionable minds. Contemporary claims about violent art attach culpability to this corrosive influence, and in order to give their blame specificity, they condemn particular artworks and artists who have supposedly exerted such influence. In 1997, Senator Joseph Lieberman — who ran unsuccessfully for the office of Vice President in 2000 — targeted the "vile, hateful, and nihilistic music" of Goth rocker Marilyn Manson in a tirade about the damage done by media violence.[4] After Columbine, many Gothic works, including the television show *Buffy the Vampire Slayer,* fell under attack, but as Gavin Baddeley observes, "The face that rose to the fore during this frenzy was that of Marilyn Manson."[5] Michael Moore interviews Manson in his 2002 documentary *Bowling for Columbine,* and when asked about why he received so much negative attention, Manson explains that he was an easy target because he is "a poster boy for fear."[6] Seeking the sources for Manson's fearsome presence, Baddeley traces elements of Manson's music all the way back to *The Castle of Otranto*.[7] Manson's alleged blameworthiness relates directly to his Gothicness. Baddeley describes Manson's reactions to the flurry of accusations against him:

> The year 2000 was not easy for Marilyn Manson. "I was attacked and felt everybody wanted to destroy me," he lamented, even after it was confirmed that the two perpetrators of the Columbine massacre were not Manson fans at all. "I thought, 'Hey, maybe now they'll call the dogs off,' but actually it had the opposite effect."[8]

Although Kass suggests that Dylan Klebold had a poster of Manson on his bedroom wall, no one has established any direct connection between Manson's Goth music and Harris and Klebold's actions.[9] Despite the lack of a clear connection, the very existence of Manson's work, and Manson's status as a poster boy for fear, made him subject to retributive attacks.

Critics who oppose media violence because of its corrosive influence describe the effects of that influence in a way that makes clear connections to particular artworks unnecessary for blaming them. The undermining of "character" that Bob Dole pins on media violence suggests that violent fictions do their work on the abstract level of normative ideals: the nation's character is the image it projects of itself, the image toward which children must aspire, and a surfeit of violent art taints that image. In his book *Hollywood Vs. America: Popular Culture and the War on Traditional Values*, Michael Medved summarily states that "the power of the entertainment industry to influence our actions flows from its ability to redefine what constitutes normal behavior in this society." His ideas about the normative power of entertainment support his general indictment of Hollywood, the center of the American film industry: "The dream factory has become the poison factory."[10] W. James Potter's *The 11 Myths of Media Violence* also rails against the norms supported by the entertainment industry:

> The body of research clearly shows that when people are exposed to violent portrayals in the media, they are more likely to behave in an aggressive manner when given an opportunity immediately following the exposure ... The belief in a connection between exposure to media violence and negative effects now seems intuitively obvious, akin to other beliefs that seem intuitively obvious to us, such that criticism of the belief seems unreasonable.[11]

The media teach people how to behave, and in views such as Potter's, violent media teach them to behave badly.

Potter calls disagreement with his view of the media's normative influence "unreasonable" because he has a "body of research" to back him up. His vehemence about the obviousness of his claim seems inadvertently to acknowledge that this body of research, though substantial, has yet to achieve definitive empirical proof that violent media cause aggressive behavior. In his 2002 study *Media Violence and Its Effect on Aggression: Assessing the Scientific Evidence*, Jonathan L. Freedman cites various organizations that claim thousands of conclusive studies support the idea that media violence causes aggression and remarks that "they must not read the research because there are not anywhere near that many studies." Freedman devotes the majority of his book to reviewing the studies that have been done, and he systematically debunks the evidence that supposedly supports the "causal hypothesis." After this review, with less dogmatism but confidence equal to Potter's, Freedman states, "exposure to media violence does not cause aggression, or if it does the effects are so weak that they cannot be detected and therefore must be vanishingly small."[12]

Those on Potter's side of the media violence debate can rebut Freedman's view of the data with arguments about how absolute certainty is nearly impossible in the social sciences, and those on Freedman's side can rebut those rebuttals. For example, Karen Sternheimer's 2003 book, polemically titled *It's Not the Media: The Truth about Pop Culture's Influence on Children*, chastises those who blame Marilyn Manson and other countercultural influences, calling the reaction to Manson "a great example of how fears of music enable worried adults, parents, and politicians to blame music for a grab bag of social problems." She goes further, warning that "ultimately the fear of bands like Marilyn Manson promotes ostracizing and further alienating many young outcasts."[13] In other words, the condemnations of the violent media that help youth sub(counter)cultures — including Goths — to define themselves might contribute to the very outcomes that anti-violence pundits fear. Gerard Jones encapsulates this perspective: "Adult anxieties about the effects of entertainment are sometimes the real causes of the very effects that we fear most."[14]

Voices like Sternheimer's and Jones's, however, remain in the minority. Scholars in psychology and sociology continue to report findings that link media violence to aggression. Without direct reference to Freedman or others like him, George Comstock, in an article published in the journal *The American Behavioral Scientist* in 2008, looks at an aggregate of studies and argues "the aggregations provide a strong and sufficient reply to the critics of any one or several studies" and concludes "the joint outcomes of experimental and survey designs make a strong case for causation."[15] The centrality of these empirical studies in the contemporary debate about violent media indicates a change from the form of the debates about the Gothic in the eighteenth century. Whereas critics such as Coleridge and Mathias relied primarily on religious authority to bolster their calls for social and legal action against violent art, critics such as Medved and Potter rely on the authority of science, an authority based on the interpretation of data that offer no judgments themselves.

Religion has not disappeared entirely from the debate. Graeme Hunter's article in *The Ottawa Citizen* segues from framing Columbine as an enactment of "gothic fantasy" to lamentations about cultural attacks on "the Christian ethic of character and responsibility." Phil Phillips and Joan Hake Robie, authors of an assault on media violence called *Horror and Violence: The Deadly Duo in the Media*, mount their entire argument in order to "'bring glory to the Lord and lift up the body of Christ.'"[16] Nevertheless, most attacks on media violence in the contemporary debate, including that of Phillips and Robie, ground whatever ethical and/or religious agendas they may have in allusions to scientific proof. The participation of "science" as such allows for the medicalization of fictional violence's corrosive influence. Fictional violence not only spreads "poison," a term that Medved uses in an echo (likely unconscious) of Coleridge's representation of *The Monk* as a source of illness, but it is literally a disease, "The Number *One* Health Threat in America Today," according to the subtitle of the *Media Violence Alert* published by the Center for Successful Parenting.[17]

In the *Alert*, which includes writings from some of the leading scholars in the anti-violence camp, the medical often slides into the pseudo-medical. John Nelson, a trustee of the American Medical Association, refers to "young people ... suffering the effects of couch potato syndrome and brain-drain," letting the word "syndrome" dress up language expressing conventional rather than medical wisdom. More poignantly, Dave Grossman grants the desensitizing effects of media violence mentioned by Clinton the name "AVIDS — Acquired Violence Immune Deficiency [Syndrome]," a name that conjures one of the deadliest epidemics in human history, borrows its medical legitimacy, and uses it to amplify the fearfulness of the media's threat.[18] The similarity between AIDS and AVIDS suggests a parallel: just as some homophobic leaders have called AIDS a symbol and proper punishment for homosexual decadence, *Stop Teaching Our Kids to Kill* suggest that AVIDS and its result, Columbine, are emblems of "what the National Funding Collaborative on Violence Prevention refers to as our 'culture of violence.'"[19] Like the medical dimension of the form of pathological reproduction attributed to the influence of homosexuality, the medicalization of media violence's supposed influence would allow its critics' "call to action" to marshal support for eradicating the influence's source. In debates about both sexuality and media violence, controlling the language of science means controlling the language of power.

The battle for the strongest claim to scientific authority, epitomized by Medved, Potter, and Grossman on one side and Sternheimer, Jones, and Freedman on the other, hinges on the definition of "causality." Critics on Grossman's side of the debate usually don't hesitate to claim that fictional violence causes aggression and real-life crimes. Freedman, on the other hand, emphasizes that, though some scientific studies do show correlations between exposure to media violence and increased aggressiveness, "correlations do not indicate causality."[20] Furthermore, as Comstock explains, "Laboratory-type experiments, of course, permit causal inference, but by themselves they are unsatisfying in this instance because their results do not clearly project to circumstances outside the laboratory." Thus, to support his claims about causation, Comstock refers to a combination of laboratory tests that support causality and field observations that strongly support correlation, arguing "individual studies supply the evidence that there is no convincing alternative explanation that wholly accounts for the correlation."[21]

The word "wholly" here is the key: though politicians' finger-pointing in the aftermath of Columbine was often simplistic, the scientific literature arguing for a causal relationship in recent years has strengthened its position through increasing references to complexity, admissions that media violence may be only part of the problem and may not act as a causal agent by itself. The concession that media violence could be only part of a complex whole keeps arguments that demonstrate other possible causes from necessarily weakening arguments blaming media violence. Potter explains this position in relation to Columbine:

> It seems like every person has his or her favorite target of blame. All of these positions are right, and they are all wrong. They are all right in the sense that these factors are likely to have contributed to the shootings—at least we cannot rule any out completely. However, they are all wrong in asserting that one factor is to blame and the others are not. The process of influence that leads up to the manifestation of a negative effect is constructed from many factors.[22]

In other words, violent fiction might not necessarily produce the real-life effect of violence by itself, but in conjunction with other forces, it might make a significant contribution to the effect's emergence. Providing more rigorous support for Potter's insight, recent publications in scientific journals by Brad J. Bushman, L. Rowell Huesmann, Paul Boxer, and others begin with references to meta-analyses that confirm a causal relationship between violent media exposure and aggression.[23] These publications then build on the foundation provided by that confirmation, arguing for differentiations between short-term and long-term effects and for ways to include violent media in analysis of broader risk factors for violent behavior. This trend in arguments linking media exposure to violence and aggression is important for two reasons: first, it represents an effort to move beyond the question of whether a causal relationship exists, taking its existence as a given, and second, it provides ways to approach and analyze multiple causation, reaffirming the idea that media violence is only one factor among many in the complex process that results in violent behavior.

Brooks Brown, a high school friend of Harris and Klebold, taps into this rhetoric of complexity in his book *No Easy Answers: The Truth Behind Death at Columbine*. Published in 2002, a year before Potter's *11 Myths of Media Violence*, *No Easy Answers* offers a distinction that supports a position quite different from Potter's: "I won't dispute the idea that some of the elements in [Harris and Klebold's] plan were derived from video games. What I disagree with is the notion that video games *caused* the shootings — as well as most of the rest of the violence that takes place in America." Brown's separation of causation from "elements ... derived from" violent media suggests resistance to the sort of retrospective causality described in this book's introduction, and his outright rejection of a causal relationship distances his view from Potter's.[24] Nevertheless, he makes an impassioned argument for complexity:

> After all, what's the easier sell for a politician: to go out there and tell people they've screwed up, that they need to take better care of their kids, that they've created an ugly, uncaring society for the next generation, and that we need to search our own souls for a solution?
> Or just tell them that the evil entertainment industry is ruining our kids?

Brown frames Harris and Klebold as products of their society, of a whole host of social factors that go far beyond violent entertainment, which he sees as a reflection of "violent culture in and of itself."[25]

Emphasis on multiple or complex cultural causation, seeded in both popular and scientific discourses by works like Brown's and Potter's, gradually became dominant in the years following Columbine, causing a change in how people respond to and represent real-world violence. In the immediate aftermath of Columbine, the finger-pointing at violent media led a movie production company to change the title of a film about kids taking revenge against a teacher from *Killing Mrs. Tingle* to *Teaching Mrs. Tingle*, seeming to concede that something as simple as a movie's title might cause violent behavior.[26] This simplistic thinking continued in the political realm as, in 2005, Hillary Clinton, Joe Lieberman, and Evan Bayh introduced the "Family Entertainment Protection Act," which reveals the lingering impact of earlier scientific statements about causality. The act sought to

> limit the exposure of children to violent video games [because] experimental research and longitudinal research conducted over the course of decades shows that exposure to higher levels of violence on television, in movies, and in other forms of media in adolescence causes people in the short-term and, after repeated exposure, even years later to exhibit higher levels of violent thoughts, anti-social and aggressive behavior, fear, anxiety, and hostility, and desensitization to the pain and suffering of others.[27]

The bill never made it out of committee, and although a similar bipartisan bill failed to get out of committee in 2006, in mid-2010, no similar bills are in circulation. Whether the failures of these bills stem from a rejection of simplistic causal connections between media and real violence is unclear, but the failures do suggest decreasing interest in simple claims about causality. For whatever reason, most politicians seem to have stopped telling the American people that the entertainment industry is single-handedly ruining their kids.

Filling the space left by the abandonment of simple finger-pointing, a different approach emerged in the works of Cullen, Kass, and Langman. Langman's approach in *Why Kids Kill: Inside the Minds of School Shooters* is perhaps the most traditional of these three books published around the ten-year anniversary of the Columbine shootings, but he nevertheless builds his investigation on the claims that "Rampage attacks are too complex to be attributed to any one cause" and that "there is no simple connection between media violence and murder."[28] To fathom this complexity, Langman provides case studies of ten individuals involved in eight different school shootings between 1997 and 2007. The case studies divide the individuals into categories — psychopathic shooters, psychotic shooters, and traumatized shooters — and tells each individual's story in ways that reveal the underlying psychological factors that led to his (they're all male) crimes.

The motif of storytelling to fathom complexity is even more formative for Cullen's totalizingly titled *Columbine* and Kass's genre-tagging *Columbine: A True Crime Story*. In his introductory note on sources, Cullen refers repeatedly "the story" his book tells, positing his mission as "setting the story right." The book begins and ends with rich description, and it often presents events with dialogue and other elements characteristic of narrative fiction. Cullen's style oscillates between pure narrative and reflective reporting and does not spare sensational, gory details, as in this description of Harris and Klebold's suicides:

> Eric raised the shotgun barrel to his mouth, like the antihero of [Nine Inch Nails's album] *The Downward Spiral*. Dylan pointed the TEC-9 at his left temple … Eric fired through the roof of his mouth, causing "evacuation of the brain." He collapsed against the books, and his torso slumped to the side. He ended that way, with his arms curled forward, as if hugging an invisible pillow.[29]

This brief passage provides one bloody detail, "'evacuation of the brain,'" with quotation marks signaling forensic reporting, alongside sympathizing, poetic description, "arms curled forward, as if hugging an invisible pillow," with "as if" signaling metaphoric, authorial imagination.

This sort of imaginative juxtaposition is even more pervasive in Kass's work, which also provides dialogue and a wealth of direct evidence from the writings of the killers, the victims, and others affected by the tragedy. Kass fragments the narrative, beginning with the massacre as a hook and returning to it repeatedly as he explores the event's precursors and aftermath. His style is comparable to Cullen's:

> Harris points a gun under the table. He fires two rounds of pellets. Nowlen is injured, and a shotgun pellet grazes Tomlin's chest. Nowlen thinks Tomlin jumps out from under the table to avoid being hit by a second gunshot. He lands on his stomach. Klebold stands over him and finishes off his life with four shots from the TEC-DC9. Nowlen's legs are now touching Tomlin's. His legs shake, then stop a moment later. … "Who is under the table?" Harris asks.[30]

Like Cullen, Kass provides forensic details, such as numbers of shots and pellets as well as the gun model TEC-DC9, and he quotes dialogue in ways that suggest direct borrowing from historical sources. Using novelistic indirect discourse, Kass gives the reader access to the thoughts of Nowlen, who survived and could provide testimony, but not Tomlin, who died in the attack; thus the dramatic language remains verifiable. Also like Cullen, Kass provides gory details, such as the death twitching of Tomlin's leg; the story is a true crime story, so violent that it borrows from the excesses of the Gothic. The biggest difference between Kass's and Cullen's styles might be Kass's use of the present tense, which abandons the sense of reflective reporting in order to give the reader an experience of the horror that feels first-hand. Significantly, the back covers of both Cullen's and Kass's books compare the works to Truman Capote's *In Cold Blood*. The styles of these books, presenting nonfiction with fictional flair, mark a significant passage for the history of Columbine: after ten years, it had become a literary, Gothic event.

Narrativizing and the Tragedy at Virginia Tech: Seung-Hui Cho's Horror Story

In *Nightmare on Main Street: Angels, Sadomasochism, and the Culture of Gothic*, a book published prior to the Columbine massacre, Mark Edmundson observes a narrativizing trend in American news media, commenting in detail on how the media presented the O.J. Simpson murder trial and other major events of the 1990s in ways that seem to come straight out of eighteenth-century Gothic novels.[31] While the narrative qualities of the O.J. Simpson coverage might have served primarily to sensationalize the case further and thus attract more viewers and readers for the media, the narrativizing tendencies of Cullen's and Kass's, and to a lesser extent Langman's, works serve a different purpose. After ten years of politicians and pundits trying to reduce Columbine to comprehensible, numerable causes, the narrative approach accommodates the complexity that more and more commentators began to emphasize as the years passed. Presenting Columbine and events like it as stories to be told, rather than effects to be traced back to causes, allows room for multiple interpretations. In the classic model of mimetic art, narrativizing holds a mirror up to nature and allows onlookers to observe the complexity of the world, judging it themselves.

Though it doesn't directly identify its narrative with Columbine, Gus Van Sant's *Elephant* (2003), a controversial, fictional film about high school that climaxes with Columbine-like shootings, provides a paradigmatic example of this mimetic approach. Van Sant's point-of-view camera takes turns following characters, whose names initially appear as titles on dark screens that announce shifts in perspective, through what seems like an ordinary day in an ordinary high school. Though a few stylistic, third-person shots appear, the film consists almost entirely of first-person camerawork, making the film's representation of events pointedly subjective. To emphasize the complexity of subjective experience, the film shows several seemingly common events — such as a boy passing a group of girls in the school hallway — multiple times, each from a different character's point of view. Through the course of its wanderings around the school, the camera picks up many of the phenomena pointed to as possible causes for Columbine, including irresponsible parents, bullying, sexual repression (both hetero- and homo-), and social ostracism. The film even provides a shot of one of the killers playing a first-person shooter video game, blend-

Top: Elephant (2003) shows a school shooter playing a video game. This pixilated image foreshadows a clearer image from an almost identical perspective on the shootings that occur at the film's climax. *Above: Elephant* (2003) provides a first-person shot almost identical to the perspective of a video game that appears earlier in the film. Though the visual correlation is strong, the film foregoes blame in favor of multi-perspective narrative.

ing the game's perspective with its own. Through this relentless subjectivity, *Elephant* posits everything and nothing as causes for its Columbine-like conclusion. The multiplicity of perspectives suggests the complexity of the seemingly ordinary, showing the high school world itself as host and generator of the film's violent climax.[32]

Emphasis on complexity and multiple causation also pervades the reports and narratives that attempted to process the tragedy that occurred April 16, 2007 at Virginia Tech. Finger-pointing at the media was notably rare. On April 28, 2007, Josh Korr published an article in *The St. Petersburg Times* entitled "Finally, Pop Culture Escapes Blame." The article celebrates Korr's observation that not every report on the tragedy included "a lazy attempt to link Seung-Hui Cho's rampage to some pop culture influence" and editorializes, "Accepting that there are no single causes for a mass shooting can be hard."

Of course the press didn't avoid finger-pointing altogether. On April 20, London's *Daily Telegraph* ran a feature by Gerald Kaufman titled "Questions film-makers must ask themselves after Virginia Tech," which leads with the claim, "The most chilling aspect of the Virginia Tech massacre is that is perpetrator, Cho Seung-hui, a South Korean, was directly inspired by a recent South Korean splatter movie, *Oldboy*." The evidence of this direct inspiration is strong: on the day of his rampage, Cho sent pictures of himself in weapon-clad poses modeled after *Oldboy* (2003) to NBC. Though Kaufman is certainly didactic in his encouragement of filmmakers to "accept that they have a wider responsibility," he also ends his tirade with the caveat, "we should not pretend that either here or in America there is a simple solution," dampening his blame of the media with the rhetoric of complexity.

This dampening is telling: whereas attacks on Marilyn Manson continued for years even after the connection between his music and the Columbine killers was disproved, the outcry against *Oldboy* was muted almost immediately. Within the Anglo/white perspective that dominates American and British news media, the Korean identities of both Cho and *Oldboy*, which Kaufman emphasizes unnecessarily, might have kept the Virginia Tech shootings from seeming as all–American as Columbine and thus, following racist logic, less important. However, race alone seems insufficient to explain the almost immediate retreat from simplistic finger-pointing at the media for Cho's crimes. The decrease in finger-pointing signals a transformation of the causal agency attributed to media violence.

The specific aspects of this transformation observable in the response to the tragedy at Virginia Tech stem at least in part from ambivalence regarding Cho's self-conscious citations of media influences. By sending the press a "multimedia manifesto" rife with film allusions, Cho seemed to beg for people to correlate his crimes with fiction. The response to Cho's self-photos and videos is virtually uniform in correlating specific images with *Oldboy* and other films, but news reporters' confidence in linking the crimes themselves to works of fiction varies. On April 20, 2007, three newspapers provided a spectrum of opinion about such a link: London's *The Independent* noted that "some have dismissed the connection as 'the most ridiculous hypothesis yet,' saying there was no apparent link between Cho and *Oldboy* besides the lone photograph among the 28 video clips, 23-page written message and 43 self-portrait photos he sent to NBC"; the U.K. *Daily Star* claimed, "Police believe the oddball loner repeatedly watched the gory movie *Oldboy* as he meticulously prepared for his killing spree"; and *The Mirror* asserted, "Cho was re-enacting scenes from a violent South Korean movie when he massacred 32 students and teachers, police believe." Whether they claimed that the link consisted of a mere photo, meticulous preparation, or all-out reenactment, such reports were not ambivalent about the newsworthiness of the references to fiction in Cho's multimedia manifesto. Together, they place Cho's references, and the multimedia manifesto itself, in a spotlight.

This spotlighting connects to an even deeper ambivalence regarding Cho's case: some commentators identify in Cho's media manifesto a desire for a spotlight that depicts him in the same manner of his favorite movies' (anti)heroes. By fulfilling this desire, reporters and other commentators risk becoming complicit in the enactment of Cho's violent fantasies. Douglas Kellner explains:

> The ensuing media spectacle apparently achieved what the crazed Cho had in mind, a spectacle of terror in the manner of the 9/11 terror attacks that attracted scores of media from all over the world to Blacksburg in saturation coverage of the event. His carefully assembled multimedia package revealed to the world who Cho was and won for him a kind of sick and perverted immortality, or at least tremendous notoriety in the contemporary moment.
> There was a fierce, albeit partially hypocritical, backlash against NBC for releasing the media dossier and making a potential hero and martyr out of Cho.[33]

Cho sought to turn himself into a spectacle and a story, to inspire people to speak and write about him in very particular ways. Numerous news sources note that Cho idolized Eric Harris and Dylan Klebold in a manner similar to Cho's idolization of the main character in *Oldboy*: not only did his crimes occur around the anniversary of the Columbine massacre, but Cho also referred to Harris and Klebold as martyrs. In *No Right to Remain Silent: The Tragedy at Virginia Tech*, Lucinda Roy considers Cho's spotlight-seeking in depth. In years prior to the attack, Roy was

Chair of Virginia Tech's English Department and had worked one-on-one with Cho, so her insight is direct, personal, and poignant. She writes, "Like Eric Harris and Dylan Klebold, [Cho] was well aware of the power he wielded; he knew that his videos would appeal to other disaffected young people."[34] Just as Harris and Klebold's writings and videos had inspired him, Cho's multimedia manifesto would immortalize Cho and perhaps inspire others.

Roy's attention to the ways Cho positioned himself as a story to be told gives her book, a memoir that narrates her own attempts to understand the tragedy, an oppositional stance. Roy divides her account into a prologue, three main parts, and an epilogue. Significantly, she titles part one "Horror Story." In these pages, she describes news reports about the crimes of a student she had known and the deaths of colleagues, students, and friends—news reports that included eager speculation about the "record-breaking death toll"—as "the glorification of murder," all part of "the horror story [Cho] crafted with himself in the starring role."[35] Roy suggests that through his murders Cho *wanted* to become a Gothic event, a spectacle of bloody excess. Authors don't need to package his murders as, following Kass's subtitle, a "true crime story" because Cho's multimedia manifesto and crimes have provided the genre-laden packaging already. By making "Horror Story" part one, followed by "Back Story" and "Dialogue," Roy's account introduces multiple perspectives and voices and thus repackages, and renarrativizes, what took place at Virginia Tech, events she pointedly calls "the tragedy at Virginia Tech" instead of adopting the media's preferred term, "the Virginia Tech massacre." She dethrones Cho as horror writer, exposing a human drama that she refuses to sensationalize.

As Roy tells her story, which she terms a "personal journey," she reflects, "Causality is supposed to make the plot credible in a tragedy like this one." Like Brooks Brown, Roy resists the notion of easy answers, but she does provide a numbered list of ten risk factors that "have the potential to contribute to education's perfect storm," and "a pop culture that routinely exposes children and youth to excessive violence" is number six on that list.[36] In his multimedia manifesto, Cho blames "the slaughter on everyone but himself—and especially rich students."[37] Thus the two writers, Cho in a Gothic mode and Roy not, both provide multiple causes in the ways they tell their stories. Their narratives present competing multiplicities, competing notions of complexity, struggling to determine how Gothic reality actually is.

Stephen King, Influence, and the Idea of a Blueprint

When Roy's search for causes prompts her to consider the roles of popular culture in school shootings, she comes upon Stephen King's novel *Rage*, noting, "The shooting rampage of Barry Loukaitis in 1996 in Moses Lake, Washington, and its connection to a novel by Stephen King have been well documented." She quotes Katherine Newman's *Rampage*:

> In fact, [Loukaitis's] actions were organized and rehearsed, according to police detectives, because Loukaitis was acting out the plot from one of his favorite novels: Stephen King's 1977 book, *Rage*, which police detectives found on Loukaitis's bedside table. In the novel, a teen holds his algebra class hostage with a revolver, kills a teacher, and talks about killing a popular student. During Loukaitis's shooting spree, classmates reported that he turned to one of them and said, "This sure beats algebra, doesn't it?"—a direct quote from the book.[38]

Loukaitis's quotation of King's novel cements Newman's claim about the direct connection between *Rage* and Loukaitis's crimes. Without *Rage*, the crimes could not have taken the form that they did, and thus *Rage* has at least a limited causal connection to the shootings.

King began *Rage* when he was in the same position as the novel's main characters—he was in high school. He finished it years later and, after the enormous success of his first published novel, *Carrie*, finally published it under the pseudonym Richard Bachman. *Rage* tells the story of Charles Decker, a disturbed teenager, alienated from his father and from his society, who brings a pistol into his algebra class, murders two teachers, and holds his classmates hostage while they form emotional bonds through a cathartic confessional ritual he calls "getting it on."[39]

Of course Stephen King didn't invent the idea of school shootings, but his novel does provide an intimate and seemingly prescient account of the high school cultures that host and arguably produce such crimes. Like other narratives about school shootings, *Rage* reflects on the complexity of the shooter's psyche and motivations, and thus it has the capacity to help disturbed teenage readers to understand, and perhaps define, themselves and their actions. Barry Loukaitis was neither the first nor the last person to take inspiration from King's novel. The September 21, 1989 edition of the *St. Louis Post-Dispatch* reports:

> A teen-ager pleaded guilty to holding 11 classmates hostage at gunpoint for up to 10 hours, then got his demand to see his father for the first time in 13 years.

7. Fictions That Kill

Dustin Pierce, 17, had said during the siege that he was angry with his distant father and wanted to see him. ... The boy apparently had been acting out the scenario of a Stephen King novel, "Rage," in which a youth takes over a classroom in pursuit of what the author describes as a "pathological rage fantasy about his father."

The entry for *Rage* in George Beahm's encyclopedia *Stephen King from A to Z* notes of this incident, "The similarities to the novel were too many to dismiss; in fact, the police combed the novel for clues on how to deal with this situation."[40] In a story by Jesse Katz headlined "A High School Gunman's Day of Rage," *The Los Angeles Times* of January 14, 1990 recounts a similar tale: on April 26, 1988, Jeffrey Lynne Cox, then age 17, brought a rifle to school and held sixty classmates hostage. He did so after discovering *Rage*, which the *Times* rightly describes as critiquing "the hypocrisy and boredom of [a] stifling small town." After reading King's novel repeatedly, Cox decided, "The message was his, too." Langman also notes that police found a copy of *Rage* in Michael Carneal's locker after Carneal shot eight people, killing three, in his high school in West Paducah, Kentucky, in 1997.

Summing up the controversy that has surrounded *Rage*, Beahm remarks, "King has expressed great concern and regret that this book was published, undoubtedly because unstable students use it as a blueprint for their own hostage-taking scenarios."[41] Calling King's novel a "blueprint" acknowledges that *Rage* gave form to the events; just as an architectural blueprint shows workers how to shape a building, *Rage* has shown several disturbed young people how to shape their crimes. Blueprints, however, do not wholly cause buildings to be, and they are not responsible for construction. Acknowledging that violent fictions provide blueprints is not the same thing as laying blame.

As a horror novelist and one of the most popular writers of the last century (recent dust jackets of his books boast that he "is the author of more than forty books, all of them worldwide bestsellers"), King is often blamed for inciting violent criminals to action, and thus he often confronts the question of whether violent art can cause real-life violence. In an entry titled "'The Evil that King Does,'" Beahm describes a letter by a disgruntled viewer of the film *Pet Sematary*, based on King's novel of that name, which accuses King of inciting "impressionable teenagers" to commit arson and claims, "What [King] did was equivalent to shouting 'Fire!' in a crowded theater."[42] This claim implies that the state could and should censor King's work according to the United States Supreme Court's 1919 decision in

Schenck v. United States, which announced the "clear and present danger" rule according to which "speech can be regulated by the government only if the content of that speech contributes immediately and proximately to the occurrence of an activity that is itself subject to government regulation."[43] American critics who call for censorship of violent media usually cite this rule, arguing that horror fiction is language with the power to contribute immediately to the occurrence of crime.

Despite the possibility of inviting censorship, King has engaged the issue of media violence without denying art's potential for a negative influence. In his study of the horror genre *Danse Macabre* (1981), King includes an indirect indictment of his own work:

> Boston, 1977. A woman is killed by a young man who uses a number of kitchen implements to effect the murder. Police speculate that he might have gotten the idea from a movie — Brian DePalma's *Carrie*, from the novel by Stephen King. In the film version, Carrie kills her mother by causing all sorts of kitchen implements — including a corkscrew and a potato-peeler — to fly across the room and literally nail the woman to the wall.

King cites several murders linked to other horrific fictions, including *Psycho* and *The Exorcist*, before stating the question himself: "What sort of burden does the writer — particularly the writer of horror fiction — have to bear in all of this?" Citing an event apparently spawned by the broadcast of the movie *Fuzz* on network television, he also provides an answer:

> I would suggest that there has been a great tendency, particularly when it comes to such popular forms as movies, television, and mainstream fiction, to kill the messenger for the message. I do not now and never have doubted that the youths who burned the lady in Roxbury got the idea from the telecast of *Fuzz* one Sunday night on ABC; if it had not been shown, stupidity and lack of imagination might have reduced them to murdering her in some more mundane way.[44]

By framing horror writers as messengers, King argues that violence in fiction merely reflects violence in the world. He grants that art about violence can influence violence, but he distinguishes correlation from causality by suggesting that, while influence can shape a "mundane" crime with "imagination," the crime itself would have happened anyway, without such an influence. Violent art reflects and shapes real violence, but it does not create or cause it. It contributes to crime's shape but not to its occurrence. The dissociation of correlation from causality that King accomplishes through a counterfactual would free violent fiction from the culpability that critics link to causality.

7. Fictions That Kill

In a 1982 interview collected in *Bare Bones: Conversations on Terror with Stephen King*, King generalizes about the possibility that someone could get an idea for a crime from one of his books: "If they didn't get an idea from something that I wrote, they would get it from something somebody else wrote."[45] This reasoning still poses a counterfactual, but instead of asserting that the hypothetical crime would have happened without the intervention of any influence, it posits that another influence would have taken the place of his own. The suggestion that an influence will always be available to shape the commission of crimes fits more neatly with the idea that the creators of violent art merely reflect the pervasive violence of the world: if criminal potential requires an ideational impetus, one will inevitably appear. The world, not the fiction, ultimately supplies the cause.

According to his first counterfactual argument, the blueprint that Loukaitis, Pierce, Cox, and Carneal might have used for their crimes only shaped events that would have happened anyway. According to the second, the school shooters would have found another blueprint and committed crimes that were at least comparable to the ones they actually committed. If King believes either line of reasoning, why has he expressed "regret" about *Rage*? Not in direct response to the crimes of Pierce, Cox, Loukaitis, and Carneal but later, after the shootings at Columbine, Stephen King asked his publisher to take *Rage* out of print. In *The Denver Post* of November 10, 1999, Tom Walker reports, "King took the unusual step of asking his publisher not to print any more copies of the book because of its striking resemblance to instances of school violence around the country, including those at Columbine." The article goes on to quote an interview with King that appeared on *Dateline*:

> King responded, "'Rage' is a book that deals with a kid who brings a gun to school, shoots a teacher, and holds a class hostage."
> He went on to say, "I took a look at 'Rage' and said to myself, 'If this book is acting as any sort of accelerant, if it's having any effect on any of these kids at all, I don't want anything to do with it, regardless of what may be the moral and legal rights and wrongs. Even talking about it makes me nervous.'"

King's choice of the word "accelerant" indicates that he had not entirely abandoned his earlier reasoning when he decided to remove *Rage* from publication. An accelerant speeds up a process that would have happened anyway. Nevertheless, King's nervousness about the book having "any effect" on school shootings reveals that he feels uncomfortable about—though not morally and legally culpable for—the power his books have had in shaping real events.

King's discomfort might stem from problems in his counterfactual arguments. Without *Rage*, the criminals *might* have committed crimes anyway, but this possibility cannot be proven, and even if it could, the crimes would be significantly different because they would lack quotations and other direct connections to the novel. The "some other influence would have come along" argument suffers from the same difficulty as the "it would have happened anyway" argument. The specifics of the crimes reflect the specifics of the story's plotline and message — a different story without those specifics would not have had the same influence. Histories that present one-to-one correlations between a fiction and the crimes of teenagers who claim inspiration from that fiction blunt the force of counterfactual generalizations. *Rage* is an integral part of these histories; no other influence, real or fictional, could take its place.

The problems with King's counterfactual arguments leave "blueprint" narratives open to attack. In his contribution to *Media Violence Alert*, Dave Grossman warns that "the media is providing our children with role models."[46] Consistent with his eighteenth-century predecessors, Grossman attacks horror fictions because they threaten to exert a negative influence by offering models for bad behavior. A fictional model, be it the main character of *Rage* or of *Oldboy*, exerts an effective influence if it offers a role with which readers can identify, taking the role and the specific ideas associated with it as their own.[47] So what sort of role model does Stephen King provide? *Rage* presents a highly sympathetic teenage character whose fantasy, message, and behavior result in slaughter. Charlie Decker strikes out against the society that oppresses him; framed as a rebel with a worthy cause, Charlie commits murderous acts of vengeance that almost appear justified.

Charlie stands at the peak of adolescent angst, tired of feeling powerless against the authority figures who alienate him. Confronting his high school principal, Charlie explains, "'You used to make me afraid and you still make me afraid but now you make me tired too, and I've decided I don't have to put up with that.'" Charlie ultimately realizes that lashing out at the principal and murdering two teachers are cases of "misplaced aggression" and that he should really direct his rage toward his father. He recalls a fight with his father during which his father lacerated his face with a belt buckle and threatened him with a rake; in response, Charlie threatened his father with a hatchet, making his father back down and learning "how you could get anyone's number with a big enough stick." Charlie remembers that his next "stick" was the pipe wrench he used to assault a teacher; he notes that when he needed an even bigger stick, he found his father's pistol. He uses his father's pistol, a source of literal power as well as a figure for reclaimed sexual power, to kill two teachers and hold his class hostage. Charlie's gun gives him the power to express his alienation, and under Charlie's new authority, his classmates get chances to describe their own feelings of social and sexual powerlessness.[48]

Most of Charlie's hostages, the witnesses of his violence, identify with him. They end up wanting his authority; his violent acts earn him the acceptance of his peers. One girl, after explaining how she often feels like a weak, unreal "'doll,'" tells the story of a night when she escaped that feeling by seeking a random sexual encounter. She describes the sex as unsatisfying but "'very real,'" and she adds, "'But this has been better, Charlie.'" The only hostage who insists on feeling like a hostage is Ted Jones, who, as Michael Collings argues, "represents the standard against which [the other hostages] are all measured."[49] Ted represents the norms that the other teens find oppressive, the model of behavior that they reject in favor of Charlie's form of violent self-expression. Ted tries to point out the horror of Charlie's violence to his classmates by shouting, "'HE IS CRAZY! HE HAS SHOT TWO PEOPLE! DEAD! HE IS HOLDING US HERE!'" A girl answers him by explaining that Charlie allowed her to leave for a bathroom visit, but she came back — she chose to be with Charlie. When Ted shouts that Charlie is a killer, another student calls Ted a "'soul killer,'" framing Charlie's murders as a lesser crime than the crime of emotional repression. The novel climaxes when the hostages complete their identification with Charlie by beating Ted until he "hardly look[s] human at all anymore," establishing their power over their oppressors by sending Ted, the symbol of the rejected norm, into an impotent, catatonic state. The teens' communal outpouring of violence and emotion casts "getting it on" with Charlie as liberating, in some ways even better than sex.[50]

While no one, not even Charlie himself, tries to justify Charlie's murders, the murders ultimately appear inconsequential beside the greater work Charlie accomplishes by bringing a gun to school. The adult lives taken by Charlie's actions pay for the redemption of teenage souls; body-killing, a lesser crime than soul-killing, appears to be worthwhile. The witnesses to Charlie's behavior within the novel, representatives of teenagers in general and diegetic stand-ins for the reader-as-witness, approve of Charlie. They model approval of Charlie for the reader, and their approval becomes identification when they adopt Charlie's penchant for violence. Through violence, Charlie gains physical power, sexual power, and the admiration of his peers. Acting out the violent fantasy of an unstable, alienated teen, Charlie achieves the fantasy of teen perfection. The only alternative the novel presents to adopting Charlie's role is adopting Ted's, and the Ted option winds up looking inhuman. The novel's ending — which briefly shows Charlie languishing in a mental hospital — reads as a footnote to Charlie's accomplishment. For a teen with the right predisposition, Charlie is a paragon, a model suggesting both that behavior like his is a reasonable response to teen alienation and that such a response might result in fantastic rewards.

This reading of King's novel shows how it might exert an influence on an impressionable reader, and attention to the crimes of several school shooters shows that it has already done so. The histories of these boys' crimes would not be in the way that they are if Stephen King had never published *Rage*. King's fiction is part of the essence of real crimes. No counterfactual can circumvent this fact's retrospectively causal relation to that essence.

A month after Columbine, Stephen King gave a keynote address called "The Bogeyboys" at the annual meeting of the Vermont Educational Media Association. "The Bogeyboys" anticipates the rhetoric that would become dominant over the course of the next decade:

> To some degree, what happened at Columbine happened because of what happened in Jonesboro, Arkansas (five murdered), Paducah, Kentucky (three murdered), and Springfield, Oregon (four murdered, two parents and two kids at a school dance). Similarly, the shootings and rumors of shootings in the weeks and months ahead will happen because of Harris and Klebold and Columbine High; because of T.J. Solomon and Heritage High. It's an amp-cult thing. Harris & Klebold may be dead, but they're going to be mighty lively for awhile. Believe me on this. I know a good deal about spooks, and more than I want to about boys who play with guns.
>
> In the wake of the shootings, film and TV and book people have pointed the finger at the gun industry and at that ever-popular bogeyman, the NRA. The gun people point right back, saying that America's entertainment industry has created a culture of violence. And, behind it all, we are bombing the living hell out of Yugoslavia, because that's the way we traditionally solve our problems when those pesky foreign leaders won't do what we think is right. So who is really to blame? My answer is all of the above. And I speak from some personal experience and a lot of soul-searching.[51]

King's "all of the above" answer is effectively the answer that Potter offered when he published *The 11 Myths of Media Violence* several years later and that social scientists and others support when they enumerate media violence among other risk factors.

In "The Bogeyboys," King returns to the idea of *Rage* as an "accelerant" and says, "I withdrew *Rage*, and I did it with relief rather than regret." King acknowledges that violent media rightly stands among many causes, and he feels the possibility strongly enough to take his own work out of print, but when he turns from questions of causation, retrospective and otherwise, to questions of moral (and legal) responsibility, he has a clear answer:

> If, on the other hand, you were to ask me if the presence of potentially unstable or homicidal persons makes it immoral to write a novel or make a movie in which violence plays a part, I would say absolutely not. In most cases, I have no patience with such reasoning. I reject it as both bad thinking and bad morals. Like it or not, violence is a part of life and a unique part of American life. If accused of being part of the problem, my response is the time-honored reporter's answer: "Hey, man, I don't make the news, I just report it."[52]

Thus he appeals to time-honored wisdom: "Don't blame the messenger." For King, inclusion of violent media among the multiple causes associated with violent events is not mutually exclusive with guiltlessness for art and artists. *Rage*, *Oldboy*, or any other fiction — Gothic or otherwise — might provide a blueprint for a deed. For most people in the media violence debate, the question of whether a violent fiction could be *a* (not *the*) cause for real violence has a clear answer: yes. As King demonstrates, however, admitting this answer, acknowledging the blueprint, does not make way for a leap from causation to responsibility. As investigations into school shootings reveal diverse causes and perspectives, they also reveal the unspannable distance such a leap would involve.

8

Violent Self-Reflection
Natural Born Killers, *Wes Craven's Nightmares,* and Torture Porn

When a fictional character like Charlie Decker, the antihero of Stephen King's *Rage*, or Dae-Su Oh, the antihero of Chan-wook Park's *Oldboy*, takes revenge against society through horrific acts of violence, his story implicitly critiques the society he attacks, suggesting that, at least from one person's perspective, the society deserves the violence it gets. Building on this premise, this chapter examines what on the surface might seem like an odd coincidence: the horrific fictions that politicians and pundits most frequently blame for inciting real-world violence take a critical stance toward the very social structures and authorities whose representatives condemn them. Specifically, the fictions that receive the greatest shares of blame tend to critique the relationships between representations of violence and the societies that produce those representations. The people who condemn these fictions don't do so out of retribution, but they do seem oblivious to the films' critiques, and in their obliviousness lies a fear that goes beyond the fear of infectious violence. The most frightening thing about these fictions is the knowledge they impart.

The NBK Effect

Eric Harris's journal reveals that there was at least one powerful fictional influence on the tragedy at Columbine. A year before the event took place, Harris was already planning it, referring to the coming carnage as "NBK," an abbreviation of *Natural Born Killers*, a 1994 film by Oliver Stone.[1] The film tells the story of Mickey and Mallory Knox, a young couple who, after escaping from abusive parents and harsh treatment by the law, go on a cross-country shooting spree, murdering more than fifty people while they celebrate the love and freedom they have found with one another. Often shown from the killers' perspectives, many of the murders look like vigilantism, and almost all of them appear to involve at least a little bit of fun.[2]

Columbine didn't need to introduce *Natural Born Killers* as a pivotal text for the media violence debate: it has been controversial since its release. In her essay "Time to Face Responsibility," Mary Whitehouse reports that the British Board of Film Classification delayed the U.K. release of Stone's film because of "claims that this film had been a factor in a number of murders in the United States," particularly in "the case of Nathan Martinez, a seventeen-year-old boy charged with killing two members of his own family after watching *Natural Born Killers* ten times."[3] John Grisham, a bestselling author of violent legal thrillers, mounted a campaign against the film after the murder of his friend Bill Savage. Grisham calls for legal action against "the likes of Oliver Stone," claiming in a piece called "Natural Bred Killers," "A case can be made that there exists a direct causal link between *Natural Born Killers* and the death of Bill Savage." According to Grisham, the killers, Benjamin Darras and Sarah Edmondson, committed murders after discussing how they wanted to behave "like Mickey and Mallory."[4] With reasoning that recalls Stephen King's, Oliver Stone writes in a brief retort called "Don't Sue the Messenger," "It is likely that, whether they had seen *Natural Born Killers*, *The Green Berets*, or a *Tom and Jerry* cartoon the night before their first crime, Darras and Edmondson would have behaved in exactly the way they did."[5] Stone's defense is disingenuous: if Grisham's claims about the killers' discussions are accurate, the killers' *exact* behavior would not have been possible without the film. Darras and Edmondson named Mickey and Mallory explicitly as their role models.[6]

As role models, Mickey and Mallory share Charlie Decker's strategy of overcoming feelings of powerlessness by taking up guns and slaughtering people in vengeful wrath. *Rage* and *Natural Born Killers* both focus on alienated youth and psychosexual trauma, but when situating them within debates about media violence, another comparison requires interpretation: they both make statements about the effects of media violence on impressionable minds. After describing the shooting of his first teacher-victim,

I Love Mallory is an imaginary television show in *Natural Born Killers* (1994) that represents the fantasy world of Mickey and Mallory Knox (Woody Harrelson and Juliette Lewis, who is pictured here). It suggests that the killers understand their lives as television fictions.

whom the students call "Book Bags," Charlie mentions that people often ask him why he thinks the students didn't run, and he explains,

> If I told them anything, it would be that they've forgotten what it is to be a kid, to live cheek-by-jowl with violence, with the commonplace fistfights in the gym, brawls at the PAL hops in Lewiston, beatings on television, murders in the movies. Most of us had seen a little girl puke pea soup all over a priest right down at our local drive-in. Old Book Bags wasn't much shakes by comparison.[7]

Charlie suggests that the extreme violence that surrounds children in modern American culture, particularly in movies such as *The Exorcist* (1973), makes real-life violence seem tolerable "by comparison." His answer agrees with Bill Clinton's statement about media and desensitization, and so *Rage*, itself a violent fiction, begins a metafictional meditation on fiction's formative influence.

When he and his hostages are just starting to "get it on," Charlie fires his gun at the floor to make a listening authority figure believe he has shot a new victim. One of the hostages applauds him, and after describing the applause, Charlie's introspective narration produces a comparison of his own homicidal impulses with the impulses fed by violent entertainment:

8. Violent Self-Reflection 187

> ... I wasn't too surprised [by the applause] ... Craziness is only a matter of degree, and there are lots of people who have the urge to roll heads. They go to the stock-car races and the horror movies and the wrestling matches they have in the Portland Expo.

He places going to a horror movie, cheering on a gunman, and murdering a teacher in the same category of phenomena, differentiated only by "degree." Taking Charlie's ruminations at face-value, *Rage* is violent entertainment that depicts youth corrupted by the influence of violent entertainment. Given Charlie's actions, one might view his ideas about fiction's role in youth violence as an attempt at exculpation, but in the light of *Rage*'s actual influence, his statement of this position, however genuine, gains powerful resonance. Charlie emphasizes the presence of reporters outside the school where the main events are taking place and develops a sense of himself as "a documented case, routine grist for the newspaper mill."[8] A claim that *Rage* is fundamentally about media violence would be an overstatement, but Charlie's occasional comments on the roles of "routine" media violence in his life do create a subtle sense of a cycle

In *Scream 2* (1996), Maureen Evans (Jada Pinkett Smith, credited as Jada Pinkett) stands dying in front of a movie screen showing a fictional representation of the killer in a ghost-face mask from *Scream*. Life seems to imitate art as real and fictional violence run parallel.

in which representations of violence in the media influence real-life violence, real-life violence earns representations in the media (fictional and non-fictional), and these representations go on to have their own influences on reality, *ad infinitum*.

While metatextual consciousness of this cycle is subtle in *Rage*, it is overwhelming in *Natural Born Killers*. The film blends recognizable television styles in a chaotic pastiche. The early romance between Mickey and Mallory appears as an episode of *I Love Mallory*, complete with a title script that mimics the title of the 1950s sitcom *I Love Lucy* (see page 186). Some of Mickey and Mallory's murders appear in quick-cut MTV style set to the tunes of the Goth-industrial band Nine Inch Nails, and others appear in the documentary style of a television show called *American Maniacs*. At times, televisions appear in buildings where windows should be, and in a particularly heavy-handed scene, a wise Native American sees the words "too much t.v." superimposed on Mickey and Mallory as they stand before him. The killings shot directly from Mickey and Mallory's point of view do not differ significantly from the fictionalized reenactments on *American Maniacs*, and thus image after image in *Natural Born Killers* indicates that television itself supplies the killers' point of view. Near the end of the film, the lead reporter from *American Maniacs*, who enjoys comparing the TV ratings of Mickey and Mallory to those of Charles Manson, joins Mickey and Mallory on their killing spree, suggesting a broad alliance between the purveyors of media violence and murderous psychopaths. When Grisham attacks Stone's claim that *Natural Born Killers* is a satire on the "media's craving" for violence as a defensive bid for the "high ground," he is taking a turn at being disingenuous.[9] Unlike *Rage*, *Natural Born Killers* is fundamentally about the effects of watching media violence; self-consciousness pervades the film in both form and content.

Considering a long list of horror films about spectatorship, Carol Clover concludes, "A strong prima facie case could be made for horror's being, intentionally or unintentionally, the most self-reflexive of cinematic genres."[10] Clover's conclusion is correct not only for horror films but for Gothic horror dating back to the eighteenth century, as this book's analyses of metafictional self-consciousness in *The Monk*, *The Mysteries of Udolpho*, and the ghost story tradition should suggest.[11] Though self-reflection has always been an important element in horror fiction, in the 1990s, it became horror's definitive attribute. Arguably the most successful horror film series of the decade, Wes Craven's *Scream* trilogy makes self-consciousness so extreme that it (self-consciously) crosses back and forth over the line between comedy and horror. The first *Scream* (1996) not only cites other horror films both in the form and in the dialogue of almost every scene, but it also tells the story of two killers who "watched a few movies, took a few notes" in order to get their calling right. *Scream 2* (1997) adds a second level: it begins with the murders of two movie patrons attending a showing of *Stab*, a movie based on the events of the first *Scream*, and ultimately tells the story of two "copycat" killers. The final film, *Scream 3* (2000), takes place on the set of *Stab 3*, where a killer murders participants in *Stab 3* in manners derived from *Stab 3*'s script.[12] The box office success of the *Scream* series spawned a host of imitators, *Urban Legend* (1998) perhaps being the most notable. These imitators were a parade of horror stories about horror stories creating horror stories.

Scream, like *Natural Born Killers*, has supposedly inspired real-life crimes. In the *Milwaukee Journal Sentinel* of August 1, 1998, Keith Edwards reports:

> Authorities found videotapes from the movies "Scream" and "Scream 2" as well as packaging for a costume that resembles that of the killers in the teen horror movies when they searched the bedroom of a 16-year-old boy accused of stabbing his ex-girlfriend's parents, officials said Friday.
>
> Thaddeus K. Swim dressed up in the costume and patterned the attack Monday after a character in the horror movie "Scream," police said.

An editorial entitled "Censorship, No; Concern, Yes When Movies Lead to Copycats" in the December 8, 1997 *Omaha World-Herald* states, "Police investigators surmise that the movie "Scream" influenced three gunmen who tried unsuccessfully to hold up two Omaha restaurants." Similarly, Andrew Brussels, in *The Observer* for November 18, 2001, refers to another brutal stabbing "motivated by the cinematic trilogy" as part of "a spate of copycat killings and attacks" inspired by the films. Curtis Schieber opines in the December 20, 1996 *Columbus Dispatch* article headlined "'Scream' like Serial Slashing 101," "Aspiring serial killers take note: Director Wes Craven has made a primer for you." W. James Potter depicts Craven as a kind of supervillain among reprehensible horror artists:

> Perhaps the most egregious example of denial of responsibility comes from Wes Craven, director of horror movies such as *Scream* and *Nightmare on Elm Street*. Following the Columbine shootings, Craven and certain other filmmakers were strongly criticized for their ultraviolent plots and graphic images. Craven said that prior to the criticism he had decided to cut down on the amount of blood in his newest film.... As a backlash against the criticism, he decided to make his film even more graphic.[13]

The image of the *Scream* series that emerges from these news reports and critiques suggests that the films not only influence crime, but they do so by design.

The *Scream* films, like *Natural Born Killers*, engage contemporary concerns about the effects of media violence, but unlike *Natural Born Killers*, they include defenses of violent fiction within their literal depictions of influence gone awry. After many references to how films have shaped his crimes, Billy Loomis, one of the killers in the first *Scream*, reveals a more mundane motive: he wants revenge against the family of the woman who broke up his parents' marriage. After this revelation he remarks, "don't blame the movies ... movies don't create psychos; movies make psychos more creative." With these crucial comments, *Scream* mobilizes the same "it would have happened anyway" defense that Stephen King and Oliver Stone use with varying degrees of success. *Scream 2* uses the same strategy more extensively. One of its two killers is Billy Loomis's mother, who also seeks revenge, and she reveals that she recruited the other killer, Mickey, from a chatroom for serial killers. Mickey doesn't offer much of a motive for his participation, but he does explain his plans:

> I've got my whole defense planned out. I'm gonna blame the movies ... it's all about the trial. The effects of cinema violence on society. I'll get Dershowitz, Cochran to represent me, Bob Dole on the witness stand in my defense. Hell, the Christian Coalition will pay my legal fees. It's air tight ... I'm the innocent victim.

Perhaps in response to attacks by the likes of Bob Dole on the first film, *Scream 2* names the cinema violence debate and shifts the blame attributed to violent art to those who cast the blame. According to Mickey, by blaming art for the crimes of people, the critics of media violence allow murderers to appear "innocent." This lack of individual culpability becomes, for Mickey, an incentive to kill.

An unauthenticated early version of the script of *Scream 2*—which circulates on the internet and in movie memorabilia shops—has a different ending with two killers, Derek and Hallie, assisting Billy Loomis's mother. When Sidney, the series' heroine, asks them why they do it, this exchange follows:

> HALLIE: Ever see *Natural Born Killers*? Well, Derek and I have this whole Mickey/Mallory ... thing going on.
> DEREK: I really don't like that comparison, honey.
> HALLIE (to Sid): He hates Oliver Stone.
> DEREK: I find his work overwrought.[14]

This version uses a specific movie to tag the media violence debate — arguably the definitive movie for contemporary arguments about the negative influence of the horror film. When Mickey, whose name might be the actual film's way of alluding more subtly to Stone's "overwrought" treatise-in-fiction, calls attention to his plans for his trial, he also suggests that he looks forward to the kind of media fanfare that Mickey and Mallory receive in *Natural Born Killers*. *Scream 2* invokes the representation-reality cycle of influence with the name of the film that, more dramatically than any other, has both represented and participated in this cycle.

When Eric Harris and Dylan Klebold planned their own NBK, they "wanted to be media stars too."[15] In the months leading up to the massacre, they speculated and fantasized, with some accuracy, about how the world would receive their crimes. The self-consciousness of *Natural Born Killers* became their own self-consciousness. Killers in *Rage*, *Natural Born Killers*, and the *Scream* series all name fictional violence as influences on their own violence, just as criminals who pattern their attacks on these works cite their influences by name. A direct line connects artistic self-consciousness with criminal consciousness, and as a result, the names of these self-conscious works have become buzzwords for the critics of media violence. In the NBK effect, fictions that reflect on the power of fiction increase both the perception and the reality of that power. Self-conscious influence becomes causal and, in the minds of some critics, culpable.[16]

Forbidden Knowledge

The NBK effect marks self-consciousness in violent fiction as one of the Gothic's most virulent threats. Models of negative behavior teach that bad behavior is possible, and self-conscious models of negative behavior make the teaching stand out as teaching, as a model for imitation. Textual self-consciousness posits a kind of textual selfhood. It creates an illusion of living consciousness, of a desire and ability for deliberate action — a textual agency. The self-aware text appears personified as a teacher ready to spread a poisonous lesson. When critics blame an influence for a crime, they name knowledge, the teacher's poison, as the murder weapon.

Belief in the poisonous power of knowledge stands out most clearly in critical attacks on non-fictional media violence. *Rage*'s self-conscious reference to Charlie Decker's story as "routine grist for the newspaper mill" highlights how a story such as his will likely proliferate within the representation-reality cycle of influence because of news reports' predilection for violent fare.[17] While *Natural Born Killers* involves both fictional and non-fictional media in its critical pastiche, it emphasizes the complicity of the sensational news shows represented by *American Maniacs* with the sort of criminals represented by Mickey and Mallory. The news shows represented by *American Maniacs* share Gothic fiction's tendency to give violence an exciting, sensational frame, and thus the style in which media present violent models might seem to bear on students' eagerness to embrace the teaching. Less sensational news stories may be equally influential, however. Dave Grossman's claim in *Media Violence Alert* that "the media is providing our children with role models" includes "not just ... the lawless sociopaths in movies and in television shows" but also the perpetrators of violence represented in the news, a point he supports by citing research showing that "local television reporting of suicides was responsible for causing numerous copycat suicides of young, impressionable teenagers."[18] Such reporting does not glamorize violence in the manner of *American Maniacs*, but it does give impressionable minds the spark of an idea, and this idea, in Grossman's view, becomes a culpable cause.

Jonathan L. Freedman, whose work debunks scientific claims for a causal relationship between media violence and real violence, states a caveat near the end of his study:

> It is important to remember that the research I have reviewed dealt almost exclusively with the effects of fictional or fictionalized programs and films. ... Although there is no systematic evidence to support it, many people believe that media coverage of horrific crimes causes some people to imitate those crimes. The killings at Columbine High School received an enormous amount of media attention and were followed by a number of similar attacks in other schools. It is possible that the later crimes were caused to some extent by coverage of the earlier one.[19]

The claim that non-fictional violence may have a causal power that fictional violence does not creates a vital role for the distinction between models represented as fact and those represented as fiction. Gerard Jones, author of *Killing Monsters: Why Children Need Fantasy, Super Heroes, and Make-Believe Violence*, tells the story of Kip Kinkel, which "dramatizes, in its most horrible form, the cost of investing fantasies with too much reality." According to Jones, the fact that Kinkel's parents forbade toy guns and violent play gave the boy an obsession with real guns and violence. He became a sad teenager whose hopelessness drove him to "put the lyrics to a Marilyn Manson song on his wall, which asserted that there could be 'no salvation.'" Forbidding fantasy put violent fantasies on the same level as violent realities for Kinkel, so in his confusion he acted out his fantasies: he shot his parents, carried his gun to school, and opened fire on his classmates.[20] The delimiting frame of fiction, in Jones's view, insulates and sanitizes fantasies of bad behavior. Jones's telling of Kinkel's story suggests that although fantasy violence cannot cause actual violence, the failure to distinguish fiction from reality can.

Freedman and Jones, who oppose those who claim that violent fictions have a deleterious effect, uphold the dangerousness of negative role models when they grant causal influence to non-fictional sources and to authorities who fail to distinguish fiction from reality. In this limited way, they agree with the leaders of the anti-violence camp. Hardly anyone on either side of the media violence debate argues against the poisonous potential of knowledge: the defenders of media violence merely emphasize how framing influential knowledge as fiction keeps it from causing unwanted effects. As the previous chapter suggests, Jones blames the media violence debate — which expresses adults' anxieties about entertainment's power to corrupt the young — for creating real violence.[21] More than anything, the debate spreads the idea that fictional violence spreads bad influences. This idea creates anxiety, and the anxiety prompts adults to make violent entertainment taboo for their children. For the children, the taboo breaks down the distinction between fiction and reality, and, as Jones explains, it also makes the tabooed subject much more attractive to some impressionable minds.[22] Considering the ways parental advisory stickers on music and movies advertise taboos, the *National Television Violence Study* concludes, "Children who reported engaging in more aggression-related behaviors showed more interest in programs with advisories."[23] Thus tabooing the knowledge helps it spread.

Few artists have benefited more from the knowledge taboo than the band led by Marilyn Manson. Gavin Baddeley observes, "the violent disapproval of 'the Establishment' only establishes the band's status." Baddeley quite rightly points out that the "parental advisory stickers" that the political influence of Joe Lieberman and company have attached to the albums of Manson and other artists end up increasing sales, and he wryly remarks, "Attempts to ban Marilyn Manson gigs are just 300-foot-tall 'parental advisory' stickers in psychedelic neon." Manson thrives on his critics' disapproval:

Marilyn enjoys his villainy, encouraging dark rumours that his enemies will repeat and amplify. Ironically, they become the best PR agents he could hope for, leaving him looking like the persecuted scapegoat and themselves like hysterical liars.

For teenagers, particularly those who would identify with *Rage*'s Charlie Decker instead of his conformist rival Ted Jones, vilification of Marilyn Manson amounts to glorification. Manson's glorification reached a peak when his vilification brought him to the attention of Michael Moore. According to Baddeley, Manson's appearance in *Bowling for Columbine* brought him critical praise and started a backlash against post–Columbine attacks on Gothic culture, and thus, "demonizing Manson only made him more powerful in the long run."[24]

In a manner comparable to the NBK effect, the media violence debate increases the power of the very things that the detractors of media violence fear. The detractors promote awareness of media violence's potential for a negative influence, and this awareness underscores the potentially bad influences as influences, making the negative models more visible as models to the parents listening to the debate. The parents, in turn, increase the visibility of these models as models for their children, many of whom find the models more attractive as a result. As the fictional models gain visibility, calling them models for real behavior blurs the line between fiction and reality. The knowledge spreads, and fiction's influential power grows. Knowledge of the influence continues to increase the influence. The critics who liken media violence to epidemics (using terms like Grossman's AVIDS — Acquired Violence Immune Deficiency Syndrome) therefore become complicit in the influence by calling attention to and therefore reifying influence's power. Spreading knowledge makes them their own enemies. Like the cultural conservatives who wag their fingers at Marilyn Manson, the enemies of fiction's influence inadvertently become its allies.

Wes Craven's Nightmares

Wes Craven was creating self-conscious horror long before he began the *Scream* series. His imagination spawned the enormously popular *Nightmare on Elm Street* series, which Grossman, Potter, Medved, and others opposed to violent art often name as a particularly pernicious influence. As of late 2009, the *Nightmare* series includes eight films, and a remake of the original was released in April 2010. The concept for the original *Nightmare on Elm Street* (1984) is deceptively simple: a boogeyman named Freddy Krueger stalks teenagers in their nightmares, and when he kills them in their nightmares, they die in reality. At their core, then, the *Nightmare* films are about blurring the distinction between the fantastic and the real, and as they play with this distinction, they involve self-consciousness comparable to, but less overt than, the self-consciousness that drives *Natural Born Killers* and *Scream*.

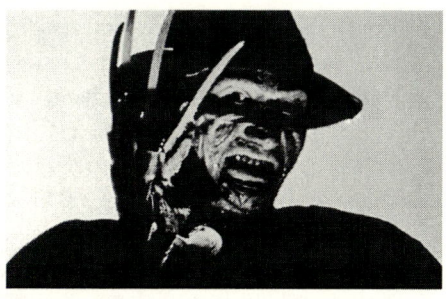

Freddy Krueger (Robert Englund), the boogeyman from *A Nightmare on Elm Street* (1984), directed by Wes Craven.

Trouble with the fantasy/reality divide marks Craven's boogeyman story at its inception because, although it wasn't marketed as such, *A Nightmare on Elm Street* was inspired by real events. Adam Rockoff explains:

> The idea for *A Nightmare on Elm Street* was gleaned from a series of articles which Craven had seen in *The Los Angeles Times*. They all involved people who had suddenly been wracked with what they described as "the worst nightmares they had ever had." They were terrified of going back to bed and, as it turned out, had good reason to be. When they eventually fell asleep, they died. Because this happened over the course of a year and a half, the paper had made no connection between the seemingly unrelated deaths.
> Craven was fascinated by these stories and came up with the idea of a killer who reached his victims in their dreams.[25]

The internet provides diverse speculations about the precise news stories that fueled Craven's creativity, but the most likely events were the deaths of 18 Laotian refugees from what doctors variously describe as bangungot, Asian Death Syndrome, Brugada Syndrome, Nightmare Death Syndrome, and, most frequently, SUNDS — Sudden Unexplained Nocturnal Death Syndrome.[26] News stories about SUNDS give the notion of killer nightmares a realism that Craven's fantasy-driven film would otherwise lack.

Building on this unusual realism, questions surrounding the reality of Freddy Krueger provide much of *Nightmare*'s narrative impetus. After the gruesome death of her friend Tina, Nancy Thompson, the film's heroine and the figure whom Carol Clover dubs "the final girl," begins to suspect the horribly burned man who has appeared in Nancy and Tina's shared dreams wielding a glove that has long razors for fingers. When Nancy grabs the boogeyman's hat during a struggle in one of her dreams, she wakes up with the hat in her hand. Nancy confronts her mother with the named etched in the hat, "Fred Krueger," and learns that Nancy's parents, as well as the parents of many other children in their neighborhood, banded together to lynch Krueger, a known child murderer, after the courts released him on a technicality. Quite theatrically, Nancy's mother Marge tells Nancy that Freddy can't come after her because he's dead, "dead because Mommy killed him." Freddy's status as both ghost and dream seems to remove him doubly from reality, so parents doubt the kids' suspicions of Freddy's involvement, and the kids doubt themselves.

During one of the film's most elaborate dream sequences, Nancy repeats to herself, "This is just a dream, it isn't real, it's just a dream, it isn't real!" After a beat Freddy responds, bursting through a full-length mirror hung on Nancy's bedroom door, gleefully attacking her with his razors. Freddy's entrance contradicts Nancy's desperate assertion about reality, and his emergence from a mirror provides apt symbolism: the mirror, which reflects reality and is central to the conception of mimetic art, is the source of the nightmare boogeyman. The dream-mirror posits Freddy as both fantasy and reality, an artwork, a Freudian dream-work, and a physical presence with which the waking world must contend.

The doubt created by Freddy's paradoxical fantasy-and-reality status becomes even greater at the film's end, when Nancy learns that the way to defeat him is to take away his power by denying his reality. Having pulled him out of her dream and into what she sees as waking reality, Nancy leads Freddy through a series of booby traps that fail to subdue him. Freddy retreats to Marge's bedroom, kills Marge, disappears, and reappears for a final confrontation with Nancy, which spurs Nancy's epiphany: "This whole thing is just a dream," she says; "You're nothing. You're shit." Freddy disappears, fading into a sparkling blue silhouette. Nancy, clad in a nightgown, opens the bedroom door, and a match cut shows her emerge through her house's front door, now dressed for school. Marge appears behind her, alive and well, and Nancy's friends who have been murdered by Freddy are waiting for her to join them in their car. At this moment, every encounter with Freddy — the whole film — seems to have been a dream from which Nancy has now awakened, but the dense fog that pervades the mise-en-scene tells viewers otherwise. Nancy joins her friends, and the car's convertible top, which looks like Freddy's red and green sweater, closes, trapping them all. The car, beyond their control,

8. Violent Self-Reflection

In *New Nightmare* (1994), Heather (Heather Langenkamp) stops her visibly traumatized son Dylan (Miko Hughes) from watching *A Nightmare on Elm Street*.

drives off. Freddy's hand bursts through the front door and grabs Marge. The film ends.

This ending thrusts the film into inescapable ontological ambiguity, recasting the entire narrative as a regression of dreams within dreams, in which reality may be everywhere, nowhere, or both. *A Nightmare on Elm Street* thus thematizes the collapse of reality into fantasy that haunts the politicians and pundits who fear that artworks have the

As Dylan (Miko Hughes) behaves like Freddy Krueger, *New Nightmare* (1994) envisions the possibility, feared by critics of media violence, that kids become what they watch.

power to become real. The next few films in the series, none of which Wes Craven directed, continue to play with this collapse in various ways. *A Nightmare on Elm Street 2: Freddy's Revenge* (1985) shows Freddy emerging from the dream-world into reality by bursting out of a victim's ravaged body. A particularly tongue-in-cheek scene from *Nightmare on Elm Street 3: Dream Warriors* (1987) shows Freddy's head and arms emerge from a television, into which he rams the head of an aspiring actress. Punning viciously as he kills her, "This is it, Jennifer — your big break in TV," Freddy literalizes the notion that the media can be deadly.[27]

Wes Craven returned to direct the seventh film in the series, *Wes Craven's New Nightmare* (1994), which features Wes Craven playing a character named Wes Craven who writes a script called *Wes Craven's New Nightmare*. The events he writes happen in the "real life" level of the film; effectively, his writing makes Freddy real. The story centers on Heather Langenkamp, the actress who plays Nancy in the original *Nightmare*, playing herself as she and her (fictional) son Dylan get caught up in the *Nightmare* movies' intrusion on reality. In an early scene, Heather catches Dylan watching *A Nightmare on Elm Street* on TV. She forbids him from watching it, but throughout the film, people accuse her of corrupting her son with her own movies (see page 197). As Freddy becomes more real, Dylan's access to the original *Nightmare* becomes stronger — the movie plays on his television even when the power cord is unplugged. Showing the effect of the bad influence, Dylan eventually tapes knives to his fingers and starts behaving like Freddy (see page 197). Ultimately, Heather and Dylan can only challenge Freddy by playing along with Wes Craven's story, battling and defeating the dream-monster on his own turf. After their victory, mother and son sit down to read Craven's script together, suggesting not that parents should keep their kids from experiencing violent fictions but that parents should guide their children through such fictions in order to help them learn and develop.[28]

The most recent (non-remake) Freddy movie pits Freddy against the nightmare character of another series critics often blame for real violence, Jason Voorhees, the maniac who slaughters teens in all but the first of the *Friday the 13th* films. This film, *Freddy vs. Jason* (2003), tells a story about how Freddy needs Jason to kill kids on Elm Street so that Freddy can gain enough power to resume his violent work himself. The adults in Freddy's home town have conspired against him by making everyone forget about him. They have removed records of his deeds; they have agreed never to speak of him. Freddy explains:

> They figured out a way to forget about me, to erase me completely ... being dead wasn't a problem, but being forgotten, now that's a bitch ... I can't come back if nobody remembers me ... I can't come back if nobody's afraid ... I found someone who'd make them remember.

As Jason hacks up kids on Elm Street, people in search of the culprit begin to stumble on Freddy's legend. A worried sheriff hears Freddy mentioned and says, "Don't even say that son of a bitch's name out loud ... we've been through too much to let this thing spread now." Knowledge of Freddy works like a disease. The more people know about him, the more powerful he becomes. Adults' suspicions become teenagers' nightmares, and teenagers start to die.[29] If Freddy were to go unchecked, he could become the number one health threat in America.

Though the DVD's "Jump to a Death" menu, complete with "Kill All" and "Random Death" options, suggests the film's primary purpose, *Freddy vs. Jason* also serves as a parable about the hunt for culpable, causal influences. Evoking the controversy still fresh in the minds of the film's original target audience, a culturally savvy teenager steps back from the events around her and comments, "It's not like this is some sort of Columbine thing or something," suggesting that paranoid adults' reactions to Freddy are misguided and blown out of proportion. Freddy, a creature of fantasy, derives his ability to cause destruction from the strength of the reputation that the adults help him build. The more people blame him for tragedies, the more people see him, and the more people see him, the more real he becomes. He emerges from the unconscious of dreams into consciousness, and from consciousness, he becomes real. Vilification of violent art ultimately vilifies the consciousness that art imbues. When influences bear the blame for the realities they inform, knowledge itself becomes the instrument of evil. In the world of *Freddy vs. Jason*, the only cure for knowledge — the only way to beat Freddy — is to live in silence and ignorance. Believing in Freddy, in the dream that can be guilty of murder, in the fiction that has the power to kill, means living in a world where ideas are boogeymen, and no one is safe.

Torture Porn and National Self-Knowledge

By going to the extreme of vilifying consciousness, *Freddy vs. Jason* holds up a mirror to the most paranoid members of the anti-media camp, showing their reasoning taken to the point of laughable absurdity. Read as a (perhaps unconscious) parody of the pundits and politicians who claim media violence is responsible for real-world violence, this film advocates absurdly for the avoidance of knowledge as the only way to stop violence, and in this absurd advocacy, it provides anti-media advocates with self-knowledge that is undoubtedly unwelcome. Pitting savvy kids versus paranoid adults, and self-aware cinema versus unreflective critics, *Freddy vs.*

Jason delivers a tamer version of the NBK effect, a critical self-knowledge that involves at least as much laughter as horror.

The critical self-knowledge offered by two of the most successful horror franchises of the 21st century so far — the *Hostel* and *Saw* series — is anything but tame. In a highly influential article from *New York Magazine*, David Edelstein dubs the trend encompassing these films "torture porn." Edelstein writes, "As a horror maven who long ago made peace, for better and worse, with the genre's inherent sadism, I'm baffled by how far this new stuff goes — and by why America seems so nuts these days about torture." Either his bafflement is disingenuous, or he fails to understand the answer that his own article provides:

> Fear supplants empathy and makes us all potential torturers, doesn't it? Post-9/11, we've engaged in a national debate about the morality of torture, fueled by horrifying pictures of manifestly decent men and women (some of them, anyway) enacting brutal scenarios of domination at Abu Ghraib. And a large segment of the population evidently has no problem with this. Our righteousness is buoyed by propaganda like the TV series *24*, which devoted an entire season to justifying torture in the name of an imminent threat: a nuclear missile en route to a major city. Who do you want defending America? Kiefer Sutherland or terrorist-employed civil-liberties lawyers?[30]

In *Hostel* (2005) and *Saw* (2004), American viewers take turns occupying the perspectives of killers and victims.[31] In short, the films replicate the viewing position of United States citizens who have paid attention to their country's foreign policy during the last decade, a foreign policy that, despite obfuscating quibbles about whether practices such as water-boarding (simulated drowning) actually qualify as torture, has put allegedly justifiable torture at the center of a global debate. The films' replication of the citizen's viewing position provides an opportunity for individual self-knowl-

In *Hostel* (2005) Paxton (Jay Hernandez) discovers an Elite Hunting business card with a price structure on the reverse side. Americans fetch the highest amount on this list. During his escape from the Elite Hunters, Paxton meets a fellow American who is preparing to enjoy a session as torturer. When Paxton claims to have just finished murdering an American, his countryman compliments him as a "big spender."

edge that the nation as a whole, in pursuing this policy, seems to lack. Edelstein need look no further than the political subtexts of the films he calls torture porn in order to understand why America became "so nuts" for torture at the box office.

Edelstein aptly summarizes *Hostel*'s premise:

> The director, Eli Roth, captures the mixture of innocence and entitlement in young American males abroad: They breeze into a former Soviet-bloc country the way teens in old sex comedies headed for Daytona, confident that their country's power and prestige will make them babe magnets.[32]

As their Slovakian hosts surround the young Americans, Paxton and Josh, with bloody chaos that is difficult, and for Josh impossible, to escape, the characters' entitlement and overconfidence in their country's power become direct reflections on not only the involvement of the United States in Eastern Europe but also on the quagmires the country has created in Afghanistan and Iraq. Commenting on the involvement of the United States in Iraq in 2003, former President George W. Bush claimed, "In this battle, we have fought for the cause of liberty, and for the peace of the world"; this statement appeared in his years-premature "Mission Accomplished" speech.[33] Claiming the entitlement to invade another country on behalf of the entire world and the overconfidence to declare the mission accomplished at least seven years before the war's end, Bush ends up looking more than a little like an ignorant college student abroad.

Hostel's mechanism for cultural critique is as deceptively simple as it is brutal. Instead of leading them to worshipful natives ready to fulfill the erotic fantasies of young American men, Paxton and Josh's travels put them in the hands of a very well-organized group of people dedicated to "Elite Hunting." After luring the young men into a hostel that promises easy sexual gratification, the Elite Hunting organization prepares to sell Paxton and Josh as objects for exploitation in the enactment of other travelers' violent — but still eroticized — fantasies. Behind the titular hostel lies a place where people with enough money can pay to participate in acts of horrific violence, much like filmgoers pay for their own tickets to *Hostel*. As Paxton eventually learns, Americans fetch some of the highest prices from the Elite Hunters, and the Elite Hunters are not war-ravaged Slovaks or fanatical Middle Eastern terrorists but the Americans, Dutch, and Japanese who benefit from the powerful economies that enable youth to engage in overconfident globe-trotting (see page 200). The positions of subject and object, torturer and tortured, and spectator and spectacle thus become confused and interchangeable, and both killers and victims at the hostel become objects of critique.

Hostel's two most elaborate set-pieces enact the interchange between torturer and tortured as pendants. The first set-piece is the torture and murder of Josh at the hands of a Dutch businessman whose façade of heterosexuality leaves him little room for the homoerotic violence that Elite Hunting allows. The film sets up the exchange carefully: in their first meeting on a train, the Dutch businessman makes a sexual advance that Josh rudely rejects; in their second meeting in a club, Josh apologizes for being rude; in their third meeting, the Dutch businessman uses his money to dominate and mutilate the unwilling object of his violent desire. While escaping from the Elite Hunters, Paxton witnesses some of the Dutch businessman's postmortem mutilation of his friend. Later, he sees the Dutch businessman on a train, and he begins to stalk him, finally trapping him in a bathroom stall and mutilating him in ways that directly echo Josh's mutilation.

In its immediate context, the punishment of the Dutch businessman can be read as a homophobic revenge fantasy in which the violence of the Dutchman's homoeroticism encodes the violation that homophobes see as intrinsic to all homosexual contact. In such a reading, heterosexual Paxton exacts poetic justice against the Gothic-ly monstrous, closeted homosexual Dutchman who has taken advantage of his friend. Read as a pendant to the first set-piece, however, Paxton's murder of the Dutch businessman puts him in the businessman's place. The role-reversal is clearest when Paxton shows the Dutch businessman an Elite Hunting business card. The hunter has become hunted and vice versa; if the Dutch businessman is monstrous, so is Paxton. The interchange allows no one to escape culpability, so the homophobic revenge fantasy becomes another object of *Hostel*'s critique of the violence embedded in American behaviors at home and abroad. As it suggests that anyone could be both killer and victim, the film represents a world devoid of absolute goodness or evil. It therefore challenges the simplicity that Bush's "Mission Accomplished" speech embeds in its characterization of those who fight for America as people who "fight a great evil, and bring liberty to others."[34] Viewers who know about the images of Abu Ghraib that Edelstein mentions — images of Arabs sexually humiliated and tortured at American hands — can know themselves as both Paxton and the Dutch businessman, as both the naïve youth who wishes to triumph over perceived evils abroad and the capitalist who perpetrates horrific violence through economic power.

8. Violent Self-Reflection

The *Saw* series makes the positions of torturer and tortured less fungible, but it takes more direct aim at the professed morality of justified torture and violence. *Saw*'s narrative follows the parallel storylines of police who are on the trail of a serial killer, Jigsaw, and the serial killer's latest victims, middle-aged surgeon Dr. Lawrence Gordon and young photographer Adam. The film begins when Dr. Gordon and Adam awake in a dirty room, each chained in a corner with a handsaw nearby that would allow him to cut not through his chains but through his feet in order to escape. Dr. Gordon soon recognizes that their captivity resembles aspects of the recent Jigsaw murders, with which he has become entangled as a (now cleared) suspect. He tells Adam what he knows about each murder the police have uncovered, and his storytelling becomes flashbacks that show the film audience Jigsaw's crimes. Each crime features a puzzle/trap that Jigsaw has set for a victim he believes to be guilty of showing insufficient appreciation for life. A man who has tried to slash his wrists ends up in a maze of razor wire, through which he must crawl, cutting himself, if he wants to avoid being trapped forever in a room set to lock on a timer. The man bleeds to death in the effort. A man who has feigned illness, "burning" his friends and colleagues in the colloquial sense, ends up in a trap that leads him to burn himself to death. Each trap metaphorically turns the victim's perceived sin against him- or herself. Technically, Jigsaw kills no one; he is a preacher, and his professed motive is to teach life lessons, not to murder.

Detective Tapp, who leads the investigation into the Jigsaw case, follows the popular press as it reveals Jigsaw's motives. A montage of newspaper clippings that Detective Tapp has obsessively collected shows headlines that read "'Killer Preaching' Says Top Cop," and "Psychopath Teaches Sick Life Lessons." The film emphasizes the press's sensational coverage of Jigsaw's didactic violence because the coverage is part of Jigsaw's design: while few who fall into Jigsaw's traps survive, his message doesn't die with his victims because it proliferates through the reports of police who reinforce Jigsaw's preaching by drawing attention to it. Thus the police and the press, like the parents, politicians, and pundits who warn about media violence, become complicit in the acts they seek to stop.

The film's inset narratives ultimately model the spread of information through this network of people complicit in Jigsaw's didactic design. Like the newspapers, Dr. Gordon reproduces Jigsaw's murders and message when he tells Adam the stories he has learned from the police. At the center of Dr. Gordon's storytelling lies another act of storytelling, the performance of Amanda, the only survivor of one of Jigsaw's traps, telling Detective Tapp and his partner about her ordeal, which the film represents as a flashback within a flashback. Amanda awakes to find herself with a device on her head that Jigsaw refers to as a "reverse bear trap." The key that she needs to remove the apparatus is hidden in the stomach of a man to whom Jigsaw refers as her "dead cell mate." Racing to remove the key before the trap on her head automatically springs, Amanda uses a knife to dig into her cell mate's body and literally retrieve the key to her salvation. The camera lingers on her hands as they expose, remove, and search through the man's innards. The gore conveys how far Amanda must go to demonstrate the extreme drive for survival that Jigsaw deems morally necessary to be worthy of life. Once she is free, Jigsaw tells her, "Most people are so ungrateful to be alive. But not you. Not anymore." His statement suggests she has learned his lesson and adopted his values.

When Amanda finishes telling her story, Detective Tapp asks her if she thinks Jigsaw picked her because she is a drug addict. Without waiting for an answer, Tapp asks, "Are you grateful, Mandy?" Amanda answers affirmatively, saying, "He helped me." Tapp's question anticipates her response, suggesting that he, too, understands the "help" offered by her experience: he may not accept them, but he at least comprehends Jigsaw's values. Jigsaw's message about the value of life passes through a storytelling chain from Amanda to Detective Tapp, to Dr. Gordon, to Adam, and finally to the film's viewers.

Jigsaw's values spread through reproductions of violent spectacles, and the ways in which these spectacles reflect on the victim's supposed crimes recalls a form of punishment through public torture that Michel Foucault describes in *Discipline and Punish*. According to Foucault, by establishing "decipherable relations" between crime and punishment in the early eighteenth century, "justice had the crime reenacted before the eyes of all, publishing it in its truth and at the same time annulling it in the death of the guilty man."[35] Because Amanda is both a participant in and a witness of physical mutilation's production of truth, she is able to carry truth from a tortured body to a wider audience. Tapp's partner, Detective Sing, explains to Dr. Gordon that the man in whose stomach Amanda found the key was actually alive but drugged, given an "opiate overdose" so that he "couldn't move or feel much of anything." That the man dies at Amanda's hands suggests how her own use of drugs is a kind of self-destruction — anyone with sufficient will to live would not make herself so vulnerable. Amanda's confrontation with the vulnerability of a body in a situation analogous to her own life endows her with the desire to be free from such vulnerability.

In *Saw 2* (2005), Jigsaw states the moral of his spectacles directly: "Those who don't appreciate life do not deserve life."[36] This message becomes a mantra for the *Saw* series, motivating the "decipherable relations" between punishment and crime delivered by trap after trap in the five sequels to date. Of course, the idea that a multiple murderer values life is paradoxical, and therefore Jigsaw appears to be profoundly hypocritical: his methods of teaching leave little opportunity for survival, so he clearly doesn't appreciate the lives of those to whom he would teach appreciation. This hypocrisy becomes the first level in the film's critique of moralizers who, like American anti-abortion activists who murder doctors, take life in the name of valuing life. However, the critique itself is vulnerable to critique: just as some anti-abortion activists use violence to make a point about the violence of abortion, the *Saw* films use violence to make a point about hypocrites who use violence to make points about violence. If the films themselves offer a critique about the excesses of moralizers, they also relish those same excesses. If the films preach about hypocritical preachers, they also *are* hypocritical preachers. This connection allows the films not to convey moral messages, but to reflect on the pervasive moral contradictions in contemporary American politics, from the anti-abortion movement to George W. Bush's "war on terror," a war fought against people who kill to spread their values in order to spread the American value of democracy. *Saw* delivers self-knowledge to American filmgoers by making Jigsaw a lens on American politics, or at least on the self-contradictory politics of the American right.

Jigsaw's use of spectacle as a means to convey values resonates further in the series' primary context of George W. Bush's America. The "Mission Accomplished" speech, for which Bush heroically flew onto an aircraft carrier, was itself a spectacle calculated to show America's value of military strength. In fact, several of Bush's most important speeches framed his government's actions as spectacles of values. In "Mission Accomplished," Bush told the troops, "you have shown the world the skill and might of the American Armed Forces"; he framed the military action in Iraq not in terms of what it accomplished for Iraqis or Americans but in terms of what it had shown the rest of the world about America.[37] The showing Bush's government did in Iraq picks up on the showing he promised in his speech before Congress on September 20, 2001, during which he focused not on healing the damage done to New Yorkers on September 11 but on how his efforts would "show the world that we will rebuild New York City."³⁸ Thus the world could learn of America's value of resilience, a theme Bush picked up again during his farewell speech on January 16, 2009, in which he promised that, as a result of his administration's actions, "We will show the world once again the resilience of America's free enterprise system."³⁹ With rhetoric emphasizing spectacles as means for conveying values, Bush created an ethos that is continuous with, if not the inspiration for, Jigsaw's didactic killings.

Although the *Saw* series as a whole is very canny about the political resonance of its story of a murderer who preaches the value of life — *Saw 3* (2006), for example, reveals that Jigsaw is at least in part motivated by the death, or accidental abortion, of his unborn child — its most profound development is perhaps the revelation that occurs at the end of *Saw 2*.⁴⁰ Though she initially claims to have been caught in another of Jigsaw's traps, the first film's survivor, Amanda, is eventually revealed to be Jigsaw's accomplice. The most direct recipient of his teaching, of the influence of his violent spectacles, thus becomes a person who stages more violent spectacles. Through Amanda's transformation from victim to killer, the *Saw* series dramatizes the spread of violence through the cycle of representation and reality. Just as Amanda ends up identifying with her torturer because she feels grateful for the lessons the torture taught, viewers who agree with Jigsaw about his victims' unworthiness of life — and the attempted suicide, the malingerer, and the heroin addict in *Saw* do not appear sympathetic — are invited to identify with a torturer. Through these identifications, Amanda becomes a cipher for the American filmgoer, complicit in the spectacles of American moralizing that the films critique. Just like *Hostel*, then, the *Saw* films allow their American audiences to occupy multiple subject positions, to feel both horrified by and identified with Jigsaw's hypocritical moralizing, and to recognize that if they, like Amanda, adopt Jigsaw's values, they could also end up reproducing his violence.

Saw 6 (2009), the first film in the series to be released in the post–Bush era, was significantly less successful at the box office than its predecessors.⁴¹ The film maintains the series' political resonance by opening on a trap Jigsaw's minions have set for predatory lenders, but if the American people vote on films' relevance to their lives with their box office dollars, the film's poor performance suggests that the connection between 2009's economic crisis and torture isn't as resonant as the torturous dimensions of previous years' political quandaries. The diminishment of the series' power to draw a wide audience suggests that people just aren't as nuts about torture as they were when Edelstein made his observations about torture porn. The political change that began with the election of Barack Obama to the American presidency might signal a turn away from the violent hypocrisy that the *Saw* films help American filmgoers to identify in themselves. If films in the mold of *Hostel* and *Saw* provided essential insight into the Gothic side of reality during the Bush era, then maybe the knowledge these films provide has become historical rather than present, and thus torture porn is neither as relevant nor as controversial as it once was. But if the likes of Freddy Krueger and Jigsaw teach us anything, they show us that some truths never really die. In some form or other, the Gothic will keep on intruding on our realities, giving shape to the violence we see, believe, and do.

Chapter Notes

Introduction

1. *A Nightmare on Elm Street*, DVD, directed by Wes Craven (1984; Los Angeles: New Line Studios, 1999).
2. Plato, *Republic*, trans. Robin Waterfield (New York: Oxford World's Classics, 2008), 344, 360.
3. T.J. Mathias, *The Pursuits of Literature* (London: Bulmer & Co., 1812), 149. Italics and capitalization in original.
4. Nancy Armstrong, *Desire and Domestic Fiction: A Political History of the Novel* (New York: Oxford University Press, 1987), 9.
5. Martin Tropp, *Images of Fear: How Horror Stories Helped Shape Modern Culture, 1818–1918* (Jefferson, NC: McFarland, 1990), 9, 1.
6. Stephen King, *Danse Macabre* (New York: Berkley Books, 1983), 16.
7. David Punter, *The Literature of Terror*, 2d ed., vol.1 (New York: Longman, 1996), 18.
8. Jean Baudrillard, *Selected Writings*, ed. Mark Poster (Stanford, CA: Stanford University Press, 1988), 166.
9. Ian Hacking, *The Social Construction of What?* (Cambridge, MA: Harvard University Press, 1999), 24, 48.
10. Ibid., 22.
11. Michel Foucault, "The Discourse on Language," *Critical Theory Since 1965*, eds. Hazard Adams and Leroy Searle (Tallahassee: Florida State University Press, 1986), 151–155.
12. David Grossman and Gloria DeGaetano, *Stop Teaching Our Kids to Kill: A Call to Action Against TV, Movie and Video Game Violence* (New York: Crown, 1999), 46.
13. William Dudley, ed., *Media Violence: Opposing Viewpoints* (San Diego: Greenhaven Press, 1999), 31–32.
14. James Potter, *The 11 Myths of Media Violence* (Thousand Oaks, CA: Sage, 2003), 52–53.
15. Ibid., 55.
16. Ibid., 158–167.
17. Michael Medved, *Hollywood Vs. America: Popular Culture and the War on Traditional Values* (New York: HarperCollins, 1992), 242.
18. Thomas Pavel, *Fictional Worlds* (Cambridge, MA: Harvard University Press, 1986), 85.
19. Michel Foucault, *Madness and Civilization*, trans. Richard Howard (New York: Vintage Books, 1988), 28–29.
20. Medved, *Hollywood Vs. America*, 115.
21. Carol Clover, *Men, Women, and Chain Saws: Gender in the Modern Horror Film* (Princeton: Princeton University Press, 1992), see especially 44–45, 211–212.
22. Gerard Jones, *Killing Monsters: Why Children Need Fantasy, Super Heroes, and Make-Believe Violence* (New York: Basic Books, 2002), 84, 160.
23. Potter, *11 Myths of Media Violence*, 65.
24. Pierre Bourdieu, *Pascalian Meditations*, trans. Richard Nice (Stanford, CA: Stanford University Press, 2000) 169, 99.
25. Pavel, *Fictional Worlds*, 89.
26. Slavoj Žižek, *For They Know Not What They Do: Enjoyment as a Political Factor* (New York: Verso, 1991), 87.
27. Bourdieu, *Pascalian Meditations*, 130, 134.
28. Ibid., 136–137, 148, 116.
29. Ibid., 118. Emphasis in original.
30. Žižek, *For They Know Not What They Do*, 222. Emphasis in original.
31. Bourdieu, *Pascalian Meditations*, 113. Emphasis in original.
32. Žižek, *For They Know Not What They Do*, 109. Emphasis in original.
33. Slavoj Žižek, *Looking Awry: An Intro-*

duction to Jacques Lacan through Popular Culture (Cambridge, MA: MIT Press, 1991), 71.
    34. Žižek, For They Know Not What They Do, 112, 220.
    35. Žižek, Looking Awry, 20.

Chapter 1

1. Horace Walpole, The Castle of Otranto, ed. W. S. Lewis (New York: Oxford University Press, 1998), 9.
    2. Horace Walpole, The Yale Edition of Horace Walpole's Correspondence, vol. 3, ed. W. S. Lewis (New Haven, CT: Yale University Press, 1937), 261. "I wanted it to pass for an ancient production, and almost the entire world was duped." Translation mine.
    3. Lennard Davis, Factual Fictions: The Origins of the English Novel (New York: Columbia University Press, 1983), 21.
    4. Ibid., 36.
    5. Review of The Castle of Otranto, by Horace Walpole, Monthly Review 32, May 1765, 394.
    6. Jerrold Hogle, "The Gothic Ghost of the Counterfeit and the Progress of Abjection," in A Companion to the Gothic, ed. David Punter (Malden, MA: Blackwell, 2000), 293–294.
    7. Crystal Lake, "Bloody Records: Manuscripts and Politics in Horace Walpole's The Castle of Otranto" (article in progress, Georgia Institute of Technology, 2009), 17.
    8. E.J. Clery, The Rise of Supernatural Fiction, 1762–1800 (New York: Cambridge University Press, 1995), 55.
    9. Clara Reeve, Preface to The Old English Baron, in Gothic Documents: A Sourcebook, 1700–1820, eds. E.J. Clery and Robert Miles (Manchester: Manchester University Press, 2000), 132–134.
    10. Review of The Castle of St. Vallery: An Ancient Story, Monthly Review 2d ser. 9, November 1792, 337.
    11. John Locke, An Essay Concerning Human Understanding, ed. Peter H. Nidditch (Oxford: Clarendon Press, 1975), section 1.2.
    12. Ibid., section 4.3.18 and section 1.3.3. Italics removed from original.
    13. David Hume, A Treatise of Human Nature, ed. Ernest C. Mossner (New York: Penguin Books, 1985), 527, 520–521.
    14. David Hume, An Enquiry Concerning Human Understanding (Amherst, NY: Prometheus Books, 1988), 73.
    15. Locke, Essay, section 2.33.9.
    16. Ibid., section 3.11.15.
    17. Ibid., section 2.33.8.
    18. Joseph Addison, "Selection from The Spectator No. 110," in Gothic Documents: A Sourcebook, 1700–1820, eds. E.J. Clery and Robert Miles (Manchester: Manchester University Press, 2000), 17. Addison is quoting Locke, Essay, section 2.33.10.
    19. Locke, Essay, section 2.22.3, and section 2.22.2. Italics removed from original.
    20. Samuel Johnson, "Preface to the Plays of William Shakespeare," in The Major Works, ed. Donald Greene (New York: Oxford University Press, 2000), 424, 420–421.
    21. James Beattie, Essay on Poetry and Music, as They Affect the Mind, in Essays on the Nature and Immutability of Truth, in opposition to sophistry and scepticism; on Poetry and Music, as they affect the mind; On Laughter, and Ludicrous Composition; and, on the Utility of Classical Learning, vol. 2 (Dublin: printed for C. Jenkin, [No. 58] Dame-Street, 1777), 23, 6.
    22. Ibid., 15.
    23. Ibid., 6.
    24. Hannah More, Strictures on the Modern System of Female Education, with A View of the Principles and Conduct Prevalent among Women of Rank and Fortune (Boston: Printed for Joseph Bumstead, 1802), 22.
    25. Fred Botting, Gothic (New York: Routledge, 1996), 28.
    26. Samuel Johnson, "Selection from The Rambler No. 4," in Gothic Documents: A Sourcebook, 1700–1820, eds. E.J. Clery and Robert Miles (Manchester: Manchester University Press, 2000), 176–178.
    27. Ibid.
    28. Clara Reeve, The Progress of Romance, through Times, Countries, and Manners, with Remarks on the Good and Bad Effects of It, on Them Respectively, in a Course of Evening Conversations, vol. 1 (Dublin: Printed for Messrs. Price, Exshaw, White, Cash, Colbert, Marchbank, and Porter, 1785), 139.
    29. Johnson, "Preface," 427.
    30. Johnson, "Selection from The Rambler No. 4," 179.
    31. Davis, Factual Fictions, 111.
    32. Review of The Exiles, by Clara Reeve, Critical Review 67, January 1789, 75.
    33. Johnson, "Selection from The Rambler No. 4," 177.
    34. Walpole, Castle of Otranto, 9.
    35. Clery, Rise of Supernatural Fiction, 59–60.

Chapter 2

1. Peter Stallybrass and Allon White, The Politics and Poetics of Transgression (Ithaca: Cornell University Press, 1986), 4.

2. David H. Richter, *The Progress of Romance: Literary Historiography and the Gothic Novel* (Columbus: Ohio State University Press, 1996), 101.

3. Review of *The Maid of the Hamlet*, by Regina Maria Roche, *Critical Review* 2d ser. 10, April 1794, 472–73.

4. Review of *Man As He Is*, by Robert Bage, *Monthly Review* 2d ser. 10, March 1793, 297.

5. "Terrorist Novel Writing," in *Gothic Documents: A Sourcebook, 1700–1820*, eds. E.J. Clery and Robert Miles (Manchester: Manchester University Press, 2000), 184.

6. John Tinnon Taylor, *Early Opposition to the English Novel: The Popular Reaction from 1760 to 1830* (New York: King's Crown Press, 1943), 75.

7. Richter, *Progress of Romance*, 83.

8. Kate Ferguson Ellis, *The Contested Castle: Gothic Novels and the Subversion of Domestic Ideology* (Chicago: University of Illinois Press, 1989), x.

9. Review of *The School for Fathers*, by Clara Reeve, *Analytical Review* 2, October 1788, 223.

10. Michael Gamer, *Romanticism and the Gothic: Genre, Reception, and Canon Formation* (Cambridge: Cambridge University Press, 2000), 61.

11. Review of *Tancred, or a Tale of Ancient Times*, by Joseph Fox, *English Review* 18, August 1791, 143.

12. Gamer, *Romanticism and the Gothic*, 53.

13. Botting, *Gothic*, 6.

14. Samuel Taylor Coleridge, review of *The Monk*, by Matthew Lewis, *Gothic Documents: A Sourcebook, 1700–1820*, eds. E.J. Clery and Robert Miles (Manchester: Manchester University Press, 2000) 188.

15. Robert Miles, "Europhobia: The Catholic Other in Horace Walpole and Charles Maturin," in *European Gothic: A Spirited Exchange, 1760–1960*, ed. Avril Horner (Manchester: Manchester University Press, 2002), 86.

16. Mathias, *The Pursuits of Literature*, 238, 236.

17. "The Rise, Progress, and Effects of Jacobinism," *Anti-Jacobin Review* 1, August 1798, 223.

18. Richter, *Progress of Romance*, 112.

19. "The Terrorist System of Novel Writing," *Gothic Readings: The First Wave, 1764–1840*, ed. Rictor Norton (New York: Leicester University Press, 2000), 300.

20. Mathias, *The Pursuits of Literature*, xxxix, 190.

21. Reviews of *Old Manor House*, by Charlotte Smith; *Caleb Williams*, by William Godwin; *Secrecy, or The Ruin of the Rock*, by Eliza Fenwick; *Hermsprong*, by Robert Bage; and *St. Leon*, by William Godwin; *British Critic* 1, June 1793, 148; 4, July 1794, 71; 6, November 1795, 545; 7, April 1796, 430; 15, January 1800, 51.

22. W.W., "On Novels and Romances," in *Gothic Documents: A Sourcebook, 1700–1820*, eds. E.J. Clery and Robert Miles (Manchester: Manchester University Press, 2000), 216.

23. Review of *The Monk*, by Matthew Lewis, *European Magazine and London Review* 31, February 1797, 114–15.

24. Andre Parreaux, *The Publication of* The Monk (Paris: M. Didier, 1960), 136.

25. Coleridge, review of *The Monk*, 188.

26. Review of *The Monk*, by Matthew Lewis, *Monthly Review* 2d ser. 23, August 1797, 451.

27. Coleridge, review of *The Monk*, 188.

28. Matthew Lewis, *The Monk*, ed. Howard Anderson (New York: Oxford University Press, 1998), 58.

29. Judith Butler, *Gender Trouble* (New York: Routledge, 1990).

30. Lewis, *The Monk*, 232.

31. Ibid., 355–356.

32. Quoted in Parreaux, *The Publication of* The Monk, 36.

33. Lewis, *The Monk*, 356.

34. Ibid., 259.

35. Mathias, *The Pursuits of Literature*, 215.

36. Parreaux, *The Publication of* The Monk, 139.

37. Ellis, *The Contested Castle*, 135.

38. See pp. 191–194, 198–199 of the present work for a discussion of critics' promotion of ignorance in a more contemporary context.

39. Lewis, *The Monk*, 198.

40. Mathias, *The Pursuits of Literature*, 306.

41. Parreaux, *The Publication of* The Monk, 119.

42. Coleridge, review of *The Monk*, 185, 187–8.

43. Beattie, *Essay on Poetry and Music*, 6.

44. Coleridge, review of *The Monk*, 187.

45. Samuel Taylor Coleridge, review of *The Mysteries of Udolpho*, by Ann Radcliffe, *Critical Review* 2d ser. 11, August 1794), 361.

46. Anna Maria Mackenzie, *Mysteries Elucidated* (London: Minerva Press, 1795), 2.

47. Review of *The Italian*, by Ann Radcliffe, *British Critic* 10, September 1797, 266.

48. Coleridge, review of *Mysteries of Udolpho*, 361, and Nathan Drake, "On Objects of Terror," in *Gothic Documents: A Sourcebook, 1700–1820*, eds. E.J. Clery and Robert Miles (Manchester: Manchester University Press, 2000), 162.

49. "On Novels," *Walker's Hibernian*, April 1797, 357.
50. Rictor Norton, *Mistress of Udolpho: The Life of Ann Radcliffe* (London: Leicester University Press, 1999), xi.
51. Mackenzie, *Mysteries Elucidated,* xii.
52. Ann Radcliffe, *The Mysteries of Udolpho,* ed. Bonamy Dobrée (New York: Oxford University Press, 1980), 102, 278, 635, 573, 662.
53. Robert Miles, *Ann Radcliffe: The Great Enchantress* (Manchester: Manchester University Press, 1995), 132.
54. Mary Poovey, "Ideology and *The Mysteries of Udolpho*," *Criticism* 21.4 , 1979, 319.
55. Radcliffe, *Mysteries of Udolpho,* 562.
56. Poovey, "Ideology and *The Mysteries of Udolpho*," 315, 318, 329.
57. Ibid., 318, 327.
58. Miles, *Ann Radcliffe*, 153.
59. April London, "Ann Radcliffe in Context: Marking the Boundaries of *The Mysteries of Udolpho*," *Eighteenth-Century Life* 10.1, January 1986, 42.
60. Michael Taylor, "Reluctant Romancers: Self-Consciousness and Derogation in Prose Romance," *English Studies in Canada* 17.1, March 1991, 95.
61. Miles, *Ann Radcliffe*, 23, 18, 176.

Chapter 3

1. Donald Lawler, "The Gothic Wilde," in *Rediscovering Oscar Wilde*, ed. George Sandulescu (Gerrards Cross, Buckinghamshire: Smythe, 1994), 250.
2. George E. Haggerty, *Queer Gothic* (Urbana: University of Illinois Press, 2006), 5.
3. Michel Foucault, *The History of Sexuality, Vol. 1: An Introduction*, trans. Robert Hurley (New York: Vintage Books, 1990), 43.
4. Michel Foucault, *The History of Sexuality, Vol. 2: The Use of Pleasure*, trans. Robert Hurley (New York: Vintage Books, 1990), 3.
5. David M. Halperin, *How to Do the History of Homosexuality* (Chicago: University of Chicago Press, 2002), 8–9.
6. Ed Cohen, *Talk on the Wilde Side: Toward a Genealogy of a Discourse on Male Sexualities* (New York: Routledge, 1993), 9, 97, 2, 211.
7. Eve Sedgwick, *Epistemology of the Closet* (Los Angeles: University of California Press, 1990), 2. Throughout the *Epistemology*, and especially in the introduction, Sedgwick wisely counsels scholars to avoid looking for a "great paradigm shift" in the history of sexuality. A new sexual paradigm did not emerge overnight; the emergence of a binary, normative system of sexualities framed in terms of object choice was centuries in the making. For a rich and informative account of sexualities in English culture in the seventeenth and eighteenth centuries, consult Rictor Norton's sourcebook *Homosexuality in Eighteenth-Century England*, http://rictornorton.co.uk/eighteen/ (last accessed December 28, 2009). What I argue here is not that in 1895 Wilde's trials suddenly and dramatically produced a homosexuality inflected by the Gothic. Instead, I argue that Wilde's trials made a formative contribution to the ways Gothic tropes became encoded within the emerging paradigm.
8. Eve Sedgwick, *Between Men: English Literature and Male Homosocial Desire* (New York: Columbia University Press, 1985), 94.
9. Max Fincher, *Queering the Gothic in the Romantic Age: The Penetrating Eye* (Basingstoke: Palgrave Macmillan, 2007). See especially the introduction and first chapter.
10. Judith Halberstam, *Skin Shows: Gothic Horror and the Technology of Monsters* (Durham: Duke University Press, 1995), 22.
11. Jeffrey Weeks, *Coming Out: Homosexual Politics in Britain, from the Nineteenth Century to the Present* (New York: Quartet Books, 1977), 101.
12. Sedgwick, *Between Men*, 94–95.
13. Alan Sinfield, *The Wilde Century: Effeminacy, Oscar Wilde and the Queer Moment* (New York: Columbia University Press, 1994), 3.
14. Laura Green, "Hall of Mirrors: Radclyffe Hall's *The Well of Loneliness* and Modernist Fictions of Identity," *Twentieth-Century Literature* 49.3 (Fall 2003): 288.
15. Louis P. Sheldon, "Homosexuals Recruit Public School Children," Traditional Values Coalition, http://www.traditionalvalues.org/pdf_files/TVCSpecialRptHomosexualRecruitChildren.PDF (accessed Dec. 28, 2009).
16. Richard G. Howe, "Homosexuality in America: Exposing the Myths," *AFA Online*, The American Family Association, http://www.afa.net/homosexual_agenda/homosexuality.pdf, 18–19 (accessed Dec. 28, 2009).
17. Lee Edelman, *No Future: Queer Theory and the Death Drive* (Durham: Duke University Press, 2004), 10–11, 7, 2, 74.
18. Howe, "Homosexuality in America," 3.
19. Edelman, *No Future*, 16.
20. H. Montgomery Hyde, ed., *The Trials of Oscar Wilde* (Birmingham, AL: The Notable Trials Library, 1989), 253.
21. Mary Shelley, *Frankenstein*, ed. J. Paul Hunter (New York: W. W. Norton, 1996), 32.
22. Anne K. Mellor, "A Feminist Critique of Science," in *Frankenstein: Mary Shelley*, ed.

Fred Botting (London: Macmillan, 1995), 120–121.

23. Shelley, *Frankenstein*, 34.

24. Ibid., 114.

25. John Rieder, "'A Filthy Type': The Motif of the Fecal Child in Mary Shelley's *Frankenstein*," *Gothic Studies* 3.1 (April 2001) 25.

26. J. Paul Hunter, ed., "Mary Shelley: A Chronology," *Frankenstein*, by Mary Shelley (New York: W. W. Norton, 1996), 334.

27. Shelley, *Frankenstein*, 115, 79, 86.

28. Ibid., 115, 146.

29. Joseph Kestner, "Narcissism as Symptom and Structure: The Case of Mary Shelley's *Frankenstein*," in *Frankenstein: Mary Shelley*, ed. Fred Botting (London: Macmillan, 1995), 73.

30. Charles Maturin, *Melmoth the Wanderer*, ed. Douglas Grant (New York: Oxford University Press, 1998), 537–538.

31. Judith Wilt, *Ghosts of the Gothic: Austen, Eliot, and Lawrence* (Princeton: Princeton University Press, 1980), 58.

32. Maturin, *Melmoth the Wanderer*, 38–39, 43, 59.

33. Eugenia C. DeLamotte, *Perils of the Night: A Feminist Study of Nineteenth-Century Gothic* (New York: Oxford University Press, 1990), 55, 61.

34. Maturin, *Melmoth the Wanderer*, 538, 511.

35. Ibid., 5.

36. J. Sheridan Le Fanu, *Carmilla*, in *Three Vampire Tales*, ed. Anne Williams (New York: Houghton Mifflin, 2003), 147, 119.

37. Tamar Heller, "The Vampire in the House: Hysteria, Female Sexuality, and Female Knowledge in Le Fanu's 'Carmilla,'" in *The New Nineteenth Century: Feminist Readings of Underread Victorian Fiction*, eds. Barbara Leah Harman and Susan Meyer (New York: Garland, 1996), 79.

38. Lillian Faderman, *Surpassing the Love of Men: Romantic Friendship and Love Between Women from the Renaissance to the Present* (New York: Triangle Classics, 1981), 289.

39. Ibid., 31.

40. Judith Butler, *Bodies that Matter* (New York: Routledge, 1993), 86.

41. Le Fanu, *Carmilla*, 145.

42. Butler, *Bodies that Matter*, 88.

43. Le Fanu, *Carmilla*, 145.

44. Heller, "The Vampire in the House," 90.

45. Edelman, *No Future*, 60.

46. Robert Louis Stevenson, *Strange Case of Dr. Jekyll and Mr. Hyde*, ed. Katherine Linehan (New York: W.W. Norton, 2003), 60–61.

47. Wilt, *Ghosts of the Gothic*, 84.

48. Stevenson, *Strange Case of Dr. Jekyll and Mr. Hyde*, 60n2, 52, 56.

49. Ibid., 55.

50. R. von Krafft-Ebing, *Psychopathia Sexualis*, 7th edition (Philadelphia: The F.A. Davis Co., 1893), 187.

51. Stevenson, *Strange Case of Dr. Jekyll and Mr. Hyde*, 49, 55.

52. Robert Louis Stevenson, letter to John Paul Bocock, November 1887, in *Strange Case of Dr. Jekyll and Mr. Hyde*, ed. Katherine Linehan (New York: W.W. Norton, 2003), 86.

53. Wayne Koestenbaum, "The Shadow on the Bed: Dr. Jekyll, Mr. Hyde, and the Labouchere Amendment," *Critical Matrix*, Special Issue No. 1, Spring 1988, 31–55; Elaine Showalter, *Sexual Anarchy: Gender and Culture at the Fin de Siecle* (New York: Viking, 1990).

54. Martha Vicinus, "The Adolescent Boy: Fin-de-Siecle Femme Fatale?" in *Victorian Sexual Dissidence*, ed. Richard Dellamora (Chicago: University of Chicago Press, 1999), 87.

55. Oscar Wilde, *The Picture of Dorian Gray*, in *The Complete Works of Oscar Wilde* (New York: Collins, 1966), 21, 23, 28–29, 165–166.

56. Holland, Merlin, ed., *The Real Trial of Oscar Wilde: The First Uncensored Transcript of the Trial of Oscar Wilde vs. John Douglas (Marquess of Queensberry), 1895* (New York: Fourth Estate, 2003), 290, 102, 78.

57. Ibid., 102–103, 281.

58. Ibid., 294.

59. Hyde, *The Trials of Oscar Wilde*, 225, 256.

60. Ibid., 339.

61. Max Nordau, *Degeneration*, trans. 1895 from 2d German edition (Lincoln: University of Nebraska Press, 1993), 260.

62. Ibid., 452.

Chapter 4

1. See, for example, Christopher Craft, *Another Kind of Love: Male Homosexual Desire in English Discourse, 1850–1920* (Los Angeles: University of California Press, 1994). For a compelling argument associating Dracula with Oscar Wilde, see Talia Schaffer, "'A Wilde Desire Took Me': The Homoerotic History of *Dracula*," in *Dracula*, ed. Nina Auerbach and David J. Skal (New York: W.W. Norton, 1997), 470–482. Though I don't agree with the amount of credit Schaffer gives to Stoker, Schaffer's claim (which preceded mine) that "Stoker recuperates the infectiousness of

the vampire myth by making it into a paradigm for homosexual procreative sex" resonates strongly with my argument about pathological reproduction.

2. *Nosferatu*, directed by F. W. Murnau (1922; Berlin: Jofa-Atelier Berlin-Johannisthal); *Frankenstein*, directed by James Whale (1931; Los Angeles: Universal Pictures); *Bride of Frankenstein*, directed by James Whale (1935; Los Angeles: Universal Pictures).

3. Robin Wood, "An Introduction to the American Horror Film," in *Planks of Reason: Essays on the Horror Film*, ed. Barry Keith Grant (Metuchen, NJ: Scarecrow Press, 1984), 172.

4. *Gods and Monsters*, DVD, directed by Bill Condon (1998; Los Angeles: Lion's Gate, 2003).

5. Foucault, *History of Sexuality, Vol. 1: An Introduction*, 101.

6. Julia Kristeva, *Powers of Horror: An Essay on Abjection*, trans. Leon S. Roudiez (New York: Columbia University Press, 1982), 2.

7. Harry M. Benshoff, *Monsters in the Closet: Homosexuality and the Horror Film* (Manchester: Manchester University Press, 1997), 232.

8. Wilde, *The Picture of Dorian Gray*, 121–122, 166.

9. Showalter, *Sexual Anarchy*, 113.

10. Edward S. Brinkley, "Homosexuality as (Anti)Illness: Oscar Wilde's *The Picture of Dorian Gray* and Gabriele D'Annunzio's *Il Piacere*," *Studies in Twentieth Century Literature* 22.1 (1998), 73.

11. Wilde, *The Picture of Dorian Gray*, 133, 122, 167.

12. Philip Jenkins, *Using Murder: The Social Construction of Serial Homicide* (New York: Aldine de Gruyter, 1994), 1–2.

13. Diana Fuss, *Identification Papers: Readings on Psychoanalysis, Sexuality, and Culture* (New York: Routledge, 1995), 98.

14. Richard Tithecott, *Of Men and Monsters: Jeffrey Dahmer and the Construction of the Serial Killer* (Madison: University of Wisconson Press, 1997), 81.

15. Halberstam, *Skin Shows*, 21, 69.

16. *Texas Chainsaw Massacre 2*, DVD, directed by Tobe Hooper (1986; Los Angeles: MGM-UA, 2000).

17. Halberstam, *Skin Shows*, 160.

18. Ibid., 188.

19. *Shrek*, directed by Vicky Jenson and Andrew Adamson (2001; Los Angeles: Dreamworks SKG). For a compelling account of how classic monsters become kid-friendly, see Harvey Roy Greenberg, "Heimlich Manuevers: On a Certain Tendency of Horror and Speculative Cinema," in *Horror Film and Psychoanalysis*, ed. Steven Jay Schneider (New York: Cambridge University Press, 2009), 122–141.

20. Halberstam, *Skin Shows*, 21.

21. "New Moon Rising," *Buffy the Vampire Slayer: The Complete Fourth Season*, DVD, created by Joss Whedon (1999; Los Angeles: Twentieth Century–Fox Home Video, 2003).

22. *Buffy the Vampire Slayer: The Complete Sixth Season*, DVD, created by Joss Whedon (2001; Los Angeles: Twentieth Century–Fox Home Video, 2004).

23. Willow is also Jewish, making the scene read eerily like a straight Christ reclaiming a wayward lesbian Jew through his unwavering love and forgiveness.

24. Paulina Palmer, *Lesbian Gothic: Transgressive Fictions* (New York: Cassell, 1999), 40.

25. "David DeCoteau Speaks," interview by Paul Freitag, *Bright Lights Film Journal*, August 1999, http://www.brightlightsfilm.com/25/decoteau.html (accessed December 30, 2009); see also Director's Commentary, in *Voodoo Academy*, DVD, directed by David DeCoteau (2000; Los Angeles: Cult Video, 2000). All subsequent references to *Voodoo Academy* refer to this DVD.

26. *The Brotherhood*, in *The Brotherhood / The Brotherhood 2: Young Warlocks*, DVD, directed by David DeCoteau (2001; Rapid Heart Pictures, 2002); *Leeches*, DVD, directed by David DeCoteau (2003; Rapid Heart Pictures, 2004). All subsequent references to these films refer to these DVDs.

27. Reviews of *The Brotherhood*, Amazon.com, http://www.amazon.com/Brotherhood-Bradley-Stryker/product-reviews/B000GBE-WLG/ref=cm_cr_dp_all_helpful?ie=UTF8&col iid=&showViewpoints=1&colid=&sortBy=by-SubmissionDateDescending (accessed December 30, 2009). Note that the authors' names cited in the text may be pseudonyms—"Alec Scudder" bears a striking resemblance to a character in E. M. Forster's *Maurice*.

28. D. A. Miller, "Anal Rope," in *Inside/Out: Lesbian Theories, Gay Theories*, ed. Diana Fuss (New York: Routledge, 1991) 124–125.

29. Mark David Guenette, *Speak Low: Towards a Theory of the Non-Discourse of Male Homosexuality in Wilde, Proust, and Beyond* (dissertation, Columbia University; Ann Arbor: UMI, 1993), 102, 106.

30. Algernon Blackwood, "Secret Worship," in *Best Ghost Stories of Algernon Blackwood* (New York: Dover, 1973), 53–78.

31. Sigmund Freud, *Three Essays on the Theory of Sexuality*, trans. James Strachey (New York: Basic Books, 1975), 6–96.

32. Blackwood, "Secret Worship," 57–80.

33. Ibid., 85–86.
34. See pp. 47–48 of this book.
35. Blackwood, "Secret Worship," 87.
36. Sedgwick, *Between Men*, 5, 92, 49.
37. This configuration of the gaze providesan alternative to the construction of the cinematic gaze as male and heterosexual, a construction that Laura Mulvey describes in her seminal essay "Visual Pleasure and Narrative Cinema," in *Film Theory and Criticism*, 7th ed., eds. Leo Braudy and Marshall Cohen (New York: Oxford University Press, 2009), 711–722.
38. Butler, *Gender Trouble*, 137–138.
39. Susan Sontag, "Notes on Camp," http://interglacial.com/~sburke/pub/prose/Susan_Sontag_-_Notes_on_Camp.html (accessed December 30, 2009).
40. See Fincher, *Queering the Gothic in the Romantic Age*, 109, for more about the Gothic's camp tradition.

Chapter 5

1. See pp. 34, 47–49 of the present work.
2. H.J. Irwin, *An Introduction to Parapsychology*, 3d ed. (Jefferson, NC: McFarland, 1999), 245.
3. Clery, *The Rise of Supernatural Fiction*, 17–18.
4. *Ghost Hunters*, *Ghost Hunters Academy*, and *Ghost Hunters International*, broadcast on the Syfy Channel, see also http://www.syfy.com/ghosthunters/index.php; *Paranormal Activity*, directed by Oren Peli (2007; Blumhouse Productions, 2009).
5. Irwin, *An Introduction to Parapsychology*, 15–17.
6. Robert F. Geary, *The Supernatural in Gothic Fiction: Horror, Belief, and Literary Change* (Lewiston, NY: Edwin Mellen Press, 1992), 102.
7. C. Nelson Stewart, "Bulwer Lytton as Occultist" (Whitefish, MT: Kessinger Publishing, 1997), 35–36, 17.
8. Irwin, *An Introduction to Parapsychology*, 20–21.
9. Peter Haining, Introduction, *The Complete Ghost Stories of Charles Dickens*, by Charles Dickens (New York: Washington Square Press, 1982), 22–23.
10. Irwin, *An Introduction to Parapsychology*, 17, 1.
11. Geary, *The Supernatural in Gothic Fiction*, 115.
12. Jack Sullivan, *Elegant Nightmares: The English Ghost Story from Le Fanu to Blackwood* (Athens: Ohio University Press, 1978), 51.
13. Edward Bulwer-Lytton Lytton, *Zanoni* (Doylestown, PA: Wildside Press, 2002).
14. Geary, *The Supernatural in Gothic Fiction*, 106.
15. "Terrorist Novel Writing," 184.
16. The term "horizon of expectations" derives from the work of Hans Robert Jauss.
17. Jay Anson, *The Amityville Horror* (Englewood Cliffs, NJ: Prentice-Hall, 1977), x–xi, 205.
18. Hans Holzer, *Ghosts: True Encounters with the World Beyond* (New York: Black Dog and Leventhal, 1997), 629.
19. Colin Wilson, *Poltergeist!: A Study in Destructive Haunting* (London: Caxton Editions, 2000), 358–359.
20. Irwin, *An Introduction to Parapsychology*, 246.
21. Ibid.
22. Tom Ogden, *The Complete Idiot's Guide to Ghosts and Hauntings* (Indianapolis: Alpha Books, 1999), 164.
23. Holzer, *Ghosts*, 57, 49.
24. Raymond Bayless, *The Enigma of the Poltergeist* (West Nyack, NY: Parker Publishing, 1967), 12–13.
25. Wilson, *Poltergeist!*, 88.
26. Irwin, *An Introduction to Parapsychology*, 175.
27. Bayless, *The Enigma of the Poltergeist*, 7.
28. William G. Roll, *The Poltergeist* (Garden City, NY: Nelson Doubleday, 1972), 159.
29. J. Sheridan Le Fanu, "Authentic Narrative of a Haunted House," in *Best Ghost Stories of J.S. Le Fanu*, ed. E.F. Bleiler (New York: Dover, 1964), 420.
30. H.P. Lovecraft, *The Annotated Supernatural Horror in Literature*, ed. S.T. Yoshi (New York: Hippocampus Press, 2000), 61, 68.
31. Anson, *The Amityville Horror*, back cover.
32. Dorothy Scarborough, *The Supernatural in Modern English Fiction* (Maple Shade, NJ: Lethe Press, 2001), 205.
33. Rhoda Broughton, "The Truth, the Whole Truth, and Nothing but the Truth," in *Victorian Ghost Stories*, ed. Michael Cox and R.A. Gilbert (New York: Oxford University Press, 1992), 82.
34. Mary Louisa Molesworth, "The Story of the Rippling Train," in *Victorian Ghost Stories*, ed. Michael Cox and R.A. Gilbert (New York: Oxford University Press, 1992), 319, 322.
35. Edward Bulwer-Lytton Lytton, "The Haunted and the Haunters," in *The Mammoth Book of Haunted House Stories*, ed. Peter Haining (New York: Carroll & Graf, 2000), 13.

36. Ibid., 30–32.
37. Addison, "Selection from *The Spectator* No. 110," 17.
38. J. Sheridan Le Fanu, "The Haunted Baronet," in *Best Ghost Stories of J.S. Le Fanu*, ed. E.F. Bleiler (New York: Dover, 1964), 127; Charles Dickens, "Captain Murderer and the Devil's Bargain," in *The Complete Ghost Stories of Charles Dickens* (New York: Washington Square Press, 1982), 26.
39. Bayless, *The Enigma of the Poltergeist*, 7, 28, vi, 102, and front and back covers.
40. Irwin, *An Introduction to Parapsychology*, 279. Lest this figure seem hopelessly outdated, consult The Pew Forum, "Many Americans Mix Multiple Faiths," December 9, 2009, http://pewforum.org/docs/?DocID=490#4 (accessed January 8, 2010): "In total, upwards of six-in-ten adults (65%) express belief in or report having experience with at least one of these diverse supernatural phenomena (belief in reincarnation, belief in spiritual energy located in physical things, belief in yoga as spiritual practice, belief in the "evil eye," belief in astrology, having been in touch with the dead, consulting a psychic, or experiencing a ghostly encounter). This includes roughly one-quarter of the population (23%) who report having only one of these beliefs or experiences. More than four-in-ten people (43%) answer two or more of these items affirmatively, including 25% who answer two or three of these items affirmatively and nearly one-in-five (18%) who answer yes to four or more. Roughly one-third of the public (35%) answers no to all eight items."
41. Trent Brandon, *The Ghost Hunter's Bible* (Mansfield, OH: Zerotime Publishing, 2002), 6.
42. Holzer, *Ghosts*, 48.
43. Ibid., 63.
44. Brandon, *The Ghost Hunter's Bible*, 124.
45. Beth Scott and Michael Norman, *Haunted Heartland: True Ghost Stories from the American Midwest* (New York: Barnes and Noble Books, 1992), 151, xiv, xi, 146.
46. Holzer, *Ghosts*, 627–629.
47. Frank DeFelitta, *The Entity* (New York: Warner Books, 1979), 7.
48. Troy Taylor, *The Ghost Hunter's Guidebook: The Essential Handbook for Ghost Research* (Alton, IL: Whitechapel Productions, 2001), 61.
49. DeFelitta, *The Entity*, 261, 311.
50. Ibid., 265.
51. Ibid., 452.
52. *Poltergeist*, DVD, directed by Tobe Hooper (1982; Los Angeles: Warner Home Video, 2007).
53. Scott and Norman, *Haunted Heartland*, 431.
54. Clery, *The Rise of Supernatural Fiction*, 18–19.
55. Geary, *The Supernatural in Gothic Fiction*, 87.
56. Taylor, *The Ghost Hunter's Guidebook*, 13.
57. Victor Sage, *Horror Fiction in the Protestant Tradition* (New York: St. Martin's, 1988), 133.
58. Irwin, *An Introduction to Parapsychology*, 1.
59. DeFelitta, *The Entity*, 280.
60. Geary, *The Supernatural in Gothic Fiction*, 50.
61. Henry James, *The Turn of the Screw*, in *The Turn of the Screw and Other Short Fiction* (New York: Bantam Books, 1981), 3–103.
62. Charlotte Riddell, "The Open Door," in *Victorian Ghost Stories*, ed. Michael Cox and R.A. Gilbert (New York: Oxford University Press, 1992), 256.
63. Amelia B. Edwards, *Monsieur Maurice*, in *Five Victorian Ghost Novels*, ed. E.F. Bleiler (New York: Dover, 1971), 281.
64. Riddell, "The Open Door," 256.
65. J. Sheridan Le Fanu, "The Familiar," in *Best Ghost Stories of J.S. Le Fanu*, ed. E.F. Bleiler (New York: Dover, 1964), 212, 225.
66. Ibid., 209.
67. Dick Donovan, "The Corpse Light," in *A Bottomless Grave and Other Victorian Tales of Terror*, ed. Hugh Lamb (Mineola, NY: Dover, 2001), 49.
68. Wilson, *Poltergeist!*, 11–13.
69. Ibid., 89–90.
70. Holzer, *Ghosts*, 247–248.
71. Arthur Myers, *The Ghostly Register* (Chicago: Contemporary Books, 1986), 1.
72. Ibid., 326–327.
73. Holzer, *Ghosts*, 51.
74. Ibid. 13, 46.
75. Radcliffe, *The Mysteries of Udolpho*, 556. For more about Radcliffe's treatment of belief in ghosts, see pp. 53–54 of the present work.
76. Michael Arlen, "The Gentleman from America," in *The Haunted Omnibus*, ed. Alexander Laing (New York: MJF Books, 1965), 465–485.
77. Ibid., 477.
78. Wilson, *Poltergeist!*, 215–216.

Chapter 6

1. This assumption stems from Lacanian ideas about how the Symbolic stands between the subject and the Real, but it might also be viewed as a variation of the Whorf-Sapir hy-

Notes — Chapter 6

pothesis, which Stephen Prince summarizes as "extreme linguistic relativity" because it suggests "that radically different language systems might organize the world in unique ways for their users." Citing cognitive psychologists, Prince argues against extreme application of the Whorf-Sapir hypothesis to considerations of how people see and understand film, providing evidence that ways of seeing and understanding images are cross-cultural and not acquired in the same manner as language. Could the seeing (and otherwise sensing) of ghosts have some biological or other basis independent from language? Maybe, but I am not concerned with the phenomenology of perception but with perception as it is articulated, even if the articulation is only between the percipient and herself through an act of reflection, i.e. through consciousness. Perception may involve some pre-discursive phenomena, but I'm only able to access perception through discourse (or the Symbolic), and therefore I'm not concerned with what I see as inaccessible universals. The 1993 article that contains Stephen Prince's argument, however, is well worth reading. It's called "The Discourse of Pictures: Iconicity and Film Studies," and it's in *Film Theory and Criticism*, 7th edition, ed. Leo Braudy and Marshall Cohen (New York: Oxford University Press, 2009), 87–105. See especially 91–100.

2. Ellis, *The Contested Castle*, 7.
3. Roll, *The Poltergeist*, 210.
4. Taylor, *The Ghost Hunter's Guidebook*, 73.
5. Charles Dickens, "A Christmas Carol," in *The Complete Ghost Stories of Charles Dickens* (New York: Washington Square Press, 1982), 115.
6. Ibid.
7. Edgar Allan Poe, The Tell-Tale Heart," *The Haunted Omnibus: The Greatest Ghost Stories of All Time*, ed. Alexander Laing (New York: MJF Books, 1965), 772.
8. Amelia B. Edwards, "Was It An Illusion?," in *Victorian Ghost Stories*, ed. Michael Cox and R.A. Gilbert (New York: Oxford University Press, 1992), 251.
9. Brandon, *The Ghost Hunter's Bible*, 6.
10. Irwin, *An Introduction to Parapsychology*, 247.
11. Wilson, *Poltergeist!*, 216; Clery, *The Rise of Supernatural Fiction*, 13; Irwin, *An Introduction to Parapsychology*, 16.
12. Le Fanu, "Authentic Narrative of a Haunted House," 424.
13. Lytton, "The Haunted and the Haunters,"20.
14. Wilson, *Poltergeist!*, 88–89.
15. Ibid.
16. Le Fanu, "The Familiar," 212.
17. M.R. James, "The Stalls of Barchester Cathedral," in *Collected Ghost Stories* (Hertfordshire: Wordsworth, 1992), 153.
18. Wilson, *Poltergeist!*, 242.
19. Irwin, *An Introduction to Parapsychology*, 157.
20. Thomas Street Millington, "No Living Voice," in *Victorian Ghost Stories*, ed. Michael Cox and R.A. Gilbert (New York: Oxford University Press, 1992), 192.
21. Lynne Sharon Schwartz, "Sound is Second Sight," in *The Omnibus of 20th Century Ghost Stories*, ed. Robert Phillips (New York: Carroll and Graf Publishers, 1989), 143.
22. Myers, *The Ghostly Register*, 303.
23. M.R. James, "Martin's Close," in *Collected Ghost Stories* (Hertfordshire: Wordsworth, 1992), 174.
24. Algernon Blackwood, "A Case of Eavesdropping," in *The Mammoth Book of Haunted House Stories*, ed. Peter Haining (New York: Carroll & Graf, 2000), 53–68; Ambrose Bierce, "The Secret of Macarger's Gulch," in *Ghost and Horror Stories of Ambrose Bierce* (New York: Dover, 1964), 134–140.
25. Scott and Norman, *Haunted Heartland*, 231.
26. Elizabeth Gaskell, "The Old Nurse's Story," in *Victorian Ghost Stories*, ed. Michael Cox and R.A. Gilbert (New York: Oxford University Press, 1992), 12.
27. Bayless, *The Enigma of the Poltergeist*, 48.
28. "Ghosts," in *Victorian and Edwardian Ghost Stories*, ed. Richard Dalby (New York: MetroBooks, 2002), 1.
29. Sullivan, *Elegant Nightmares*, 54.
30. My play with "present absence" and "absent presence" might conjure the specter of Jacques Derrida; for an approach to ghostliness that considers Derrida with more than mere wordplay, see Julian Wolfreys, *Victorian Hauntings: Spectrality, Gothic, the Uncanny and Literature* (New York: Palgrave, 2002).
31. Clery, *The Rise of Supernatural Fiction*, 18.
32. Wilson, *Poltergeist!*, 155.
33. Arthur Conan Doyle, "Playing with Fire," in *The Mammoth Book of Haunted House Stories*, ed. Peter Haining (New York: Carroll & Graf, 2000), 504.
34. Ogden, *The Idiot's Guide to Ghosts and Hauntings*, 107.
35. Scarborough, *The Supernatural in Modern English Fiction*, 91–92.
36. Ambrose Bierce, "The Middle Toe of the Right Foot," in *Ghost and Horror Stories of Ambrose Bierce* (New York: Dover, 1964), 182;

Dinah Maria Mulock, "M. Anastasius," in *Victorian and Edwardian Ghost Stories*, ed. Richard Dalby (New York: Metro Books, 2002), 33.
37. Ellen Wood, "Reality or Delusion?" in *Victorian Ghost Stories*, ed. Michael Cox and R.A. Gilbert (New York: Oxford University Press, 1992), 129.
38. Scott and Norman, *Haunted Heartland*, 189.
39. Taylor, *The Ghost Hunter's Guidebook*, 10.
40. Holzer, *Ghosts*, 249.
41. Louisa Baldwin, "The Real and the Counterfeit," in *The Mammoth Book of Haunted House Stories*, ed. Peter Haining (New York: Carroll & Graf, 2000), 247; John Harwood, "Underground Ghost," in *Victorian and Edwardian Ghost Stories*, ed. Richard Dalby (New York: Metro Books, 2002), 212.
42. Le Fanu, "Authentic Narrative of a Haunted House," 423.
43. Algernon Blackwood, "The Listener," in *Best Ghost Stories of Algernon Blackwood* (New York, Dover, 1973), 260–272.
44. Charlotte Riddell, *The Uninhabited House*, in *Five Victorian Ghost Novels*, ed. E.F. Bleiler (New York: Dover, 1971), 98.
45. Scarborough, *The Supernatural in Modern English Fiction*, 100.
46. Wilkie Collins, *The Haunted Hotel* (New York: Dover, 1982), 77, 97.
47. Ibid., 97.
48. Wilson, *Poltergeist!*, 121.
49. Brandon, *The Ghost Hunter's Bible*, 153.
50. Ralph Cram, "No. 252 Rue M. Le Prince," in *The Mammoth Book of Haunted House Stories*, ed. Peter Haining (New York: Carroll & Graf, 2000), 123.
51. Wilson, *Poltergeist!*, 158.
52. Nigel Kneale, "The Patter of Tiny Feet," in *The Mammoth Book of Haunted House Stories*, ed. Peter Haining (New York: Carroll & Graf, 2000), 486.
53. E.F. Benson, "Bagnell Terrace," in *The Mammoth Book of Haunted House Stories*, ed. Peter Haining (New York: Carroll & Graf, 2000), 541, 546.
54. Peter Haining, Foreword, *The Mammoth Book of Haunted House Stories*, ed. Peter Haining (New York: Carroll & Graf, 2000), 3.
55. Algernon Blackwood, "The Wendigo," in *Best Ghost Stories of Algernon Blackwood* (New York: Dover, 1973), 191.
56. Holzer, *Ghosts*, 26.
57. Irwin, *An Introduction to Parapsychology*, 251.
58. Ibid.; Wilson, *Poltergeist!*, 95.
59. Shirley Jackson, *The Haunting of Hill House* (New York: Penguin, 1987), 120.

60. Jean Rhys, "I Used To Live Here Once," in *The Omnibus of Twentieth-Century Ghost Stories*, ed. Robert Phillips (New York: Carroll & Graf, 1991), 146.
61. Irwin, *An Introduction to Parapsychology*, 20.
62. *The Haunting in Connecticut*, Blu-ray, directed by Peter Cornwell (2009; Los Angeles: Lionsgate, 2009).
63. Irwin, *An Introduction to Parapsychology*, 185.
64. Scott and Norman, *Haunted Heartland*, 455.
65. H.P. Lovecraft, *The Annotated Supernatural Horror in Literature*, 68.
66. Charles Willing Beale, *The Ghost of Guir House*, in *Five Victorian Ghost Novels*, ed. E.F. Bleiler (New York: Dover, 1971), 383.
67. Scarborough, *The Supernatural in Modern English Fiction*, 101–102.
68. Ogden, *The Idiot's Guide to Ghosts and Hauntings*, 123.
69. Irwin, *An Introduction to Parapsychology*, 3.
70. *The Sixth Sense*, DVD, directed by M. Night Shyamalan (1999; Walt Disney Video, 2000).
71. Holzer, *Ghosts*, 53.
72. Benson, "Bagnell Terrace," 541.
73. J. Sheridan Le Fanu, "The Haunted Baronet"; Ambrose Bierce, "The Death of Halpin Frayser," in *Ghost and Horror Stories of Ambrose Bierce* (New York: Dover, 1964), 1–14.
74. Myers, *The Ghostly Register*, 77.
75. Scarborough, *The Supernatural in Modern English Fiction*, 29.
76. Ibid., 95.

Chapter 7

1. Carol Siegel, *Goth's Dark Empire* (Bloomington: Indiana University Press, 2005), 1.
2. Quoted in William Dudley, ed., *Media Violence: Opposing Viewpoints* (San Diego: Greenhaven Press, 1999), 160.
3. Grossman and DeGaetano, *Stop Teaching Our Kids to Kill*, 1.
4. Quoted in Dudley, *Media Violence*, 57.
5. Potter, *11 Myths of Media Violence*, 17; Gavin Baddeley, *Dissecting Marilyn Manson*, 2d ed. (London: Plexus, 2003), 53.
6. *Bowling for Columbine*, DVD, directed by Michael Moore (2002; Los Angeles: Metro-Goldwyn-Mayer, 2004).
7. Baddeley, *Dissecting Marilyn Manson*, 54.
8. Ibid., 173.

Notes—Chapter 7

9. Jeff Kass, *Columbine: A True Crime Story, A Victim, The Killers, and the Nation's Search for Answers* (Denver: Ghost Road Press, 2009), 21.
10. Michael Medved, *Hollywood Vs. America*, 261, 3.
11. Potter, *11 Myths of Media Violence*, 27.
12. Jonathan L. Freedman, *Media Violence and Its Effect on Aggression: Assessing the Scientific Evidence* (Toronto: University of Toronto Press, 2002), 9, 200–201.
13. Karen Sternheimer, *It's Not the Media: The Truth about Pop Culture's Influence on Children* (Boulder, CO: Westview Press, 2003), 130–131.
14. Jones, *Killing Monsters*, 16.
15. George Comstock, "A Sociological Perspective on Television Violence and Aggression," *The American Behavioral Scientist*, 51.8 (2008): 1188–1189.
16. Phil Phillips and Joan Hake Robie, *Horror and Violence: The Deadly Duo in the Media* (Lancaster, PA: Starburst, 1988), back cover.
17. Center for Successful Parenting, *Media Violence Alert: Informing Parents about the Number ONE Health Threat in America Today* (Zionsville, IN: DreamCatcher Press, 2000).
18. Ibid., 19, 54.
19. Grossman and DeGaetano, *Stop Teaching Our Kids to Kill*, 9, 64.
20. Freedman, *Media Violence and Its Effect on Aggression*, 44. In the original, this phrase is in bold type.
21. Comstock, "A Sociological Perspective on Television Violence and Aggression," 1188.
22. Potter, *11 Myths of Media Violence*, 54.
23. See, for example, Brad J. Bushman and L. Rowell Huesmann, "Short-term and Long-term Effects of Violent Media on Aggression in Children and Adults," *Archives of Pediatrics & Adolescent Medicine* 160.4 (2006): 348–352; Paul Boxer, L. Huesmann, B. Bushman, M. O'Brien, and D. Moceri, "The Role of Violent Media Preference in Cumulative Developmental Risk for Violence and General Aggression," *Journal of Youth and Adolescence* 38.3 (2009): 417–428.
24. For an explanation of retrospective causality, see pp. 8–11 of the present work.
25. Brooks Brown and Rob Merritt, *No Easy Answers: The Truth Behind Death at Columbine* (New York: Lantern Books, 2002), 38, 16, 18.
26. Potter, *11 Myths of Media Violence*, 17.
27. Hillary Clinton, Joe Lieberman, and Evan Bayh, "Family Entertainment Protection Act," *Govtrack.us*, http://www.govtrack.us/congress/billtext.xpd?bill=s109-2126 (accessed May 21, 2010).
28. Peter Langman, *Why Kids Kill: Inside the Minds of School Shooters* (New York: Palgrave Macmillan, 2009), 5–9.
29. Dave Cullen, *Columbine* (New York: Hachette Book Group, 2009), ix–x, 353.
30. Kass, *Columbine: A True Crime Story*, 15.
31. Mark Edmundson, *Nightmare on Main Street: Angels, Sadomasochism, and the Culture of Gothic* (Cambridge, MA: Harvard University Press, 1999).
32. *Elephant*, DVD, directed by Gus Van Sant (2003; Los Angeles: HBO Home Video, 2004).
33. Douglas Kellner, *Guys and Guns Amok: Domestic Terrorism and School Shootings from the Oklahoma City Bombing to the Virginia Tech Massacre* (Boulder, CO: Paradigm, 2008), 42.
34. Lucinda Roy, *No Right to Remain Silent: The Tragedy at Virginia Tech* (New York: Harmony Books, 2009), 89.
35. Ibid., 22, 28.
36. Ibid. 9, 226–227.
37. This quote comes from the April 20, 2007, article from the U.K.'s *Daily Star* already cited in the text.
38. Roy, *No Right to Remain Silent*, 197.
39. Stephen King, *Rage*, in *The Bachman Books: Four Early Novels by Stephen King* (New York: Plume, 1985), 1–131.
40. George Beahm, *Stephen King from A to Z* (Kansas City: Andrew McMeel, 1998), 169.
41. Ibid.
42. Ibid., 69.
43. David E. Newton, *Violence and the Media: A Reference Handbook* (Santa Barbara: ABC-CLIO, 1996), 58.
44. Stephen King, *Danse Macabre* (New York: Berkley Books, 1983), 388–393.
45. Tim Underwood and Chuck Miller, eds., *Bare Bones: Conversations on Terror with Stephen King* (New York: McGraw-Hill, 1988), 185.
46. Grossman, in *Media Violence Alert*, 59.
47. See pp. 12–15 of the present work for a theoretical account of role models and influences.
48. King, *Rage*, 18, 119.
49. Michael Collings, *Stephen King as Richard Bachman* (Mercer Island, WA: Starmont House, 1985), 36.
50. King, *Rage*, 97, 99, 36, 121, 124.
51. Stephen King, "The Bogeyboys," *Horrorking.com*, http://www.horrorking.com/interview7.html (accessed November 15, 2009).
52. Ibid.

Chapter 8

1. Brown, *No Easy Answers*, 95.
2. *Natural Born Killers: The Director's Cut*, DVD, directed by Oliver Stone (1994; Los Angeles: Vidmark/Trimark, 2000). All subsequent references to *Natural Born Killers* refer to this DVD.
3. Mary Whitehouse, "Time to Face Responsibility," in *Screen Violence*, ed. Karl French (London: Bloomsbury, 1996), 60.
4. John Grisham, "Natural Bred Killers," in *Screen Violence*, ed. Karl French (London: Bloomsbury, 1996), 231–235.
5. Oliver Stone, "Don't Sue the Messenger," in *Screen Violence*, ed. Karl French (London: Bloomsbury, 1996), 238.
6. For an extended theoretical discussion of role models in fiction, see pp. 12–15 of the present work.
7. King, *Rage*, 32.
8. Ibid., 61, 28.
9. Grisham, "Natural Bred Killers," 233.
10. Clover, *Men, Women, and Chain Saws*, 168.
11. See chapter 2 and chapter 5 of the present work.
12. *Scream*, DVD, directed by Wes Craven (1996; Los Angeles: Dimension, 2000); *Scream 2*, DVD, directed by Wes Craven (1997; Los Angeles: Dimension, 2000); *Scream 3*, DVD, directed by Wes Craven (2000; Los Angeles: Dimension, 2000). All subsequent references to the *Scream* trilogy refer to these DVDs.
13. Potter, *11 Myths of Media Violence*, 13–14. Potter is wrong on this point — if anything, *Scream 3* is less graphic than its predecessors.
14. If this script is authentic, it is by Kevin Williamson. In my dissertation, I cited a version of the script from a website called *Scr3am.net*, http://www.silverwing.net/scream/scream2/earlyscream2.txt (accessed Nov. 20, 2004). That site no longer exists, but a similar, if not identical, script was available on *Horrornews.net*, http://www.horrornews.net/horror_scripts/scripts/scream2.txt, January 5, 2010.
15. James P. Steyer, *The Other Parent: The Inside Story of the Media's Effect on Our Children* (New York: Atria Books, 2002), 70.
16. For a crucial distinction between causality and culpability, see pp. 8–11 of the present work.
17. King, *Rage*, 28.
18. Grossman, in *Media Violence Alert*, 59.
19. Freedman, *Media Violence and Its Effect on Aggression*, 209–210.
20. Jones, *Killing Monsters*, 118–120.
21. See p. 165 of the present work.
22. See pp. 29–32 of the present work, which grounds the still-popular conception of the mind as impressionable in the philosophy of John Locke.
23. Quoted in Dudley, *Media Violence*, 22.
24. Baddeley, *Dissecting Marilyn Manson*, 8, 17, 176.
25. Adam Rockoff, *Going to Pieces: The Rise and Fall of the Slasher Film, 1978–1986* (Jefferson, NC: McFarland, 2002), 152.
26. See Wayne King, "Nightmares Suspected in the Deaths of 18 Laotians," *New York Times*, May 10, 1981, Special section, Late City final edition; Annie Riordan, "Cinematic Haunts: The Facts Behind 'A Nightmare on Elm Street,'" *Brutal as Hell: Horror without Mercy*, http://www.brutalashell.com/2009/10/cinematic-haunts-the-facts-behind-a-nightmare-on-elm-street/ (accessed November 25, 2009).
27. *A Nightmare on Elm Street 2: Freddy's Revenge*, DVD, directed by Jack Sholder (1985; Los Angeles: New Line Studios, 1999); *A Nightmare on Elm Street 3: Dream Warriors*, DVD, directed by Chuck Russell (1987; Los Angeles: New Line Studios, 1999).
28. *Wes Craven's New Nightmare*, DVD, directed by Wes Craven (1994; Los Angeles: New Line Studios, 1999).
29. *Freddy Vs. Jason*, DVD, directed by Ronny Yu (2003; Los Angeles: New Line Home Video, 2004). All subsequent references to this film refer to this DVD.
30. David Edelstein, "Now Playing at Your Local Multiplex: Torture Porn," *New York*, January 28, 2006, http://nymag.com/movies/features/15622/ (accessed December 6, 2009).
31. *Hostel*, DVD, directed by Eli Roth (2005; Los Angeles: Lions Gate Films, 2006); *Saw*, DVD, directed by James Wan (2004; Lions Gate Films, 2005). All subsequent references to these films refer to these DVDs.
32. Edelstein, "Now Playing."
33. Jarrett Murphy, "President Declares End to Major Combat in Iraq, *CBS News: World*, http://www.cbsnews.com/stories/2003/05/01/iraq/main551946.shtml (accessed December 6, 2009).
34. Ibid.
35. Michel Foucault, *Discipline and Punish: The Birth of the Prison*, trans. Alan Sheridan (New York: Vintage Books, 1995), 44–45.
36. *Saw 2*, DVD, directed by Darren Lynn Bousman (2005: Lions Gate Films, 2006). All subsequent references to this film refer to this DVD.
37. Murphy, "President Declares End to Major Combat in Iraq."
38. George W. Bush, "Address to a Joint Session of Congress Following 9/11 Attacks," *American Rhetoric*, http://www.americanrhetoric.

com/speeches/gwbush911jointsessionspeech.htm (accessed December 15, 2009).

39. George W. Bush, "Bush's Farewell Speech," *CNN.com*, http://www.cnn.com/2009/POLITICS/01/15/bush.speech.text/index.html (accessed December 15, 2009).

40. *Saw 3*, DVD, directed by Darren Lynn Bousman (2006; Los Angeles: Lions Gate Films, 2007).

41. *Saw 6*, directed by Kevin Greutert (A Bigger Boat, 2009). According to *Yahoo! Movies* (http://movies.yahoo.com, accessed January 7, 2010), *Saw 6* grossed only $14,118,444 at the U.S. Box Office. In stark contrast *Saw 5* grossed $56,729,973, *Saw 4* grossed $63,270,259, and *Saw 3* grossed $80,150,343. These figures indicate a steady drop typical of film sequels, but the drop between *Saw 5* and *Saw 6* is particularly sharp. The recession in the U.S. at the time could be a significant factor, of course, but since *Paranormal Activity*, its major box office competition, ended up grossing $107,603,100, the recession alone seems an insufficient cause.

Selected Bibliography

Addison, Joseph. "Selection from *The Spectator No. 110.*" In *Gothic Documents: A Sourcebook 1700–1820*, edited by E.J. Clery and Robert Miles, 16–19. Manchester: Manchester University Press, 2000.

Anolik, Ruth Bienstock. *The Gothic Other: Racial and Social Constructions in the Literary Imagination*. Jefferson, NC: McFarland, 2004.

———. *Horrifying Sex: Essays on Sexual Difference in Gothic Literature*. Jefferson, NC: McFarland, 2007.

Anson, Jay. *The Amityville Horror*. Englewood Cliffs, NJ: Prentice-Hall, 1977.

Armstrong, Nancy. *Desire and Domestic Fiction: A Political History of the Novel*. New York: Oxford University Press, 1987.

Baddeley, Gavin. *Dissecting Marilyn Manson*, 2d ed. London: Plexus, 2003.

Baldwin, Louisa. "The Real and the Counterfeit." In *The Mammoth Book of Haunted House Stories*, edited by Peter Haining, 231–248. New York: Carroll & Graf, 2000.

Baudrillard, Jean. *Selected Writings*. Edited by Mark Poster. Stanford, CA: Stanford University Press, 1988.

Bayless, Raymond. *The Enigma of the Poltergeist*. West Nyack, NY: Parker Publishing, 1967.

Beahm, George. *Stephen King from A to Z*. Kansas City: Andrew McMeel, 1998.

Beale, Charles Willing. *The Ghost of Guir House*. In *Five Victorian Ghost Novels*, edited by E.F. Bleiler, 341–420. New York: Dover, 1971.

Beattie, James. *Essay on Poetry and Music, as They Affect the Mind. Essays on the Nature and Immutability of Truth, in opposition to sophistry and scepticism; on Poetry and Music, as they affect the mind; On Laughter, and Ludicrous Composition; and, on the Utility of Classical Learning, Volume Two*. Dublin: printed for C. Jenkins (No. 58) Dame-Street, 1777.

Benshoff, Harry M. *Monsters in the Closet: Homosexuality and the Horror Film*. Manchester: Manchester University Press, 1997.

Benson, E.F. "Bagnell Terrace." In *The Mammoth Book of Haunted House Stories*, edited by Peter Haining, 533–546. New York: Carroll & Graf, 2000.

Bierce, Ambrose. *Ghost and Horror Stories of Ambrose Bierce*. New York: Dover, 1964.

Blackwood, Algernon. *The Best Ghost Stories of Algernon Blackwood*. Edited by E.F. Bleiler. New York: Dover, 1973.

———. "A Case of Eavesdropping." In *The Mammoth Book of Haunted House Stories*, edited by Peter Haining, 53–68. New York: Carroll & Graf, 2000.

Botting, Fred. *Gothic*. New York: Routledge, 1996.

Bourdieu, Pierre. *Pascalian Meditations*. Translated by Richard Nice. Stanford, CA: Stanford University Press, 2000.

Bowling for Columbine. DVD. Directed

by Michael Moore. 2002. Los Angeles: Metro Goldwyn Mayer, 2004.

Brandon, Trent. *The Ghost Hunter's Bible*. Mansfield, OH: Zerotime, 2002.

Brinkley, Edward S. "Homosexuality as (Anti)Illness: Oscar Wilde's *The Picture of Dorian Gray* and Gabriele D'Annunzio's *Il Piacere*." *Studies in Twentieth Century Literature* 22.1 (1998): 61–82.

Brooks, Peter. "What is a Monster? (According to *Frankenstein*)." In *Frankenstein: Mary Shelley*, edited by Fred Botting, 81–106. London: Macmillan, 1995.

The Brotherhood / The Brotherhood 2: Young Warlocks. DVD. Directed by David DeCoteau. 2001. Rapid Heart Pictures, 2002.

Broughton, Rhoda. "The Truth, the Whole Truth, and Nothing but the Truth." In *Victorian Ghost Stories*, edited by Michael Cox and R.A. Gilbert, 74–82. New York: Oxford University Press, 1992. 74–82.

Brown, Brooks, and Rob Merritt. *No Easy Answers: The Truth Behind Death at Columbine*. New York: Lantern Books, 2002.

Buffy the Vampire Slayer: The Complete Television Series. DVD. Created by Joss Whedon. Twentieth Century-Fox Home Video, 2006.

Butler, Judith. *Bodies That Matter*. New York: Routledge, 1993.

_____. *Gender Trouble*. New York: Routledge, 1990.

Center for Successful Parenting. *Media Violence Alert: Informing Parents about the Number ONE Health Threat in America Today*. Zionsville, IN: DreamCatcher Press, 2000.

Clery, E.J. *The Rise of Supernatural Fiction, 1762–1800*. New York: Cambridge University Press, 1995.

Clover, Carol J. *Men, Women, and Chain Saws: Gender in the Modern Horror Film*. Princeton, NJ: Princeton University Press, 1992.

Cohen, Ed. *Talk on the Wilde Side: Toward a Genealogy of a Discourse on Male Sexualities*. New York: Routledge, 1993.

Colavito, Jason. *Knowing Fear: Science, Knowledge, and the Development of the Horror Genre*. Jefferson, NC: McFarland, 2008.

Coleridge, Samuel Taylor. Review of *The Monk*, by Matthew Lewis. In *Gothic Documents: A Sourcebook, 1700–1820*, edited by E.J. Clery and Robert Miles, 185–189. Manchester: Manchester University Press, 2000.

_____. Review of *The Mysteries of Udolpho*, by Ann Radcliffe. *Critical Review* 2d series 11 (Aug. 1794): 361–63.

Collings, Michael. *Stephen King as Richard Bachman*. Mercer Island, WA: Starmont House, 1985.

Collins, Wilkie. *The Haunted Hotel*. New York: Dover, 1982.

Comstock, George. "A Sociological Perspective on Television Violence and Aggression." *The American Behavioral Scientist* 51.8 (2008): 1188–1189.

Conan Doyle, Arthur. "Playing with Fire." In *The Mammoth Book of Haunted House Stories*, edited by Peter Haining, 497–511. New York: Carroll & Graf, 2000.

Craft, Christopher. *Another Kind of Love: Male Homosexual Desire in English Discourse, 1850–1920*. Los Angeles: University of California Press, 1994.

Craig, Siobhan. "Monstrous Dialogues: Erotic Discourse and the Dialogic Constitution of the Subject in *Frankenstein*." In *A Dialogue of Voices: Feminist Literary Theory and Bakhtin*, edited by Karen Hohne and Helen Wussow, 83–96. Minneapolis: University of Minnesota Press, 1994.

Cram, Ralph. "No. 252 Rue M. Le Prince." In *The Mammoth Book of Haunted House Stories,* edited by Peter Haining, 109–124. New York: Carroll & Graf, 2000.

Cullen, Dave. *Columbine*. New York: Hachette Book Group, 2009.

Danahay, Martin A. Introduction to *The Strange Case of Dr. Jekyll and Mr. Hyde*, by Robert Louis Stevenson, edited by Martin A. Danahay, 11–25. Orchard Park, NY: Broadview, 2001.

Davidson, Guy. "Sexuality and the Degenerate Body in Robert Louis Stevenson's *The Strange Case of Dr. Jekyll and Mr. Hyde*." *Australasian Victorian Studies Journal* 1 (1995): 31–40.

Davis, Lennard J. *Factual Fictions: The Origins of the English Novel*. New York: Columbia University Press, 1983.

DeFelitta, Frank. *The Entity*. New York: Warner Books, 1979.

DeLamotte, Eugenia C. *Perils of the Night: A Feminist Study of Nineteenth-Century Gothic*. New York: Oxford University Press, 1990.

Dickens, Charles. *The Complete Ghost Stories of Charles Dickens*. Edited by Peter Haining. New York: Washington Square Press, 1982.

Donovan, Dick. "The Corpse Light." In *A Bottomless Grave and Other Victorian Tales of Terror*, edited by Hugh Lamb, 49–59. Mineola, NY: Dover, 2001.

Drake, Nathan. "On Objects of Terror." In *Gothic Documents: A Sourcebook, 1700–1820*, edited by E.J. Clery and Robert Miles, 154–163. Manchester: Manchester University Press, 2000.

Dudley, William, ed. *Media Violence: Opposing Viewpoints*. San Diego: Greenhaven Press, 1999.

Edelman, Lee. *No Future: Queer Theory and the Death Drive*. Durham: Duke University Press, 2004.

Edelstein, David. "Now Playing at Your Local Multiplex: Torture Porn." *New York Magazine*, January 28, 2006. http://nymag.com/movies/features/15622/ (accessed December 6, 2009).

Edmundson, Mark. *Nightmare on Main Street: Angels, Sadomasochism, and the Culture of Gothic*. Cambridge, MA: Harvard University Press, 1999.

Edwards, Amelia B. *Monsieur Maurice*. In *Five Victorian Ghost Novels*, edited by E.F. Bleiler, 245–296. New York: Dover, 1971.

———. "Was It An Illusion?" In *Victorian Ghost Stories*, edited by Michael Cox and R.A. Gilbert, 239–255. New York: Oxford University Press, 1992.

Elephant. DVD. Directed by Gus Van Sant. 2003. Los Angeles: HBO Home Video, 2004.

Ellis, Kate Ferguson. *The Contested Castle: Gothic Novels and the Subversion of Domestic Ideology*. Chicago: University of Illinois Press, 1989.

Faderman, Lillian. *Surpassing the Love of Men: Romantic Friendship and Love Between Women from the Renaissance to the Present*. New York: Triangle Classics, 1981.

Fincher, Max. *Queering the Gothic in the Romantic Age: The Penetrating Eye*. Basingstoke: Palgrave Macmillan, 2007.

Foldy, Michael S. *The Trials of Oscar Wilde: Deviance, Morality, and Late-Victorian Society*. New Haven, CT: Yale University Press, 1997.

Foucault, Michel. *Discipline and Punish: The Birth of the Prison*. Translated by Alan Sheridan. New York: Vintage Books, 1995.

———. "The Discourse on Language." In *Critical Theory Since 1965*, edited by Hazard Adams and Leroy Searle, 148–162. Tallahassee: Florida State University Press, 1986.

———. *The History of Sexuality, Vol. 1: An Introduction*. Translated by Robert Hurley. New York: Vintage Books, 1990.

———. *The History of Sexuality, Vol. 2: The Use of Pleasure*. Translated by Robert Hurley. New York: Vintage Books, 1990.

———. *Madness and Civilization*. Translated by Richard Howard. New York: Vintage Books, 1988.

———. "Nietzsche, Genealogy, History." In *The Foucault Reader*, edited by Paul Rabinow, 76–100. New York: Pantheon Books, 1984. 76–100.

———. *The Order of Things*. New York: Vintage Books, 1994.

Freddy Vs. Jason. DVD. Directed by Ronny Yu. 2003. Los Angeles: New Line Home Entertainment, 2004.

Freedman, Jonathan L. *Media Violence and Its Effect on Aggression: Assessing the Scientific Evidence*. Toronto: University of Toronto Press, 2002.

Freud, Sigmund. *Three Essays on the Theory of Sexuality*. Translated by James Strachey. New York: HarperCollins, 1962.

Fuss, Diana. *Identification Papers: Readings on Psychoanalysis, Sexuality, and Culture*. New York: Routledge, 1995.

Gamer, Michael. *Romanticism and the Gothic: Genre, Reception, and Canon Formation*. Cambridge: Cambridge University Press, 2000.

Gaskell, Elizabeth. "The Old Nurse's Story." In *Victorian Ghost Stories*, edited by Michael Cox and R.A. Gilbert, 1–18. New York: Oxford University Press, 1992.

Geary, Robert F. *The Supernatural in Gothic Fiction: Horror, Belief, and Literary Change*. Lewiston, NY: Edwin Mellen Press, 1992.

Ghostbusters. DVD. Directed by Ivan Reitman. 1984. Los Angeles: Columbia Pictures, 2006.

Givner, Jessie. "The Revolutionary Turn: Mary Shelley's *Frankenstein*." *Gothic Studies* 2.3 (2000): 274–291.

Glassner, Barry. *The Culture of Fear: Why Americans Are Afraid of the Wrong Things*. New York: Basic Books, 1999.

Green, Laura. "Hall of Mirrors: Radclyffe Hall's *The Well of Loneliness* and Modernist Fictions of Identity." *Twentieth-Century Literature* 49.3 (Fall 2003): 288.

Grisham, John. "Natural Bred Killers." In *Screen Violence*, edited by Karl French, 227–236. London: Bloomsbury, 1996.

Grossman, Dave, and Gloria DeGaetano. *Stop Teaching Our Kids to Kill: A Call to Action Against TV, Movie and Video Game Violence*. New York: Crown, 1999.

Guenette, Mark David. *Speak Low: Towards a Theory of the Non-Discourse of Male Homosexuality in Wilde, Proust, and Beyond*. Dissertation, Columbia University, 1993.

Hacking, Ian. *The Social Construction of What?* Cambridge, MA: Harvard University Press, 1999.

Haggerty, George E. *Queer Gothic*. Urbana: University of Illinois Press, 2006.

Haining, Peter. Foreword to *The Mammoth Book of Haunted House Stories*, edited by Peter Haining, 3–6. New York: Carroll & Graf, 2000.

———. Introduction to *The Complete Ghost Stories of Charles Dickens*, by Charles Dickens, 1–23. New York: Washington Square Press, 1982.

Halberstam, Judith. *Skin Shows: Gothic Horror and the Technology of Monsters*. Durham: Duke University Press, 1995.

Harwood, John. "Underground Ghost." In *Victorian and Edwardian Ghost Stories*, edited by Richard Dalby, 204–217. New York: Metro Books, 2002.

Heller, Tamar. "The Vampire in the House: Hysteria, Female Sexuality, and Female Knowledge in Le Fanu's 'Carmilla.'" In *The New Nineteenth Century: Feminist Readings of Underread Victorian Fiction*, edited by Barbara Leah Harman and Susan Meyer, 77–95. New York: Garland, 1996.

Hogle, Jerrold. "The Gothic Ghost of the Counterfeit and the Progress of Abjection." In *A Companion to the Gothic*, edited by David Punter, 293–304. Malden, MA: Blackwell, 2000.

Holland, Merlin. *The Real Trial of Oscar Wilde: The First Uncensored Transcript of the Trial of Oscar Wilde vs. John Douglas (Marquess of Queensberry), 1895*. New York: Fourth Estate, 2003.

Holzer, Hans. *Ghosts: True Encounters with the World Beyond*. New York: Black Dog and Leventhal, 1997.

Homans, Margaret. "Bearing Demons: Frankenstein's Circumvention of the Maternal." In *Frankenstein: Mary Shelley*, edited by Fred Botting, 140–165. London: Macmillan, 1995.

Hostel. DVD. Directed by Eli Roth. 2005. Los Angeles: Lions Gate Films, 2006.

Howe, Richard G. "Homosexuality in America: Exposing the Myths." American Family Association. http://www.afa.net/homosexual_agenda/homosexuality.pdf (accessed Dec. 28, 2009).

Selected Bibliography

Hume, David. *An Enquiry Concerning Human Understanding.* Amherst, NY: Prometheus Books, 1988.
_____. *A Treatise of Human Nature.* Edited by Ernest C. Mossner. New York: Penguin Books, 1985.
Hurley, Kelly. *The Gothic Body: Sexuality, Materialism, and Degeneration at the Fin de Siecle.* Cambridge: Cambridge University Press, 1996.
Hyde, H. Montgomery, ed. *The Trials of Oscar Wilde.* Birmingham, AL: The Notable Trials Library, 1989.
Irwin, H.J. *An Introduction to Parapsychology,* 3d edition. Jefferson, NC: McFarland, 1999.
Jackson, Rosemary. *Fantasy: The Literature of Subversion.* New York: Methuen, 1981.
Jackson, Shirley. *The Haunting of Hill House.* New York: Penguin, 1987.
James, Henry. *The Turn of the Screw.* In *The Turn of the Screw and Other Short Fiction.* New York: Bantam Books, 1981.
James, M.R. *Collected Ghost Stories.* Hertfordshire: Wordsworth, 1992.
Jenkins, Philip. *Using Murder: The Social Construction of Serial Homicide.* New York: Aldine de Gruyter, 1994.
Johnson, Samuel. "Preface to the Plays of William Shakespeare." In *The Major Works,* edited by Donald Greene, 419–456. New York: Oxford University Press, 2000.
_____. "Selection from *The Rambler No. 4.*" In *Gothic Documents: A Sourcebook, 1700–1820,* edited by E.J. Clery and Robert Miles, 175–179. Manchester: Manchester University Press, 2000.
Jones, Gerard. *Killing Monsters: Why Children Need Fantasy, Super Heroes, and Make-Believe Violence.* New York: Basic Books, 2002.
Kass, Jeff. *Columbine: A True Crime Story, a victim, the killers, and the nation's search for answers.* Denver: Ghost Road Press, 2009.
Kellner, Douglas. *Guys and Guns Amok: Domestic Terrorism and School Shootings from the Oklahoma City Bombing to the Virginia Tech Massacre.* Boulder, CO: Paradigm Publishers, 2008.
Kestner, Joseph. "Narcissism as Symptom and Structure: The Case of Mary Shelley's *Frankenstein.*" In *Frankenstein: Mary Shelley,* edited by Fred Botting, 68–80. London: Macmillan, 1995.
Kilgour, Maggie. *The Rise of the Gothic Novel.* New York: Routledge, 1995.
King, Stephen. *Danse Macabre.* New York: Berkley Books, 1983.
_____. *Rage.* In *The Bachman Books: Four Early Novels by Stephen King.* New York: Plume, 1985. 1–131.
Kneale, Nigel. "The Patter of Tiny Feet." In *The Mammoth Book of Haunted House Stories,* edited by Peter Haining, 477–488. New York: Carroll & Graf, 2000.
Koestenbaum, Wayne. "The Shadow on the Bed: Dr. Jekyll, Mr. Hyde, and the Labouchere Amendment." *Critical Matrix, Special Issue No. 1* (Spring 1988): 31–55.
Krafft-Ebing, R. *Psychopathia Sexualis,* 7th Edition. Philadelphia: F.A. Davis, 1893.
Kristeva, Julia. *Powers of Horror: An Essay on Abjection.* Translated by Leon S. Roudiez. New York: Columbia University Press, 1982.
Lake, Crystal. "Bloody Records: Manuscripts and Politics in Horace Walpole's *The Castle of Otranto.*" Article in progress, Georgia Institute of Technology, 2009. 17.
Langman, Peter. *Why Kids Kill: Inside the Minds of School Shooters.* New York: Palgrave Macmillan, 2009.
Lawler, Donald. "The Gothic Wilde." In *Rediscovering Oscar Wilde,* edited by George Sandulescu, 249–268. Gerrards Cross, Buckinghamshire: Smythe, 1994.
Leeches. DVD. Directed by David DeCoteau. 2003. Rapid Heart Pictures, 2004.
Le Fanu, J.S. *Best Ghost Stories of J.S. Le Fanu.* Edited by E.F. Bleiler. New York: Dover, 1964.
_____. *Carmilla.* In *Three Vampire Tales,*

edited by Anne Williams, 86–148. New York: Houghton Mifflin, 2003.

Lewis, Matthew. *The Monk*. Edited by Howard Anderson. New York: Oxford University Press, 1998.

Locke, John. *An Essay Concerning Human Understanding*, edited by Peter H. Nidditch. Oxford: Clarendon Press, 1975.

London, April. "Ann Radcliffe in Context: Marking the Boundaries of *The Mysteries of Udolpho*." *Eighteenth-Century Life* 10.1 (January 1986): 35–47.

Lovecraft, H.P. *The Annotated Supernatural Horror in Literature*. Ed. S.T. Yoshi. New York: Hippocampus Press, 2000.

Lowenstein, Adam. *Shocking Representation: Historical Trauma, National Cinema, and the Modern Horror Film*. New York: Columbia University Press, 2005.

Lytton, Edward Bulwer-Lytton. "The Haunted and the Haunters." In *The Mammoth Book of Haunted House Stories*, edited by Peter Haining, 9–37 New York: Carroll & Graf, 2000.

———. *Zanoni*. Doylestown, PA: Wildside Press, 2002.

Mackenzie, Anna Maria. *Mysteries Elucidated*. London: Minerva Press, 1795.

Mathias, T.J. *The Pursuits of Literature*. London: Bulmer, 1812.

Maturin, Charles. *Melmoth the Wanderer*. Edited by Douglas Grant. New York: Oxford University Press, 1998.

Medved, Michael. *Hollywood Vs. America: Popular Culture and the War on Traditional Values*. New York: HarperCollins, 1992.

Miles, Robert. *Ann Radcliffe: The Great Enchantress*. New York: Manchester University Press, 1995.

———. "Europhobia: The Catholic Other in Horace Walpole and Charles Maturin." In *European Gothic: A Spirited Exchange, 1760–1960*, edited by Avril Horner, 84–103. Manchester: Manchester University Press, 2002.

———. *Gothic Writing, 1750–1820: A Genealogy*. New York: Routledge, 1993.

Miller, D. A. "Anal Rope." In *Inside/Out: Lesbian Theories, Gay Theories*, edited by Diana Fuss, 124–125. New York: Routledge, 1991.

Molesworth, Mary Louisa. "The Story of the Rippling Train." In *Victorian Ghost Stories*, edited by Michael Cox and R.A. Gilbert, 319–327. New York: Oxford University Press, 1992.

More, Hannah. *Strictures on the Modern System of Female Education, with A View of the Principles and Conduct Prevalent among Women of Rank and Fortune*. Boston: Printed for Joseph Bumstead, 1802.

Moretti, Franco. "Dialectic of Fear." In *Signs Taken for Wonders: Essays in the Sociology of Literary Forms*, translated by Susan Fischer, David Forgacs and David Miller, 83–108. New York: Verso, 1988.

Mortimer, John. Foreword to *The Real Trial of Oscar Wilde: The First Uncensored Transcript of the Trial of Oscar Wilde vs. John Douglas (Marquess of Queensberry), 1895*, by Merlin Holland, xi–xiii. New York: Fourth Estate, 2003.

Mulock, Dinah Maria. "M. Anastasius." In *Victorian and Edwardian Ghost Stories*, edited by Richard Dalby, 28–54. New York: Metro Books, 2002.

Mulvey, Laura. "Visual Pleasure and Narrative Cinema." In *Film Theory and Criticism*, 7th ed., edited by Leo Braudy and Marshall Cohen, 711–722. New York: Oxford University Press, 2009.

Myers, Arthur. *The Ghostly Register*. Chicago: Contemporary Books, 1986.

Natural Born Killers: The Director's Cut. DVD. Directed by Oliver Stone. 1994. Vidmark/Trimark, 2000.

Newton, David E. *Violence and the Media: A Reference Handbook*. Santa Barbara: ABC-CLIO, 1996.

Nightmare on Elm Street, A. DVD. Directed by Wes Craven. 1984. Los Angeles: New Line Studios, 1999.

Nightmare on Elm Street 2: Freddy's Revenge. DVD. Directed by Jack Sholder.

1985. Los Angeles: New Line Studios, 1999.
Nightmare on Elm Street 3: Dream Warriors. DVD. Directed by Chuck Russell. 1987. Los Angeles: New Line Studios, 1999.
Nordau, Max. *Degeneration.* Lincoln: University of Nebraska Press, 1993.
Norton, Rictor. *Mistress of Udolpho: The Life of Ann Radcliffe.* London: Leicester University Press, 1999.
Ogden, Tom. *The Complete Idiot's Guide to Ghosts and Hauntings.* Indianapolis: Alpha Books, 1999.
"On Novels." *Walker's Hibernian* (April 1797): 356–358.
Palmer, Paulina. *Lesbian Gothic: Transgressive Fictions.* New York: Cassell, 1999.
Parreaux, Andre. *The Publication of The Monk.* Paris: M. Didier, 1960.
Pavel, Thomas G. *Fictional Worlds.* Cambridge, MA: Harvard University Press, 1986.
Phillips, Phil and Joan Hake Robie. *Horror and Violence: The Deadly Duo in the Media.* Lancaster, PA: Starburst, 1988.
Plato. *Republic.* Translated by Robin Waterfield. New York: Oxford World's Classics, 2008.
Poe, Edgar Allan. "The Tell-Tale Heart." In *The Haunted Omnibus: The Greatest Ghost Stories of All Time*, edited by Alexander Laing, 769–775. New York: MJF Books, 1965.
Pollack, William S. *Real Boys' Voices.* New York: Random House, 2000.
Poltergeist. DVD. Directed by Tobe Hooper. 1982. DVD. Warner Home Video, 2004.
Poovey, Mary. "Ideology and *The Mysteries of Udolpho.*" *Criticism* 21.4 (1979): 307–330.
Potter, W. James. *The 11 Myths of Media Violence.* Thousand Oaks, CA: Sage Publications, 2003.
Prince, Stephen. "The Discourse of Pictures: Iconicity and Film Studies." In *Film Theory and Criticism*, 7th ed., edited by Leo Braudy and Marshall Cohen, 87–105. New York: Oxford University Press, 2009.
Punter, David. *The Literature of Terror*, 2d ed., 2 volumes. New York: Longman, 1996.
Radcliffe, Ann. *The Mysteries of Udolpho.* Edited by Bonamy Dobrée. New York: Oxford University Press, 1980.
Reeve, Clara. "Preface to *The Old English Baron*." In *Gothic Documents: A Sourcebook, 1700–1820*, 132–134. Eds. E.J. Clery and Robert Miles. Manchester: Manchester University Press, 2000.
———. *The Progress of Romance, through Times, Countries, and Manners, with Remarks on the Good and Bad Effects of It, on Them Respectively, in a Course of Evening Conversations.* Dublin: Printed for Messrs. Price, Exshaw, White, Cash, Colbert, Marchbank, and Porter, 1785.
Review of *Caleb Williams*, by William Godwin. *British Critic* 4 (July 1794): 70–71.
Review of *The Castle of Otranto*, by Horace Walpole. *Monthly Review* 32 (May 1765): 394.
Review of *The Castle of St. Vallery: An Ancient Story. Monthly Review* 2d series 9 (Nov. 1792): 337.
Review of *The Exiles*, by Clara Reeve. *Critical Review* 67 (Jan. 1789): 75.
Review of *Hermsprong*, by Robert Bage. *British Critic* 7 (April 1796): 430.
Review of *The Italian*, by Ann Radcliffe. *British Critic* 10 (Sept. 1797): 266.
Review of *The Maid of the Hamlet*, by Regina Maria Roche. *Critical Review* 2d series 10 (April 1794): 472–73.
Review of *Man As He Is*, by Robert Bage. *Monthly Review* 2d ser. 10 (March 1793): 297.
Review of *The Monk*, by Matthew Lewis. *European Magazine and London Review* 31 (Feb. 1797): 111–15.
Review of *The Monk*, by Matthew Lewis. *Monthly Review* 2d series 23 (Aug. 1797): 451.

Review of *Old Manor House*, by Charlotte Smith. *British Critic* 1 (June 1793): 148–49.

Review of *The School for Fathers*, by Clara Reeve. *Analytical Review* 2 (Oct. 1788): 223.

Review of *Secrecy, or The Ruin of the Rock*, by Eliza Fenwick. *British Critic* 6 (Nov. 1795): 545.

Review of *St. Leon*, by William Godwin. *British Critic* 15 (Jan. 1800): 47–51.

Review of *Tancred, or a Tale of Ancient Times*, by Joseph Fox. *English Review* 18 (Aug. 1791): 143.

Rhys, Jean. "I Used To Live Here Once." In *The Omnibus of Twentieth-Century Ghost Stories*, edited by Robert Phillips, 145–146. New York: Carroll & Graf, 1991.

Richter, David H. *The Progress of Romance: Literary Historiography and the Gothic Novel*. Columbus: Ohio State University Press, 1996.

Riddell, Charlotte. "The Open Door." In *Victorian Ghost Stories*, edited by Michael Cox and R.A. Gilbert, 256–282. New York: Oxford University Press, 1992.

———. *The Uninhabited House*. In *Five Victorian Ghost Novels*, edited by E.F. Bleiler, 1–112. New York: Dover, 1971.

Rieder, John. "'A Filthy Type': The Motif of the Fecal Child in Mary Shelley's *Frankenstein*." *Gothic Studies* 3.1 (April 2001) 25.

Riquelme, John Paul. "Oscar Wilde's Aesthetic Gothic: Walter Pater, Dark Enlightenment, and *The Picture of Dorian Gray*." *Modern Fiction Studies* 46.3 (2000): 609–31.

"Rise, Progress, and Effects of Jacobinism, The." *Anti-Jacobin Review* 1 (Aug. 1798): 223.

Rockoff, Adam. *Going to Pieces: The Rise and Fall of the Slasher Film, 1978–1986*. Jefferson, NC: McFarland, 2002.

Roll, William G. *The Poltergeist*. Garden City, NY: Nelson Doubleday, 1972.

Roy, Lucinda. *No Right to Remain Silent: The Tragedy at Virginia Tech*. New York: Harmony Books, 2009.

Sage, Victor. *Horror Fiction in the Protestant Tradition*. New York: St. Martin's, 1988.

Saw. DVD. Directed by James Wan. 2004. Lions Gate Films, 2005.

Saw 2. DVD. Directed by Darren Lynn Bousman. 2005. Los Angeles: Lions Gate Films, 2006.

Saw 3. DVD. Directed by Darren Lynn Bousman. 2006. Los Angeles: Lions Gate Films, 2007.

Saw 6. Directed by Kevin Greutert. 2009. Toronto: A Bigger Boat, 2009.

Scarborough, Dorothy. *The Supernatural in Modern English Fiction*. Maple Shade, NJ: Lethe Press, 2001.

Schaffer, Talia. "'A Wilde Desire Took Me': The Homoerotic History of *Dracula*." In *Dracula*, edited by Nina Auerbach and David J. Skal, 470–482. New York: W.W. Norton, 1997).

Scott, Beth and Michael Norman. *Haunted Heartland: True Ghost Stories from the American Midwest*. New York: Barnes and Noble Books, 1992.

Scream. DVD. Directed by Wes Craven. 1996. Los Angeles: Dimension, 2000.

Scream 2. DVD. Directed by Wes Craven. 1996. Los Angeles: Dimension, 2000.

Scream 3. DVD. Directed by Wes Craven. 1996. Los Angeles: Dimension, 2000.

Sedgwick, Eve Kosofsky. *Between Men: English Literature and Male Homosocial Desire*. New York: Columbia University Press, 1985.

———. *The Coherence of Gothic Conventions*. New York: Arno Press, 1980.

———. *Epistemology of the Closet*. Los Angeles: University of California Press, 1990.

Sheldon, Louis P. "Homosexuals Recruit Public School Children." Traditional Values Coalition. http://www.traditionalvalues.org/pdf_files/TVCSpecialRptHomosexualRecruitChildren.PDF (accessed Dec. 28, 2009).

Shelley, Mary. *Frankenstein*. Edited by J. Paul Hunter. New York: W.W. Norton, 1996.

Showalter, Elaine. *Sexual Anarchy: Gender and Culture at the Fin de Siecle*. New York: Viking, 1990.

Shrek. Directed by Vicky Jenson and Andrew Adamson. 2001. Los Angeles: Dreamworks SKG, 2001.

Siegel, Carol. *Goth's Dark Empire*. Bloomington: Indiana University Press, 2005.

Sinfield, Alan. *The Wilde Century: Effeminacy, Oscar Wilde and the Queer Moment*. New York: Columbia University Press, 1994.

Sixth Sense, The. DVD. Directed by M. Night Shyamalan. 1999. Buena Vista Home Entertainment, 2000.

Smith, Andrew. *Gothic Radicalism: Literature, Philosophy and Psychoanalysis in the Nineteenth Century*. New York: St. Martin's Press, 2000.

Sontag, Susan. "Notes on Camp." http://interglacial.com/~sburke/pub/prose/Susan_Sontag_-_Notes_on_Camp.html (accessed December 30, 2009).

Stallybrass, Peter and Allon White. *The Politics and Poetics of Transgression*. Ithaca: Cornell University Press, 1986.

Sternheimer, Karen. *It's Not the Media: The Truth about Pop Culture's Influence on Children*. Boulder, CO: Westview Press, 2003.

Stevenson, Robert Louis. *The Strange Case of Dr. Jekyll and Mr. Hyde*. Edited by Martin A. Danahay. Orchard Park, NY: Broadview, 2001.

Stewart, C. Nelson. "Bulwer Lytton as Occultist." Whitefish, MT: Kessinger Publishing, 1997.

Steyer, James P. *The Other Parent: The Inside Story of the Media's Effect on Our Children*. New York: Atria Books, 2002.

Stone, Oliver. "Don't Sue the Messenger." In *Screen Violence*, edited by Karl French, 237–239. London: Bloomsbury, 1996.

Sullivan, Jack. *Elegant Nightmares: The English Ghost Story from Le Fanu to Blackwood*. Athens: Ohio University Press, 1978.

Taylor, John Tinnon. *Early Opposition to the English Novel: The Popular Reaction from 1760 to 1830*. New York: King's Crown Press, 1943.

Taylor, Michael. "Reluctant Romancers: Self-Consciousness and Derogation in Prose Romance." *English Studies in Canada* 17.1 (March 1991): 89–106.

Taylor, Troy. *The Ghost Hunter's Guidebook: The Essential Handbook for Ghost Research*. Alton, IL: Whitechapel Productions, 2001.

"Terrorist Novel Writing." In *Gothic Documents: A Sourcebook, 1700–1820*, edited by E.J. Clery and Robert Miles, 182–184. Manchester: Manchester University Press, 2000.

"Terrorist System of Novel Writing, The." In *Gothic Readings: The First Wave, 1764–1840*, edited by Rictor Norton, 300–302. New York: Leicester University Press, 2000.

Texas Chainsaw Massacre 2. DVD. Directed by Tobe Hooper. 1986. Los Angeles: MGM-UA, 2001.

Tithecott, Richard. *Of Men and Monsters: Jeffrey Dahmer and the Construction of the Serial Killer*. Madison: University of Wisconsin Press, 1997.

Tropp, Martin. *Images of Fear: How Horror Stories Helped Shape Modern Culture, 1818–1918*. Jefferson, NC: McFarland, 1990.

Underwood, Tim, and Chuck Miller, eds. *Bare Bones: Conversations on Terror with Stephen King*. New York: McGraw-Hill, 1988.

Vicinus, Martha. "The Adolescent Boy: Fin-de-Siecle Femme Fatale?" In *Victorian Sexual Dissidence*, edited by Richard Dellamora, 83–106. Chicago: University of Chicago Press, 1999.

Voodoo Academy. DVD. Directed by David DeCoteau. 2000. Los Angeles: Cult Video, 2000.

Walpole, Horace. *The Castle of Otranto*. Edited by W. S. Lewis. New York: Oxford University Press, 1998.

———. *The Yale Edition of Horace Walpole's Correspondence*. 48 volumes. Ed. W. S. Lewis. New Haven, CT: Yale University Press, 1937.

Weeks, Jeffrey. *Coming Out: Homosexual Politics in Britain, from the Nineteenth Century to the Present*. New York: Quartet Books, 1977.

Wes Craven's New Nightmare. DVD. Directed by Wes Craven. 1994. Los Angeles: New Line Studios, 1999.

Whitehouse, Mary. "Time to Face Responsibility." In *Screen Violence*, edited by Karl French, 52–61. London: Bloomsbury, 1996.

Wilde, Oscar. *The Picture of Dorian Gray*. In *The Complete Works of Oscar Wilde*, 17–167. London: HarperCollins, 1966.

Wilson, Colin. *Poltergeist! A Study in Destructive Haunting*. London: Caxton Editions, 2000.

Wilt, Judith. *Ghosts of the Gothic: Austen, Eliot, and Lawrence*. Princeton: Princeton University Press, 1980.

Wolfreys, Julian. *Victorian Hauntings: Spectrality, Gothic, the Uncanny and Literature*. New York: Palgrave, 2002.

Womack, Kenneth. "'Withered, Wrinkled, and Loathsome of Visage': Reading the Ethics of the Soul and the Late-Victorian Gothic in *The Picture of Dorian Gray*." In *Victorian Gothic: Literary and Cultural Manifestations in the Nineteenth Century*, edited by Ruth Robbins and Julian Wolfreys. New York: Palgrave, 2000.

Wood, Ellen. "Reality or Delusion?" In *Victorian Ghost Stories* edited by Michael Cox and R.A. Gilbert, 115–129. New York: Oxford University Press, 1992.

Wood, Robin. "An Introduction to the American Horror Film." In *Planks of Reason: Essays on the Horror Film*, edited by Barry Keith Grant, 164–200. Metuchen, NJ: Scarecrow Press, 1984.

W.W. "On Novels and Romances." In *Gothic Documents: A Sourcebook, 1700–1820*, edited by E.J. Clery and Robert Miles, 210–218. Manchester: Manchester University Press, 2000.

Žižek, Slavoj. *For They Know Not What They Do: Enjoyment as a Political Factor*. New York: Verso, 1991.

——. *Looking Awry: An Introduction to Jacques Lacan through Popular Culture*. Cambridge, MA: MIT Press, 1991.

Index

Numbers in ***bold italics*** indicate pages with photographs.

accountability 9–10, 14
Addison, Joseph 31–32, 34, 38, 128
aesthetics 25, 29, 32–33, 36–39, 47, 50, 53–54, 79, 112
Afghanistan (war in) 201
agency 2, 8–11, 13–18, 20, 138, 167, 173, 191
American Family Association (AFA) 64–65, 68, 71, 74, 80, 83
The Amityville Horror 122, 126, 131–132
The Analytical Review 42
Anson, Jay 122, 131–132
Arlen, Michael 142–143, 147
Armstrong, Nancy 3
Austen, Jane 125
authenticity 44, 111, 118, 120–136, 144–148

Baddeley, Gavin 163, 193–194
Bage, Robert 41, 46
Baldwin, Louisa 151
Barbauld, Anna Laetitia 52
Bare Bones: Conversations on Terror with Stephen King 179
Baudrillard, Jean 6
Bayh, Evan 168
Bayless, Raymond 124–125, 128–130, 149
Beahm, George 177
Beale, Charles Willing 156
Beattie, James 33, 50
Benshoff, Harry M. 83–84
Benson, E.F. 153, 157
Between Men 62, 98
Bierce, Ambrose 148, 150, 158
Blackwood, Algernon 96–99, 102, 121, 148, 151, 154
blame *see* culpability
Botting, Fred 43
Bourdieu, Pierre 13–14, 16–19
Bowling for Columbine 163, 194
Brandon, Trent 129, 131, 136, 145, 153
Bride of Frankenstein 81
Brinkley, Edward S. 84
The British Critic 46, 51

Brontë, Emily 5
The Brotherhood 94–96, 98–103, ***99***, ***100***, ***101***, 111–112, 117
Broughton, Rhoda 126
Brown, Brooks 168, 175
Browning, Elizabeth 120
Browning, Robert 120
Buffy the Vampire Slayer (TV) 89–93, ***91***, ***92***, ***93***, 163
Burris, Chad ***104***
Busch, Adam ***93***
Bush, George W. 201–202, 205–207
Butler, Judith 48, 73, 111

Caleb Williams 46
camp (as a sensibility) 112–113
Capote, Truman 170
Carmilla 71–76, 79, 81, 84, 88
Carneal, Michael 177, 179
Carrie 176, 178
Carson, Edward 77–78
The Castle of Otranto 4–5, 26–29, 37–38, 43, 62, 118–119, 146, 163
The Castle of St. Vallery, an Ancient Story 28–29
Catholicism 44, 47, 53; *see also* Christianity; Protestantism; religion
causality (fiction's potential to cause phenomena) 2–5, 7–19, 30, 32, 41, 123, 141–143, 162–185, 191–193, 199
children (at risk) 1–2, 8, 12, 31, 33, 40–42, 48, 61, 64–71, 74–76, 96–97, 106–107, 128, 132, 155, 163–165, 169, 175, 180, 186, 192–194, 197–198
Cho, Seung-Hui 173–174
Christianity 34, 44–45, 63, 69, 75, 117–119, 135, 166; *see also* Catholicism; Protestantism; religion
clear and present danger 10, 177–178
Clery, E.J. 28, 38, 118–119, 135, 150
Clinton, Bill 163, 166, 186
Clinton, Hillary 168

233

Clover, Carol 12, 188, 195
Cohen, Ed 61
Coleridge, Samuel Taylor 44, 47–48, 50–51, 117, 165–166
Collings, Michael 181
Collins, Wilkie 5–6, 152
Columbine 2, 4, 8, 161–163, 165–174, 179, 182, 184–185, 189, 192, 194, 199
Columbine (book) 161, 169
Columbine: A True Crime Story 161, 169
Comstock, George 165, 167
Conan Doyle, Arthur 120, 150
Confessions of a Justified Sinner 4–5
The Contested Castle 42
convention 5–6, 52, 90–91, 111–113, 117, 120–123, 126–133, 144, 149, 152–153, 157–158, 162, 166; *see also* genre
conversion 64, 68–73, 80, 136–141, 143, 150, 156
Cox, Jeffrey Lynne 177, 179
Cram, Ralph Adam 153
Craven, Wes 2, 10, 188–189, 194–198
crime 4, 8–11, 18–21, 29, 37, 46, 53, 60, 65, 74, 78, 85–86, 108, 136, 139–140, 147, 161, 163, 167, 169–170, 173–182, 189, 190–192, 203–205; *see also* law
Criminal Man 139–140
The Critical Review 36, 40, 44, 47, 51
critics 2–6, 19, 25–29, 33, 36, 38–55, 59–60, 76, 81, 83–84, 117, 142–143, 161, 163–166, 178, 190–194, 197–199; *see also* media violence debate; reviews
Cullen, Dave 161, 169–171
culpability 3–5, 8–21, 33, 85, 91, 163–165, 173, 177–178, 184, 190–192, 194, 198–199, 202

Danse Macabre 178
Darras, Benjamin 185
Darwin, Erasmus 66
Davis, Lennard 26, 36
DeCoteau, David 94–114
DeFelitta, Frank 132–134
Defoe, Daniel 26, 126
Degeneration 79, 139
DeLamotte, Eugenia 170
Derrida, Jacques 217n30
de Sade, Marquis 48
determinism 8–11, 16–17
Dickens, Charles 5, 120, 128–129, 145, 147
Discipline and Punish 204
disease 25, 61–82, 85–86, 88–89, 91, 94, 97, 100, 136, 138, 162, 166, 177, 199, 214n1
Dole, Bob 163–164, 190
domesticity 3, 33, 42, 62, 119
Donovan, Dick 139
Douglas, Alfred Lord 78
Dracula 4, 6, 81, 213n1
Drake, Nathan 51

Edelman, Lee 64–65, 74, 82
Edelstein, David 200–202, 207
Edmondson, Sarah 185
Edmundson, Mark 171
Edwards, Amelia B. 137, 145
Elephant 171–**172**
The 11 Myths of Media Violence 164, 168, 182
Eliot, George 5
Ellis, Kate Ferguson 42, 49, 144
The English Review 43, 47
Englund, Robert **195**
The Enigma of the Poltergeist 124
Enlightenment 5, 20, 25–29, 38, 43
The Entity 132–136
epistemology 4, 7–8, 26, 144–158
Epistemology of the Closet 61
An Essay Concerning Human Understanding 29
Essay on Poetry and Music, as They Affect the Mind 33
The European Magazine and London Review 46
EVP (electronic voice phenomenon) 148
The Exiles 36
The Exorcist 126, 178, 186
explained supernatural 51–52

Factual Fictions 26
Faderman, Lillian 72
Fenwick, Eliza 46
Fictional Worlds 12
Fielding, Henry 35
Forster, E.M. 63, 214n27
Foucault, Michel 7, 12, 19–20, 60, 72, 82, 204
Fox, John 119, 146, 148, 150
Fox, Joseph 43
Frankenstein (book) 66–75, 80–81
Frankenstein (film) 81
Freddy vs. Jason 198–199
free will 9–11, 16–18
Freedman, Jonathan 164–167, 192–193
French Revolution 40, 44, 46–47, 48, 54
Freud, Sigmund 12, 96–100, 196
Friday the 13th 198
Fuss, Diana 86
Fuzz 178

Gamer, Michael 43
Gaskell, Elizabeth 149
Gaynor, Kerry 132–133
Geary, Robert F. 119, 121, 135–136
gender 12, 40, 42–43, 47–48, 53, 59, 61–62, 111–112, 117
genre 2, 4–5, 62, 89, 169, 175, 178, 188, 200; *see also* convention
Ghost Hunters 119, 148
The Ghost Hunter's Bible 129, 136
The Ghost Hunter's Guidebook 132

Index

The Ghost of Guir House 156
Ghostbusters 155
The Ghostly Register 140
ghosts 4, 7–8, 19, 26–27, 31–32, 43, 53, 96, 98, 117–158, 162, 187–188, 196
Ghosts: True Encounters with the World Beyond 124
Gill, Charles 65, 78–79
Glanvil, Joseph 124
Gods and Monsters 81–82
Godwin, William 45–46, 53
Gothic, definiition of 5–6
Goth's Dark Empire 161
Grisham, John 185, 188
Grossman, David 8, 163, 166, 180, 192, 194
Guenette, Mark David 95

Hacking, Ian 7
Haggerty, George 60
Haining, Peter 154
Halberstam, Judith 62–63, 82, 86–89, 93
Hall, Radclyffe 62
Halperin, David 60–61
Hamlet 139, 148
Hannigan, Alyson *91*
Harrelson, Woody 186
Harris, Eric *see* Columbine
Harwood, John 151
Haunted Heartland: True Ghost Stories of the American Midwest 131–132, 135, 148, 151, 156
The Haunted Hotel 152–153
The Haunting in Connecticut 155
The Haunting of Hill House 155
Hays, Mary 52
Heller, Tamar 72–73
Henderson, Josh *106*
Hermsprong 46
Hernandez, Jay 200
heteronormativity *see* normativity
high and low culture 19, 39–41, 49–52
Hitchcock, Alfred 95
Hogg, James 4
Hogle, Jerrold 27
Hollywood vs. America: Popular Culture and the War on Traditional Values 164
Holzer, Hans 122, 124, 127, 129–132, 140–141, 151, 154, 157
Home, Daniel 120
homophobia 63, 65, 73–74, 80, 85–86, 89, 92, 95, 98, 102, 106–107, 109–113, 166, 202
homosexuality 7–8, 50, 59–113, 162, 166, 202, 212*n*7
Hopper, Dennis 87
Horror and Violence: The Deadly Duo in the Media 166
Horror Fiction in the Protestant Tradition 136
Hostel **200**–202, 206–207

Hughes, Miko *197*
Hume, David 30

idealization 35–39
identification 11–15, 18, 20–21, 37, 59, 63, 88, 90, 93, 96–97, 109, 150, 180–181, 194, 203, 206
The Idiot's Guide to Ghosts and Hauntings 123, 135
impressions 12, 29–35, 41, 51, 53, 96, 132, 138, 154–156, 158, 163, 177, 182, 185, 192–193
In Cold Blood 170
Inchbald, Elizabeth 52
Indra, Ben *103*
influence 1–21, 29–30, 36, 41, 46, 50, 52–53, 55, 69–72, 75–80, 96–98, 112, 120, 127, 139, 158, 161–167, 173, 176, 178–194, 198–199, 206
instruction 8, 11, 32–38, 41, 45, 50, 53, 155, 163–164, 191–192, 203, 205–207
intersectionality 62–63
An Introduction to Parapsychology 118, 136
Iraq (war in) 201, 205
Irwin, H.J. 118–120, 123–124, 127–129, 136, 139, 146, 148, 154–155, 157
The Italian 5, 51
It's Not the Media: The Truth about Pop Culture's Influence on Children 165

Jackson, Shirley 155
Jacobinism 44–45, 47–48
James, Henry 137
James, M.R. 126, 147–148, 156
John Silence 96
Johnson, Samuel 32–38, 50, 118–119, 150
Jones, Gerard 12, 165–166, 192–193
Judaism 214*n*23
judgment 15, 19, 31, 33, 39, 49, 79, 84–85, 90, 94, 105, 127–128, 131, 137, 145–146, 158, 165, 171

Karloff, Boris 81
Kass, Jeff 161, 164, 169–171, 175
Kellner, Douglas 174
Kestner, Joseph 68
Killing Monsters: Why Children Need Fantasy, Super Heroes, and Make-Believe Violence 192
King, Stephen 5, 6, 176–185, 190
Kinkel, Kip 192–193
Klebold, Dylan *see* Columbine
Kneale, Nigel 153
Koestenbaum, Wayne 76
Krafft-Ebing, R. von 61, 75–76, 79
Kristeva, Julia 83

Lacan, Jacques 15, 20, 216*n*1
Lake, Crystal 28

Langenkamp, Heather *197*
Langman, Peter 161, 169, 171, 177
law 9–11, 30, 42, 46, 48–50, 53, 59–60, 62, 76, 82, 111, 140, 148–149, 151, 165, 179, 183, 185, 190, 192, 200
Lawler, Donald 60
Leather Jacket Love Story 94
Leeches! 94, 102–112, *106*
Le Fanu, J. Sheridan 71–75, 121, 125–126, 128, 138, 147–149, 151, 158
Levine, Madeline 8
Lewis, Juliette *186*
Lewis, Matthew 40, 44, 46–51, 53, 59, 98
Lieberman, Joseph 163, 168, 193
The Literature of Terror 6
Locke, John 29–39, 41, 96, 128, 150, 210n18
Lombroso, Cesare 139–140
Loukaitis, Barry 176, 179
Lovecraft, H.P. 126, 156
Lutz, George 132
Lutz, Kathleen 132
Lytton, Edward Bulwer 120–121, 127–128, 137, 147

Machen, Arthur 121
Mackenzie, Anna Maria 51–52
Madness and Civilization 12
The Maid of the Hamlet 40–41
The Mammoth Book of Haunted House Stories 154
Man as He Is 41
Manson, Charles 188
Manson, Marilyn 6, 163, 165, 173, 193–194
Martinez, Nathan 185
materialism 121, 125, 135, 139–140
Mathias, T.J. 3, 44–50, 53, 165
The Matrix 6
Maturin, Charles 5, 44, 63, 69–72
Maurice 63, 214n27
Media Violence Alert 166, 180, 192
Media Violence and Its Effect on Aggression: Assessing the Scientific Evidence 164
media violence debate 8–15, 162–175, 183–185, 190–194, 199, 203
Medved, Michael 11–12, 164–166, 194
Mellor, Anne K. 66
Melmoth the Wanderer 5, 63, 69–76
Men, Women, and Chain Saws 12
metafiction 142–143, 186, 188
Miles, Robert 44, 53–54
Miller, D.A. 95
Millington, Thomas Street 148
Mistress of Udolpho: The Life of Ann Radcliffe 52
models *see* role models
Molesworth, Mary Louisa 127
The Monk 40, 44, 46–52, 55, 59, 98, 166, 188
Monsieur Maurice 137

Monsters in the Closet 83–84
The Monthly Review 26–29, 41, 43, 47
Moore, John 46
Moore, Michael 163, 194
morality 25, 28–39, 46, 50, 65, 71, 75, 84, 97–98, 100, 102, 161, 163, 179, 183, 200, 203–206
More, Hannah 34, 40
Mulock, Dinah Maria 150
multiple causation *see* causality
murder 1, 3, 9, 32, 43, 46–47, 77, 79, 84–86, 91–93, 105, 113, 129, 142, 145, 147–149, 152, 161, 169, 171, 175–178, 180–182, 185–191, 196, 199–206
Murnau, F.W. 81
music 6, 77, 96, 108, 129, 148, 163–165, 173, 193
Myers, Arthur 140, 148, 158
The Mysteries of Udolpho 40, 51–55, 142–143, 188

National Rifle Association (NRA) 10, 182
National Television Violence Study 193
Natural Born Killers 185–*186*, 188–195
Nelson, John 166
neo–Gothic 5–6
New Nightmare see *Wes Craven's New Nightmare*
Newman, Katherine 176
A Nightmare on Elm Street 1–2, 189, 194–198, *195*
Nightmare on Elm Street 2: Freddy's Revenge 197
Nightmare on Elm Street 3: Dream Warriors 197–198
Nightmare on Main Street: Angels, Sadomasochism, and the Culture of Gothic 171
No Easy Answers: The Truth Behind Death at Columbine 168
No Future: Queer Theory and the Death Drive 64–65
No Right to Remain Silent: The Tragedy at Virginia Tech 174
Nordau, Max 79, 139
Norman, Michael 131
normativity 29, 40, 59–64, 73–74, 80, 82–83, 88–90, 98, 101–102, 109–110, 112–113, 117, 164, 212n7
norms 3, 11, 28, 35, 42–43, 45, 47, 53, 59, 61–65, 68, 71, 74, 80, 82, 112, 121, 145–147, 149, 158, 164, 181
Northanger Abbey 125
Norton, Rictor 52, 212n7
Nosferatu 81

Obama, Barack 207
Ogden, Tom 123–125, 150
The Old English Baron 28–29, 52
The Old Manor House 46

Oldboy 173–174, 180, 183–184
The Omen 126
ontology 4, 7–8, 118, 133, 144, 156, 197

Page, Sam **99, 100, 101**
Paine, Thomas 45
Paranormal Activity 119, 148
parapsychology 19, 118, 120, 122–125, 128–136, 139, 143, 145, 155, 157
parental advisories 193
Park, Chan-wook 184
Parreaux, Andre 47–50
Pascalian Meditations 13
pathology *see* disease
patriarchy 42–43, 48, 53–54, 72–73, 92
Pavel, Thomas 12–14
performativity 111–112
Pet Sematary 177
Phillips, Phil 166
Philosophical Considerations considering the existence of Sorcerers and Sorcery 124
The Picture of Dorian Gray 6, 59–62, 65, 76–80, 84–86, 95
Pierce, Dustin 177, 179
Pinkett, Jada **187**
Plato 2
The Plays of William Shakespeare 32–33
Poe, Edgar Allan 5–6, 145
poison 33–34, 47, 50, 164, 166, 191, 193
politics 3, 28, 39, 44–46, 50, 52, 64, 111, 161, 165, 167–168, 171, 184, 193, 197, 199, 201–207
The Politics and Poetics of Transgression 39
Poltergeist (film) 134–135, 156, 158
The Poltergeist 125, 129
Poltergeist!: A Study in Destructive Haunting 122, 129
Poovey, Mary 53–54
Potter, W. James 9–11, 13, 16, 164–168, 182, 189, 194
The Progress of Romance (Reeve) 35–36
Protestantism 44, 47, 49, 53, 117, 136, *see also* Catholicism; Christianity; religion
psychics 166–167, 226n40
Psycho 178
Psychopathia Sexualis 61, 75–76
The Publication of the Monk 47
Punter, David 6
The Pursuits of Literature 3, 44, 49

Queensberry, Marquess of 77–78
Queer Gothic 60

Radcliffe, Ann 5–6, 40, 51–55, 142
Rage 176–188, 191, 194
The Rambler 34–37
Rampage 176
ratings (of films and television) 1, 188
reality, definition of 6, 7, 52

Reeve, Clara 28, 35–36, 42, 52, 55
Reitman, Ivan 155
religion 34, 42–49, 53, 104, 117, 119, 165; *see also* Catholicism; Christianity; Judaism; Protestantism
reproduction *see* children
Republic 2
Resident Evil (video game) 6
responsibility 2, 4–5, 9–21, 25, 32–33, 46, 166, 171, 173, 177, 183, 185, 189, 192, 199
retrospective causality 9–11, 14, 18, 168, 182–183; *see also* causality
reverse discourse 82–86, 89
reviews (of film and literature) 26–31, 36, 39–55, 94, 132
Rhys, Jean 155
Richter, David 40
Riddell, Charlotte 137, 152
Rieder, John 67
The Rise of Supernatural Fiction 118–119
Robie, Joan Hake 166
Roche, Regina Maria 40
Rockoff, Adam 195
role models 3, 11–13, 15, 35, 138–140, 143, 173, 180–182, 185, 191–194
Roll, William G. 125, 128–129, 139, 145
Romanticism 5, 43
Romanticism and the Gothic 43
Rope 95
Rosemary's Baby 126
Roy, Lucinda 174–176
RSPK (recurrent spontaneous psychokinesis) 125, 133, 157
Rubinstein, Zelda 135
The Ruin on the Rock 46

Sage, Victor 136
St. Leon 46
Saw 200, 203–207
Saw 2 205
Saw 3 206
Saw 6 206
Scarborough, Dorothy 126, 152, 156, 158
Schaffer, Talia 213n1
The School for Fathers 42
school shootings *see* Carneal, Michael; Columbine; Cox, Jeffrey Lynne; *Elephant*; Harris, Eric; Kinkel, Kip; Klebold, Dylan; Loukaitis, Barry; Pierce, Dustin; Virginia Tech
Schwartz, Lynne Sharon 148
science 19, 30, 65–6, 69, 74, 82, 104, 119–125, 129, 133, 140, 152, 165–166
science fiction 5
Scott, Beth 131
Scream 187–191, 194–195
Scream 2 **187**, 189–191
Scream 3 189
séances 119–120, 130, 143, 150, 155

Sedgwick, Eve 61–63, 98, 212n7
sensation novel 5
sensibility 52–54, 112, 129
sentimentality 42, 53
sexuality 7–8, 59–113, 117, 166, 202, 212n7
Shakespeare, William 32–36, 51
Shelley, Mary 5–6, 66–68, 81
Showalter, Elaine 76, 84
Shrek 89
Shyamalan, M. Night 157
Siegel, Carol 161
Simpson, O.J. 171
The Sixth Sense 157
Skin Shows 86
Smith, Charlotte 46
The Social Construction of What 7
Society for Psychical Research *see* parapsychology
Sontag, Susan 112
South Park 83
The Spectator 31
Speed Demon 102
Spiritualism 119–120, 127, 147
Stallybrass, Peter 39
Stephen King from A to Z 177
Sternheimer, Karen 165
Stevenson, Robert Louis 5–6, 74–76, 78–79
Stewart, C. Nelson 120
Stoker, Bram 4–6, 81, 213n1
Stone, Oliver 185, 188, 190
Stop Teaching Our Kids to Kill 8, 163
The Strange Case of Dr. Jekyll and Mr. Hyde 5, 74–76, 81, 84, 86
Strictures on the Modern System of Female Education 34
Stryker, Bradley 99, **100**, **101**
Sullivan, Jack 121, 149
supernatural *see* explained supernatural; ghosts; religion; superstition
Supernatural (television show) 148
The Supernatural in Modern Fiction 126
superstition 27, 29, 43–45, 47, 52–53, 117, 127–128, 136
Swim, Thaddeus K. 189

Taff, Barry 132–133
Tancred, or a Tale of Ancient Times 43, 47
Taylor, John Tinnon 41
Taylor, Michael 54
Taylor, Troy 132, 136, 145, 151
teaching *see* instruction
Teaching Mrs. Tingle 168

terrorism 41, 45, 121, 200–201
The Texas Chainsaw Massacre 2 86–89, **87**, **88**, 93
Three Essays on the Theory of Sexuality 96
torture porn 200–207
Traditional Values Coalition (TVC) 64, 68, 71, 74, 80, 83
A Treatise of Human Nature 30
Tropp, Martin 3–4
The Turn of the Screw 137

The Uninhabited House 152
the unspeakable 63, 69, 99
urban horror 6, 162
Urban Legend 189

Vampyros Lesbos 102
Van Sant, Gus 171
Vicinus, Martha 76–77
Victorian (Age) 60, 85, 119, 126
video games 6, 163, 168–169, 171–**172**
Virginia Tech 161–162, 171–175
Voodoo Academy 94, 102–107, **103**, **104**, 110, 112

Walker's Hibernian 51–51
Walpole, Horace 2, 4–6, 26–29, 32, 37–38, 44, 51, 62, 118–119
Walton, Kendall 12
Weeks, Jeffrey 62
The Well of Loneliness 62–63
Wes Craven's New Nightmare **197**–198
Wesley, John 135
Whale, James 81–82
White, Allon 39
White Noise 148
Whitehouse, Mary 185
Why Kids Kill: Inside the Minds of School Shooters 161, 169
Wilde, Oscar 6, 59–63, 65, 68, 71–81, 84–85, 89, 95–96, 111, 212n7
Williams, Caroline **87**, **88**
Wilson, Colin 122, 124, 129–130, 139–140, 143, 147, 150, 153, 155
Wilt, Judith 69
Wollstonecraft, Mary 52
Wood, Ellen 150
Wood, Robin 81
Wuthering Heights 5–6

Zanoni 120–121
Zeluco 46
Žižek, Slavoj 15, 18–20